SOFT FURNISHINGS
for your home

SOFT FURNISHINGS
for your home

Written and compiled by
Sharyn Skrabanich

A J.B. Fairfax Press Publication

EDITORIAL
Managing Editor: Judy Poulos
Editorial Assistant: Ella Martin
Editorial Coordinator: Margaret Kelly
US Editor: Trisha Malcolm

PHOTOGRAPHY
Andrew Payne
Additional photography by Andrew Elton

ILLUSTRATIONS
Carol Dunn

DESIGN AND PRODUCTION
Production Managers: Sheridan Carter,
Anna Maguire
Cover design and book design concept:
Michelle Withers
Cover Art Direction: Christine Davis
Layout: Margie Mulray, Lulu Dougherty

Published by J.B. Fairfax Press Pty Limited
80-82 McLachlan Ave
Rushcutters Bay, NSW 2011
Australia
A.C.N 003 738 430

Formatted by J.B. Fairfax Press Pty Limited
Printed by Toppan Printing Co, Singapore

First printed in this edition 1995
Reprinted 1997

JBFP 476 US

SOFT FURNISHINGS FOR YOUR HOME
Includes Index
ISBN 1 86343 125 X

DEDICATION

*This book is dedicated to my husband, Phillip;
my parents, Robert and Shelagh Dounan; and
Ivy Skrabanich. Without their love and support,
this book would not have been possible. I would
also like to thank Graeme Dann, Tim Starkey,
Joanne Potts, Frank Kerklaan and my colleagues
at Maurice Kain Textiles.*

Introduction

Fabric designers must create a master artwork that combines the elements of color, scale, pattern and proportion, uniting them with harmony and balance to create a finished design that is interesting and pleasing to the eye. In approaching this task, these designers take into account the proposed function of the fabric.

The designer will experiment with different forms of color, pattern, scale and proportion in order to compose their final artwork. This design process is quite lengthy and complex, passing through planned steps – and unplanned hiccups. When all the elements are working in unison, the artwork is finally completed.

The home decorator must also make decisions about mood or style and faces a similar challenge. Like the designer, the home decorator must consider all the design elements and how they will affect the final result. The elements then take shape in the form of fabric choices and color schemes, which in turn are converted into individual projects, such as those in this book.

As you see your planning taking shape, then comes the feeling of satisfaction in being able to say "I did it myself". **Soft Furnishings for Your Home** not only shows you how to achieve seven enticing and wonderful room settings, it also encourages you to combine elements from the various chapters to create a unique look for your home.

The first section of the book "Creating Your Style", covers the planning process involved in combining all the design elements to create a master plan. Before you cut your first length of fabric or sew your first stitch, you are made fully aware of the many things to consider when you design and make your own soft furnishings: the effects of color and texture, the choice of an appropriate fabric, the selection of trims and accessories to adorn and define your projects, and the essential equipment you will need for sewing for the home. Individual chapters, based on soft furnishing groupings – such as curtains, pillows or table accessories – will give you more specific instructions for making those particular items. Each project has step-by-step instructions and the details in "Creating Your Style" can be used as a quick and easy reference to help you achieve a professional result.

Soft Furnishings for Your Home presents many different design styles, each project so inviting and so easy that you will want to attempt them all. There are no hidden secrets or tricks used in this book. As long as you are able to sew a straight line and have the basic equipment to achieve a professional finish, you will be able to conjure up new and unique creations in a matter of hours!

Contents

❖

Creating Your Style 10
❖ Trims ❖ Fastenings
❖ Equipment ❖ Stitch Guide

Curtains 34
❖ Unlined Curtains
❖ Tie-On Curtains ❖ Lined Curtains
❖ Café Curtains ❖ Shirred Curtain
Panel
❖ Decorator Scarf ❖ Curtain Trims
❖ Swags and Jabots ❖ Tiebacks
❖ Valances

Shades 72
❖ Bonded Roller Shades
❖ Roman Shades ❖ Austrian Shades
❖ Tie-up Shades

Pillows 88
❖ Piped Pillows
❖ Heirloom Pillows
❖ Stenciled Pillows ❖ Bolsters
❖ Chair Cushions
❖ Round Buttoned Pillows

Slipcovers 112
❖ Edge Treatments ❖ Armchair Cover
❖ Drop-in Seat Cover
❖ Director's Chair Covers ❖ Tailored
Chair Cover ❖ Ruffled Chair Cover
❖ Instant Sofa Cover-up

Bed Linen 132

❖ Bed Sheets ❖ Duvet Covers ❖ Ruffled Bed Skirt ❖ Box-pleated Bed Skirt ❖ Tiered Bed Skirt ❖ Pillowcases ❖ Comforter ❖ Quilted Spread ❖ Tent Canopy ❖ Sheer Canopy ❖ Fringed Bedspread ❖ Upholstered Headboard ❖ Nursery Linen

Table Linen 160

❖ Stenciled Linens ❖ Circular Tablecloths ❖ Table Toppers ❖ Place Mats And Napkins ❖ Quilted Linens ❖ Festive Setting ❖ Scalloped Linens ❖ Fringed Table Set

The Finishing Touch 180

❖ Lined Basket ❖ Wastepaper Basket ❖ Band Boxes ❖ Lampshades ❖ Decorative Screen ❖ Towels With Flair ❖ Picture Bows ❖ Photo Frames ❖ Drawstring Bag ❖ Fabric-Covered Box

Index 199

Creating Your Style

Making major changes to home decor can perplex the most enthusiastic home decorator. A few wrong choices and you could end up with something that is not how you intended it to be. What's more, the time and effort involved in making major changes can be very disruptive to the entire family.

Style

❖

Planning to change your entire decor can be an expensive exercise. Sentiment also plays a major part in deciding what to change and what to keep. Imagine having to part with your favorite comfortable chair because the color won't work with your new scheme or because the arms and seat are too worn and you have been told it is beyond salvation! This is where the decorator in you must take control and overcome sentiment.

How to begin

Making the decision to do something may leave you asking, "So, where do I begin?". In fact, you have already begun! You have been influenced by things you have seen that you like and you know what you want to change about your existing decor. A good way to prepare yourself is to collect pictures from magazines with color schemes, ideas and projects that you like. Keep them in a folder or scrapbook for easy reference. Make a list of the positive and negative elements of each room and make a note of the things you like and dislike in other homes you visit. Soon you will see a pattern forming in your selection process. You may be drawn to a certain color scheme, to the grandeur of high ceilings or the plushness of rich vibrant fabrics. It may be the simplicity of a room that pleases your eye, where the texture of the fabrics and furnishings are more important than the use of color.

Once you have selected the features you like about an interior, try to analyze the decorating style. Is it the richness of pattern commonly used in the Victorian style? Is it the modern clean lines of the minimalist approach? Is it the simplicity of materials and objects more commonly associated with French provincial decorating? It is imperative that once you have decided what you like about a room you make a commitment that this is what you want to create.

Do not slavishly follow the current trends in decorating. If you do not like the currently fashionable look, don't feel obliged to incorporate it into your new scheme. If clean minimalistic decorating lines are in, but you feel that gathering your personal treasures around you makes you feel relaxed and happy, then follow your heart.

Once you have set your goals in the direction of the style you want to achieve, it is time to consider the other elements that will help bring your plans to fruition.

Left: The sample board
Below: The uncluttered simplicity of this living room is enhanced by the choice of fabrics

Color

Color provides the basis for any room setting. Your color selections will invoke a certain atmosphere within a room, so it is important to work with colors that reflect the mood you are trying to create. Ruby red, for example, creates a feeling of warmth and passion, while subtle, refreshing blue gives a sense of calm and coolness.

Working with color

Decorating with soft furnishings often means that a color scheme is already in place for the walls and floor of your room. The fabrics you select for soft furnishings will either transform your room into something totally new and unique, work with your existing furnishings and ornaments to create a fresh look, or blend and harmonize with your general color scheme to ensure that other focal points, such as paintings or objets d'art, take pride of place in your room setting.

Not only will fabric color create a mood, but the pattern and texture of the fabric will also play a very important role in the overall style of the room. The tactile qualities of fabric absorb and reflect light to create varying degrees of warmth.

The effect of one color in relation to another can also have a major bearing on your final color scheme. In some instances, heavily patterned and dyed fabrics absorb surrounding colors into them, leaving them looking washed out. This phenomenon is further emphasized by variations in light. Light and shadow have a major bearing on the effect of color in a room: a light color in a sunlit room will be washed

Above: Create a romantic bedroom setting
Top: The sample board

out even further by strong light and make your walls or fabrics appear lighter; dark colors in rooms with little natural light will often appear darker and in some places, such as corners, will often appear as black.

To decide on the effect you want to create, you must consider the features of your room. The positive features should be highlighted and brought to the forefront through the use of suitably colored or textured fabrics. A beautifully shaped bay window or an elegant chaise longue would be ideal focal points, highlighted with patterned fabric or vibrant colors.

It may be that the only positive features of a room are structural, such as the height of the ceiling or decorative moldings, and the

other parts will need to be changed. This is where the principles of color should be applied in order to emphasize ceiling height and enhance decorative moldings without letting the room becoming too austere and overpowering.

Color can also be used to play clever tricks and remedy faults that would otherwise require major alterations. For example, a long hallway will seem shorter painted in a warm color with the far back wall painted in a stronger or lighter tone of the wall color.

The color wheel

❖

Using a color wheel allows you to experiment with color without losing control of your decorative objectives or having to deal with the cost of expensive failures.

Warm and cool colors
Warm and cool colors play very important roles in the visual effect we can create in a room. Blues and greens, found on the right-hand side of the color wheel, are cool, calming colors, creating the illusion of space and distance. For this reason, they are ideal for giving a feeling of spaciousness to a small or awkwardly shaped room.

Red, orange and violet, with the inclusion of yellow, are warm colors. Yellow and violet are in interesting positions at the top and bottom of the wheel. Their effect can be varied depending on whether they tend to the cool or warm side of the wheel.

When a greater proportion of one primary color is combined with another, its partner, a warm or cool toning of the resulting secondary color, is formed. For example, seventy percent blue and thirty percent yellow make blue/green, a cool color. If the proportions were altered to seventy percent yellow and thirty percent blue, the resultant yellow/green would be a warm color.

Neutral colors
Black and white, described as neutral colors, are often used as tints to vary the strength of a primary or secondary color. Neutral colors can

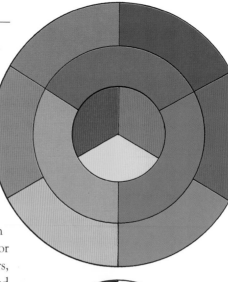

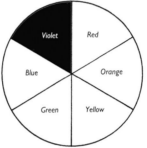

Monochromatic color scheme

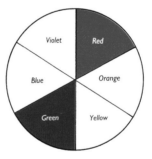

Complementary color scheme

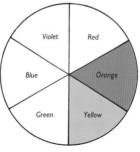

Harmonious color scheme

also be warm or cool. Browns and grays are also neutral colors and they can also be tinted with black or white to give the impression of coolness or warmth.

Monochromatic color schemes
In a monochromatic color scheme, various tones of a single base color are used together to produce a subtle color scheme. Quite often, monochromatic schemes are based on neutral shades, such as cream or ivory. In such a scheme, you might find pillows in cream raw silk, curtains in off-white handloomed cotton, and embossed furnishing fabrics in a creamy-beige; all serve to create very exciting textural effects, even though there are only slight variations in the overall color scheme.

Harmonious or analogous color schemes
These colors are grouped together on the color wheel and, when used together, are the easiest and safest color choices for decorating.

Complementary color schemes
Complementary colors are found directly opposite one another on the color wheel, for example red and green, or blue and yellow. While most of us would not be comfortable in a room decorated in red and green, the softer tonings on the outer ring of the color wheel can provide interesting decorative effects.

Accent colors
Accent colors are just that – a way of providing an accent or highlight in an overall color scheme; such as a light color against a dark one or a cool color against a warm one.

Fabrics & fabric selection

Today, home decorators have a vast selection of fabric styles from which to select soft furnishing treatments. This endless variety of fabric is very exciting and even awe-inspiring when it comes to making choices.

Remember when purchasing fabric, do not skimp on the amount. A full-bodied curtain which flows on to the floor below makes a statement of grandeur. If you feel the cost of making such a statement could be out of your price range, shop around! Fabric suppliers are usually happy to help you compare prices and quality and you will be surprised at the amount of variation. Visiting showrooms will enable you to see a range of the latest fabrics so you can select the best in your price range. This is also an opportunity to be very creative – slipcovers and window treatments of unbleached muslin or cotton, used extravagantly, will often create as much ambience as a more expensive fabric.

The beauty of decorating with fabric is that it can, for example, adorn a window for a few years and then be cut down to make pillow covers. It can then be used with other fabrics to create a patchwork masterpiece for your bed or sofa.

Pattern and texture

When people think of fabric they immediately think of pattern. Pattern, although the most noticeable feature of some fabrics, is by no means the only one. The texture and 'hand' or feel of a fabric are elements which should not be overlooked. Many natural fabrics, such as silk or wool, are natural fibers spun into uneven yarns which are woven together to form a cloth, giving an uneven slub-like texture to the finished fabric. Crisp linens and polished cotton chintzes have pleasing textural qualities, while hand-loomed cottons also have a rough uneven texture due to the unevenness of the natural fibers.

Know your fabric

Today, manufacturers often have helpful information printed on sample cards, telling you about the washability of a fabric. Fabrics are only guaranteed by the manufacturer if they are used and cleaned as recommended.

Hints for choosing fabric

1 Be sure the fabric you choose is suitable for its intended purpose. For example, don't expect a shiny chintz to be long-lasting in a child's bedroom or lace curtains to block out the sunlight.

2 Be sure you are making an economically sound purchase. Don't spend a lot of money on areas that don't warrant the expense, but do invest in good quality fabric for high-traffic areas or for furnishings of classic design.

3 If you are going to sew soft furnishings, be sure that your machine can sew the fabric you choose.

4 Look into how you plan to care for the fabric and make sure the one you have chosen is suitable for this regime. For example, if you are going to wash your curtains at home rather than have them professionally cleaned, be sure that your fabric is washable and will not shrink or distort.

Below: The sample board
Bottom: Rich fabrics and trims enhance this formal dining room

Fabric types & qualities

❖

Today, you still have the choice of natural fibers, but you also have access to a very wide range of synthetic fibers. This variety can sometimes be confusing so it is useful to know a little about the properties of various fibers and the fabrics made from them.

The four natural fibers (cotton, wool, silk and linen) are all commonly used to make home furnishing fabrics.

Natural fibers

• *Cotton* has long been the most popular for sheets, towels and most curtains. It is mass-produced, making it relatively inexpensive to manufacture into fabrics of many weights and textures.

• *Wool* is commonly the basis of traditional and modern floor coverings. It has strong insulating properties, as well as being hard-wearing, flame-retardant, light, and fairly waterproof. It is long-lasting, but needs special care when laundering.

• *Silk* is the glamor fiber, used traditionally for upholstery fabric, tassels and braids, pillow covers and luxury rugs. Silk is a very fine and soft fiber and is a good insulator, but it is quite expensive compared to other natural fibers. It is the most lustrous fiber of all.

Linen is the world's oldest domestic fiber. There have always been sheets and household accessories made from linen, with its main appeal being its sheer endurance – it never seems to wear out!

Natural fibers and fabrics are very easy to clean but, due to their often loose or uneven weave, they are prone to shrink, crease or distort if laundered incorrectly. This unevenness can only be rectified if the natural fiber is interwoven with a synthetic fiber.

Decorating with fabric is like painting a picture

Synthetic fibers

Synthetic fibers are becoming increasingly popular and are often blended with natural fibers in fabrics. This serves two purposes: the cost is reduced, and very often the synthetic fibers give added strength. Synthetic fabrics usually wash very well, the fibers do not absorb dirt and moisture, and they are long-wearing. They also provide insulation and effective light control.

The most commonly used synthetic fibers are acetate, polyester, acrylic and viscose – all produced by chemical processes and all with valuable qualities.

• *Acetate* is created by treating cotton linters or cotton fibers. It is often used as a substitute for silk in moirés or brocades, and feels soft to the touch with good draping qualities. An acetate works best in a tightly woven fabric because it tends to sag in looser weaves.

• *Acrylics* are bulky pile fabrics which also feel soft to the touch. They have excellent draping qualities and are crease-resistant. Acrylic fibers are often blended with polyester, cotton or wool for lasting strength and easy maintenance.

• *Nylon* is a by-product of coal. While not as soft as polyester, it is still drapable and is often found mixed with other fibers to form synthetic laces, net or satin. Washing is easy and the fabric can be drip-dried, requiring little ironing.

• *Polyester* is the hardest wearing of the synthetic fabrics. It combines well with many natural fibers, such as cotton, to provide an easy-care, wrinkle-free fabric which has excellent draping qualities.

Pattern

❖

Patterns have been used throughout the centuries to adorn the walls of caves, primitive shelters, houses, and stately castles. Ancient civilizations were inspired by the patterns found in nature and often copied the markings on insects and reptiles when painting their bodies.

The printing of patterns onto fabric by screen printing or stenciling are techniques still commonly used today for both hand-crafted and mass-produced items. During the eighteenth century, copper rollers were engraved with patterns that were rolled over a fabric to form a repetitive pattern (known as a repeat), giving birth to the printed patterns that are still used, such as the motifs on highly polished chintz.

The effects of pattern

Pattern can be used in different ways to achieve different effects. In a small room, a bold floral chintz drape can be used as a focal point;

in a larger room, the pattern of one fabric can be used with other patterned fabrics as part of the overall decorative rhythm or theme.

Coordination of patterns is now a breeze for home decorators with many fabric manufacturers providing totally coordinated ranges to choose from.

While there are no set rules for

Top left: The sample board
Above: Combine several prints with a common color theme for an interesting visual effect

coordinating fabrics there are some general guidelines for you to refer to. For example, larger scale prints work best when used for larger pieces, such as couches or sofas, or for drapes in larger rooms; vertical stripes will emphasize the height of a wall or window area; smaller florals are ideal for pillows and accents; and plain fabrics in complementary colors make ideal trims.

Scale and proportion

The next element to consider when selecting patterned fabrics is the size and scale of the pattern. Wall coverings are usually best suited to smaller scale prints, while larger scale elaborate designs work better when draped into folds for curtains (fig. 1).

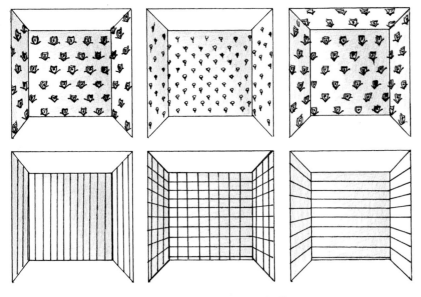

Fig. 1: Patterns create different visual effects

If you are working with a fabric manufacturer's coordinated range, always purchase large samples showing a full repeat. It is important to see how a fabric will drape, as opposed to just being stretched over a chair or pillow.

Mixing patterns

Usually people prefer to use just one pattern and mix it with solids or other coordinating fabrics in a room. To add more interest, you can select a similar pattern to the first one, in either a larger or smaller scale, or in reversed colorations.

However, very different patterns can also be used right next to each other, in balance, and will produce very interesting effects. To mix patterns confidently, there should be a common element, such as color, to tie them together.

Sample boards

A sample board is the ideal way to consider whether color, scale, pattern and

Left: The sample board
Below: Combinations of pattern and texture work in a two-color scheme

proportion are working harmoniously. Most importantly, a sample board provides a working space which can be altered – much less expensive than scrapping the new curtains and starting again.

You must ensure that the elements of your sample board are in proportion to one another and to the scale of the room. The swatch of your sofa fabric must be much larger than the contrasting sofa piping or trim that you are using with it. Paint swatches showing wall colors, or a piece of board painted in your wall colors, allows for better matching to curtain fabrics. Present your fabrics as they will appear in the room. For example, try to fold or drape your curtain sample as it will appear on your window.

We made up sample boards for each of our room settings before we began the design process. You can see from the sample boards shown with each picture how the final effects have evolved from the design stage to the final presentation in the room.

Top left: The sample board
Left: Rich colors and strong patterns are a feature of this stylish bedroom

Pattern matching

When you are using patterned fabric where lengths are joined across the width, you must take care to match the patterns. To do this, you must determine the pattern repeat. A pattern repeat is the length of the pattern from beginning to end, running down the length of a fabric. If your fabric has a strong motif running across, it is a good idea to place a complete motif at the top and, if possible, another one at the bottom. If there is a strong motif running vertically through the fabric, this should be centered, as far as possible, in the finished project.

Obviously, you will not always be able to have a complete pattern repeat at both the top and bottom. The broken repeat should be where it is least visible – at the top in a shorter curtain and at the bottom in a floor length one (fig. 1).

Each print poses a different challenge when it comes to pattern matching

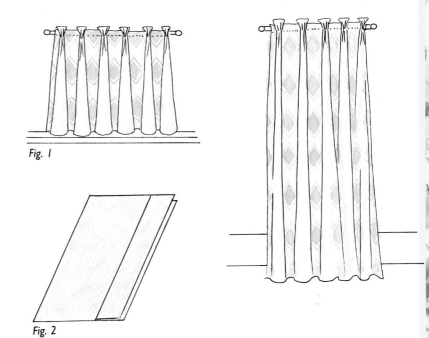

Fig. 1

Fig. 2

Joining panels

Ideally, fabric panels should be joined in such a way that the stitching is as unobtrusive as possible.

1 Place the two panels together with right sides facing. Stitch them together with a $5/8"$ (1.5cm) seam and press the seam flat (fig. 2).

2 Trim one seam allowance to $1/8"$ (3mm) and turn $1/8"$ (3mm) to the wrong side along the raw edge of the other seam allowance (figs. 3 and 4).

3 Press the folded edge over to the seam line enclosing the raw edges. Slipstitch the folded edge over the previous stitching (fig. 5).

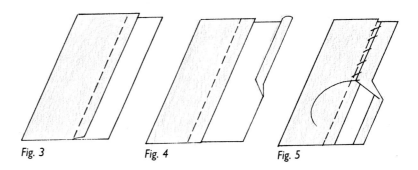

Fig. 3

Fig. 4

Fig. 5

Trims

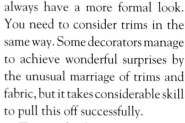

Decorative trims provide the perfect finishing touch to many soft furnishing projects. Interior designers have always valued the "extra something" given to a piece of furniture or accessory by the addition of well-chosen trims. In this book, we feature a variety of trims and show how the same trim can be applied to different projects to achieve a totally different look.

It may be the color or texture of the trim selected, or the extravagance of rich bullion trims, feminine ruffles and lace, or the defined lines of bias and piping details that provide stylish finishes.

Today's furnishings are increasingly ornate and generous in proportion. This trend is exemplified in the softness and fullness of a well-padded sofa with feather-

filled pillows, or in generous lengths of fabric draped across curtains to form swagged valances or gathered into festoon shades. These generous lines are often accentuated by the choice of trims. Equally, if you prefer the look of straight sharp edges, the well-defined lines of a bonded shade or the crispness of starched bed linen, the selection of the perfect trim or braid will underline the effect you are trying to create.

Most stores that sell furnishing fabrics have a good range of trims for you to choose from, and many are surprisingly inexpensive. While cost is a most important consideration, if only because it is possible to overembellish an inexpensive fabric, there are several other considerations to bear in mind when selecting your borders and trims. While creativity frequently challenges rules of color and suitability, your eye will tell you if a trim suits a fabric. Fabrics that are generally dull rather than lustrous tend to look casual, while shimmery fabrics will always have a more formal look. You need to consider trims in the same way. Some decorators manage to achieve wonderful surprises by the unusual marriage of trims and fabric, but it takes considerable skill to pull this off successfully.

Too much of a contrasting trim will become the focal point of a project. This is not generally a problem if the trim is the same color as the fabric, so the trim will not compete with the fabric; rather it will add interesting textured effects.

Wearability

For the best results when selecting trims, ensure that the trims and the fabric are similar or compatible in weight; delicate lace will not work with a heavy velvet. This is particularly important when it comes to the care and cleaning of your soft furnishings. If you are making pillow covers that you plan to wash, make sure that the trim you use is washable and whether the color will run in water. If you are planning to wash a trimmed item, you should wash the trim and the fabric separately before you begin. This also applies if you are trimming an existing item. It may seem like a lot of extra work, but checking shrinkage and color fastness will save you heartache later. Sometimes a handful of salt thrown into cold rinsing water will help to set the dyes in trims.

Will the braid be as long-wearing as the fabric? This may not be a major consideration, but if your fabric is expensive you will

The choice of trims available to the home stitcher is rich and wide

have to consider the life expectancy of your trims. Be mindful of where you use the trim – arm rests and head rests are more prone to wearing than the back of a sofa. If a pillow cover will be used on the family-room couch much-loved by the kids and the family dog, do not choose a delicate lace ruffle.

It is usually a good idea to purchase more braid, ribbon or lace than you need to allow for adjustments and for replacement of worn areas later on.

Applying trims

When applying trims to fabric, pins may pucker, stretch or distort the fabric and trim. To avoid this problem, use a fabric or craft glue to temporarily secure the trim to the fabric while you stitch. (Make sure the glue is dry before you begin sewing.) There are also a number of products available that bond both fabric and trim, without sewing. Many of these bonds can also be laundered regularly, while remaining quite secure.

Always try to work with a continuous length of trim, but if cutting is necessary, allow enough excess for seams and corners. When working the trim or braid around a corner, baste the trim at the corner before sewing. When applying a ruffle to a corner, such as on a pillow cover, allow extra fullness at the corner to prevent pulling. (See how to sew corners on page 22.)

Binding

Making and joining strips of bias binding

1 To find the bias on a piece of fabric, fold one corner so that the top edge is parallel to the selvage. Press the fold. This pressed line is the bias. Draw lines parallel to the pressed line, the desired width of the bias strip plus $1/2$" (1.2cm) seam allowances apart. Cut along the marked lines to make bias strips.

2 Join strips by placing two lengths of bias right sides together across each other at a 45 degree angle, and with side edges meeting $1/4$" (6mm) from the end (fig. 1).

3 Stitch the ends together. Press the seam open (fig. 2).

How to make continuous bias binding

1 Cut a piece of fabric (fig. 3). Decide on the width of your bias strip, including $1/2$" (1.2cm) seam allowances, and mark strips on the bias as shown. Cut away side areas.

2 Fold the fabric with the right sides together, so that both points A and B are matching. Note that one strip width extends on each side. Stitch together with a $1/4$" (6mm) seam. Press the seam open. Cut along the marked line to make one continuous strip of bias fabric (fig. 4).

Attaching bias binding

By machine

If you are using bias binding you have made yourself, press $1/4$" (6mm) seam allowances under with a bias strip pressing guide. Fold the bias strip in half lengthwise with the wrong sides together and place it over both raw edges of the seam.

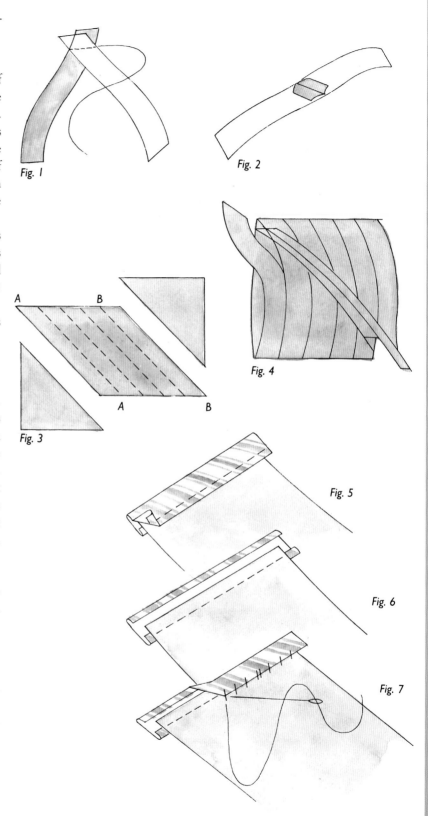

Fig. 1

Fig. 2

Fig. 3

Fig. 4

Fig. 5

Fig. 6

Fig. 7

A   B

A   B

Pin and stitch the bias strip in place ⅛" (3mm) from the edge, catching both sides of the bias strip (fig. 5).

By hand
Open out the bias binding. With the right sides together, match fabric and bias binding raw edges. Pin and stitch them together, stitching along the fold line of the bias binding (fig. 6). Fold the binding to the wrong side of the fabric, enclosing the raw edges. Slipstitch the binding in place, covering the stitching line (fig. 7).

Piping

❖

Piping differs from binding in that lengths of bias fabric cover a length of purchased cording, which is in turn sewn into a flat seam so that the covered cord or piping is sandwiched between the layers of fabric. Piping cords can be purchased in various thicknesses so that a number of different styles can be achieved for different end uses, such as for upholstery, pillow covers or table accessories.

Cut and join lengths of bias fabric in the same way as for making continuous bias binding on page 20. Remember, the bias strip must be wide enough to wrap around the piping cord, with sufficient seam allowances on both sides for stitching.

To make piping
1 Measure the length of piping you will need for your project. Cords can be joined if necessary by butting two ends together and binding them with matching thread or by carefully intertwining the strands (figs. 8 to 10).

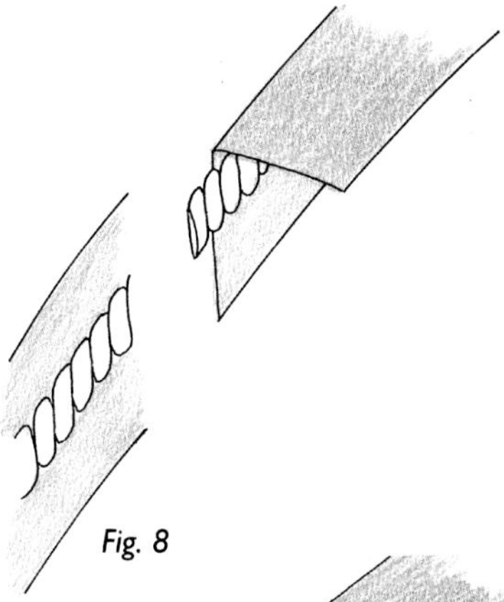

Fig. 8

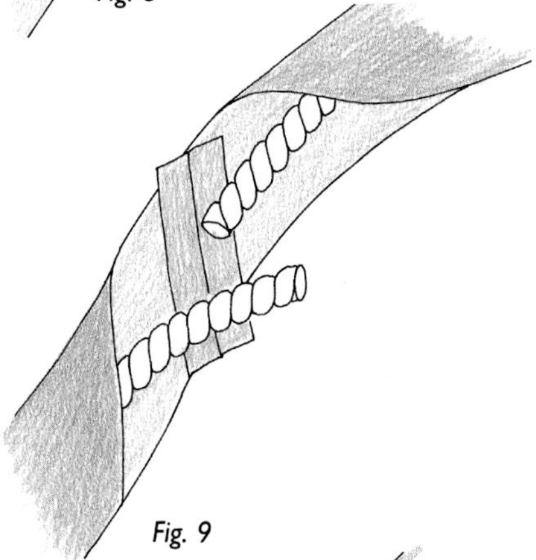

Fig. 9

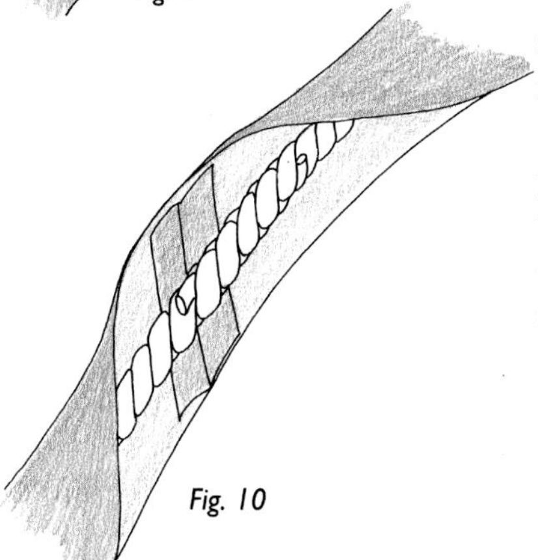

Fig. 10

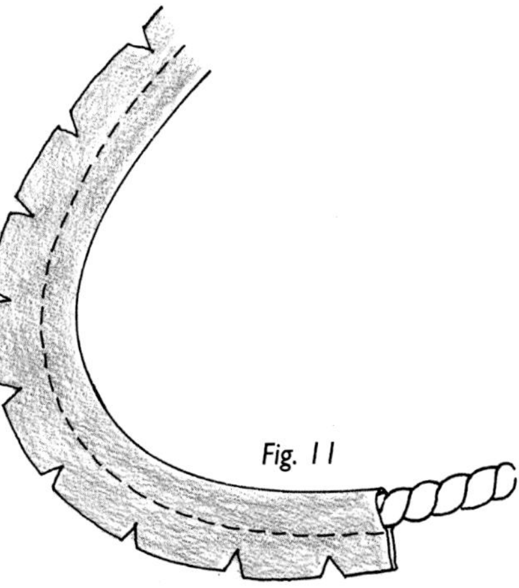

Fig. 11

2 Fold the bias strip over the piping cord. Using matching sewing thread and the zipper foot on your sewing machine, stitch through the bias strip close to the cord.

Attaching piping
1 Lay the piping on the right side of one fabric piece with raw edges even. Baste in place.
2 Place the other piece of fabric right side down, over the top of the basted fabric and piping, with raw edges even. With a zipper foot, stitch along the seam line through all layers of fabric and piping, stitching close to the cord. If necessary, trim the seam allowances to remove excess bulk.
3 Fold right side out with the piping fixed securely between the layers of fabric.

Piping around a curve
To allow the piping to lie neatly around a curved edge, slash the raw edge of the bias strip at 1¼" (3cm) intervals before attaching the piping (fig. 11). This creates a very flexible working piece that can be moulded around corners, such as on pillows.

Corners

❖

Corners can be a little difficult to sew neatly, so it's worth taking time to learn a trick or two.

Sewing a right-angled corner
1 Stitch until the needle is ⅝" (1.5cm) from the fabric edge (or the distance of your seam allowance). Lift the machine presser foot and turn the fabric to an angle of 90 degrees. Lower the presser foot so that it is parallel to the raw edge of the fabric and continue sewing.
2 To allow the corner to be turned right side out, cut diagonally across the seam allowance at the corner. You can also trim the seams to remove any excess fabric bulk (fig. 1).

Sewing a sharp corner
Work in the same way as for the right-angled corner, but add one or two stitches across the corner for extra strength. Trim the corner across the diagonal as for the right-angled corner (fig. 2).

Sewing a mitered corner
Mitered corners give a particularly neat square finish to corners, particularly on table linen and where piping is a feature.
1 To sew a mitered corner, such as on a tablecloth, press in ⅛" (3mm) to the wrong side on both raw edges to finish them, then press under the seam allowances (fig. 3).
2 Open out the corner and press it in toward the center so that the pressed lines are matching. Press the diagonal; this will be your stitching line (fig. 4).
3 Open out the corner again and refold it diagonally through the corner. Stitch along the pressed diagonal line. Trim the excess fabric

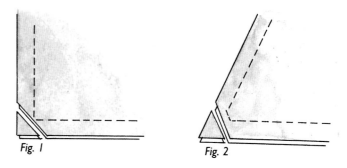

Fig. 1

Fig. 2

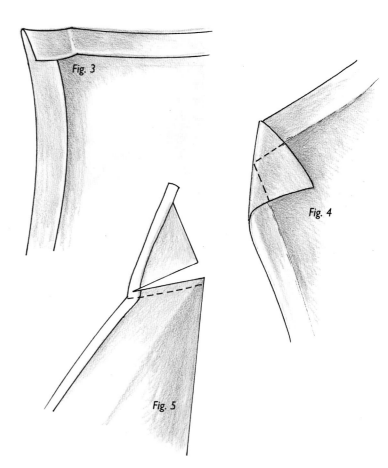

Fig. 3

Fig. 4

Fig. 5

(fig. 5). Turn the corner right side out and press carefully.

Sewing a mitered corner on a trim
1 Fold the trim over double with the wrong sides together and raw edges matching. Pick up the top piece and fold it to one side, so the edges are now at right angles to each other and you have formed a diagonal fold. Finger-press the fold (fig. 6).
2 On the wrong side, pin and stitch diagonally from the corner to the edge along the fold, then cut away the excess trim, so that the corner lies flat. Press the seam open (figs. 7 and 8).

To miter a corner with piping, pin and baste the piping in place up to the corner. At the corner, snip into the seam allowance of the piping so that the snip forms an L-shape. Bend the piping.

To miter a corner on a border where there is a raw edge on both sides, before you stitch the corner, turn under the seam allowance on the raw edge which will remain visible.

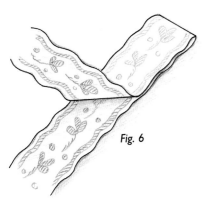

Fig. 6

Ruffles can really dress up a collection of pillows

Ruffles

❖

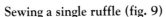

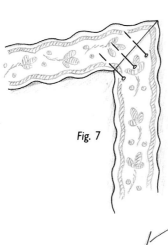

Fig. 7

Fig. 8

Ruffles are one of the easiest decorating finishes for a variety of soft furnishing projects, including pillows, curtains, shades and bed linen. Whether used singly or in layers, they add a soft, luxurious touch to a project. How full you make the ruffle will depend on the fabric weight and where it is to be used. Usually, the lighter the fabric, the fuller the ruffle. As a general rule, allow about twice the finished length when cutting a strip of fabric for the ruffle.

Sewing a single ruffle (fig. 9)
1 Cut out a strip for the ruffle, adding 1¹/₄" (3cm) for the hem. If you need to join strips, add ⁵/₈" (1.5cm) for each joining seam allowance.
2 Make a double hem on one long edge. To gather the ruffle, hand- or machine-sew two parallel rows of gathering stitches close to the raw edge (figs. 10 and 11).

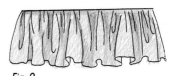

Fig. 9

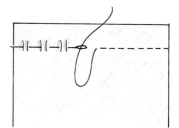

Fig. 10

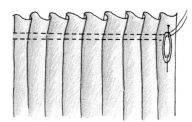

Fig. 11

Add a ruffle to the lower edge of an Austrian shade

3 Pin the gathered edge of the ruffle to the raw edge of the fabric piece with right sides together, adjusting the gathering for an even fit. Machine-sew the ruffle in place, stitching very close to the gathering stitches.

Sewing a ruffle with a heading (figs. 1 and 2)

Generally, this attractive ruffle is used to finish the bottom edge of a curtain, where the upper ruffle is narrower than the lower one.

1 Cut the ruffle strip with additional width for the upper ruffle or heading and 2¹/₂" (6cm) for upper and lower hems. Join strips as necessary to achieve the correct length.

2 Double hem both the upper and lower raw edges. Mark a line where the heading is to be attached and hand- or machine-sew two parallel rows of gathering stitches along either side of the marked line.

3 Pin the ruffle in place along the gathering line, adjusting the gathers evenly. Stitch between the two rows of gathering. Remove the gathering threads after stitching.

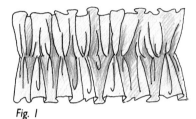

Fig. 1

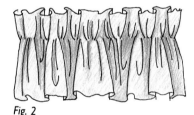

Fig. 2

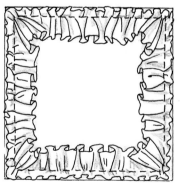

Fig. 3

Sewing a double ruffle

This ruffle has more body than a single ruffle, and eliminates the need for a lower hem.

1 Cut the ruffle double the required width and add 1¹/₄" (3cm) for seam allowances.

2 Fold the ruffle in half with wrong sides together and press. Gather up the ruffle with two rows of gathering stitches inside the seam allowance.

3 Attach the ruffle in the same way as the single ruffle.

Applying a ruffle

1 This technique ensures that ruffling looks even on a finished project. Divide the length of the ruffle into equal parts and mark with pins. Divide the edge to which it will be applied into the same number of equal parts. For smaller projects, four sections are usual, but for larger projects and circles, six may be required. If you are attaching the ruffle to a pillow, use the four corners as your marks.

2 Pin the ruffle in place, matching the pin marks and adjusting the gathering evenly between them. Pin and baste, then stitch the ruffle in place (fig. 3).

Fastenings

Today, we are able to choose from a number of alternatives for closures on projects such as duvet covers and pillows. Take into account not only the appearance of your fastenings but their practicality, particularly on pieces that will be laundered.

Snaps (either singly or on tape), Velcro®, zippers, and hooks and eyes are all excellent methods for securing openings. Knowing how to apply these products will add to the success of your project.

Hooks and eyes

Where the edges overlap, stitch the hook on the underside of the overlapping edge and the eye on the outside of the opposite edge (fig. 4). Where fabrics meet edge to edge, stitch the eye on the wrong side, slightly over the edge, and stitch the hook so that the end is flush with the fabric's edge (fig. 5).

Making a thread eye

A thread eye is less obvious than a metal one, so there may be times when you prefer to use it. Mark the required length for the eye and sew, long continuous loose stitches along that length (fig. 6). Stitch over the loose stiches with blanket stitches for extra strength and a neat finish (fig. 7). Remember that a thread eye is not as strong as a metal one.

Fastening tapes

Hook-and-loop fastenings, such as Velcro®, come in various shapes and sizes. The most common is in the form of long continuous strips,

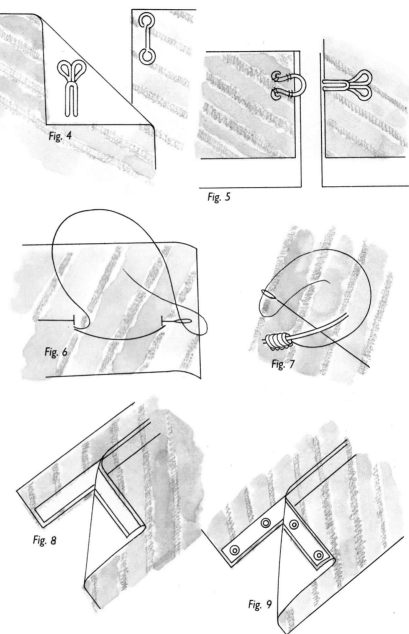

Fig. 4

Fig. 5

Fig. 6

Fig. 7

Fig. 8

Fig. 9

purchased by the yard or meter (fig. 8). Precut Velcro® circles can also be used for closures, such as on a duvet cover. These fastenings are easy to attach by simply stitching close to the outside edges.

Another type of fastening tape is snap tape (fig. 9). Attach this tape using the zipper foot on your sewing machine which will enable you to stitch quite close to the snaps.

Buttons

Buttons can be both functional and decorative. On duvet covers, pillowcases and pillow covers, they provide a very decorative fastening method. Select buttons in shell or wood to provide interesting texture and scale.

Creating a button shank

When attaching a button to thick fabric it is useful to make a shank for the button.

1 Secure the thread in the fabric where the button is to be attached and bring the needle to the right side of the fabric. Pass the needle and thread through the first hole in the button.

2 Place a matchstick on top of the holes in the button and work several stitches over the matchstick, through the holes in the button and through the fabric (fig. 1).

3 Remove the matchstick and pull up the button. Wind the thread around the shank about six to eight times, then secure it.

Work several stitches through the fabric and shank before fastening off the stitching.

Zippers

Zippers are most commonly used for loose covers. A concealed zipper allows a pillow to be used on both sides.

Choose a good quality zipper to ensure the long life of your project. It can be very frustrating to make a beautiful pillow only to have the zipper fail not long after.

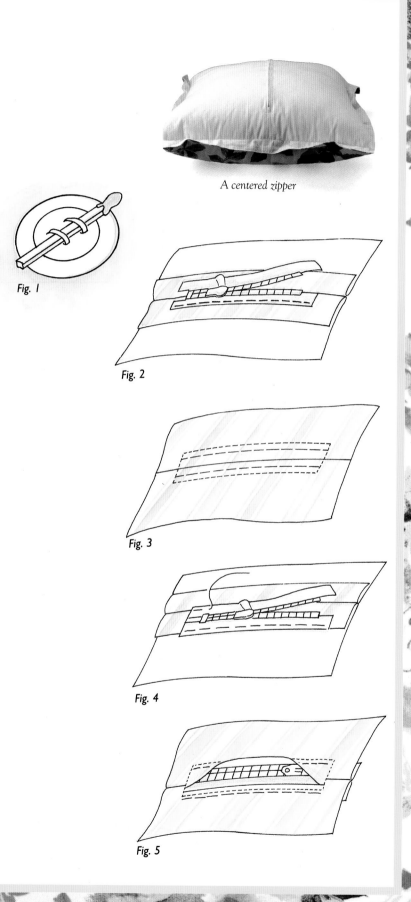

A centered zipper

Fig. 1

Fig. 2

Fig. 3

Fig. 4

Fig. 5

Inserting a centered zipper

1 Mark the length of the zipper opening, plus 2" (5cm). Stitch the two ends of the seam and baste the zipper opening closed. Press the seam open.

2 Open the zipper and place it face down on the seam allowance so that the zipper teeth are along the seam line. Pin and baste one side of the zipper tape to the fabric. With a zipper foot, stitch through all thicknesses approximately $\frac{1}{8}$" (3mm) from the zipper teeth (fig. 2).

3 Close the zipper and place the zipper tape on the opposite seam allowance. Pin and baste in place as before.

4 Turn the fabric right side up with the zipper beneath. Starting at the top of the zipper and with the zipper foot on your sewing machine, top-stitch down one side approximately $\frac{1}{4}$" (6mm) away from the zipper teeth. Continue to stitch across the bottom of the zipper close to the end, then up to the top of the zipper and across the top. Remove the basting stitches and press carefully (fig. 3).

To insert an offset zipper

If you wish the zipper to be more concealed, you can insert it offset, by the following method.

1 Mark the zipper opening as for the centered zipper. Stitch the ends of the zipper opening seam and baste the zipper opening closed.

2 With the zipper open and face down, position it over the seam so that the teeth are centered over the right-hand seam allowance. Baste the right-hand side of the zipper tape in place close to the zipper teeth (fig. 4).

3 Close the zipper and baste the

An offset zipper

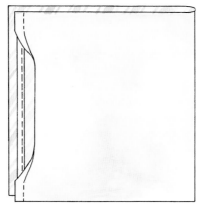

Fig. 6

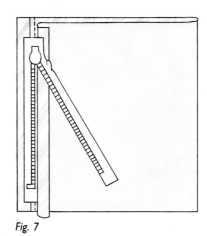

Fig. 7

A zipper in the side seam

other side in place, closer to the edge of the zipper tape.

4 On the right side and with the zipper foot of your sewing machine, topstitch through all the layers of fabric down both sides of the zipper and across both ends. Remove the basting stitches (fig. 5).

Lapped zipper in a piped seam

Occasionally, you will need to insert a zipper into a seam which already has piping in it, such as on one side of a pillow cover. This can be quite bulky and difficult to manage.

1 On the side without the piping, press the seam allowance of the zipper opening to the wrong side.

2 Pull back the top seam allowance to expose the piping seam allowance (fig. 6). Open the zipper and lay it face down over the extended seam allowance with the zipper teeth resting on the top of the piping. Baste in place (fig. 7). Check that the zipper will open and close easily before stitching. Using the zipper foot on your sewing machine, stitch the zipper tape close to the zipper teeth, then remove the basting stitches.

3 Stitch the other side of the zipper tape to the seam allowance on the other side.

If you want to avoid the bulk, cut the fabric for the back of the pillow in two halves, adding 1" (2.5cm) at the center back for the seam allowances. Insert the zipper into the center back seam, using the method for applying a centered zipper, then make up the pillow cover in the usual way.

Equipment

One of the nicest things about decorating with soft furnishings is that you do not need to invest a lot of money in hardware to complete your projects. When creating soft furnishings, the majority of home sewers have already made the investment in the number one timesaver: a sewing machine.

Cutting table

A clean work surface is also necessary to achieve a professional finish in your sewing. If you do not have a table large enough, invest in a cutting board that has a grid marked in 1" (2.5cm) squares. A cutting board will be very valuable when you are working with large pieces of fabric where straight, even cutting is essential. In a project such as a bonded shade, having a cutting table could make the difference between an average job and a truly professional one.

Needles and pins

Just as you need a variety of machine needles, it is helpful to have a variety of handsewing needles.

Medium Sharps are useful for everyday sewing projects. A curved upholstery needle should be used for heavy fabric and can also be useful for sewing buttons on to pillows. In addition to these, choose needles that are appropriate to specific jobs, such as quilting, embroidery and tapestry.

There are also a variety of pins available. Stainless steel dressmaking pins are the most common; some have colored plastic heads which make them very easy to see. Quilters pins are longer than most other pins and are useful for pinning fabric to a padded surface.

Glues, adhesives and fusible webs

There are a large number of glues, adhesives and fusible webs available at most craft and fabric suppliers. Their use in appliqué, hemming and bonding fabric and trims to a variety of surfaces means that many decorative applications can now be done quickly and easily to complete projects that, in the past, you might have thought too difficult or time consuming to attempt.

Iron

A good steam iron is an essential piece of equipment for achieving a truly professional finish. All seams should be pressed with a warm steam iron. A pressing cloth is a good investment, especially for use with delicate or coated fabrics.

Turning tool

A long wire-like object with a hook at the end makes turning fabrics for loops and decorative cording much easier than old-fashioned methods.

Scissors

Make sure your scissors are sharp. Fabrics can be damaged by blunt scissors. Dressmaking shears are the most commonly used and are ideal for everyday projects. Embroidery scissors are useful for appliqué and cutting out intricate shapes. Pinking shears are a useful timesaving device for finishing seam allowances.

Sewing machine

You do not necessarily need a top-of-the-line machine for sewing soft furnishings. It is important that your sewing machine is able to handle a range of tension variations for sewing different weights of fabric, and that it can sew a basic straight stitch, a zigzag stitch, insert a zipper and make a buttonhole. The latest electronic machines feature many embroidery stitch variations which are wonderful for adding decorative interest to your project.

Regular oiling of machine parts and cleaning with a fine brush may be all that is required to keep your sewing machine in top working order for many years.

Specialized machine feet are available for a variety of specific tasks, such as attaching a zipper, sewing a buttonhole, ruffling and darning. A zipper foot is also a great asset for inserting piping. Rufflers are a great timesaver for adding long lengths of ruffles while hemming, and blind stitch feet make hems a breeze. A quilting foot, which has marked stitching guidelines is very handy for sewing quilting patterns on table napkins, quilts and pillow covers.

A variety of machine needle sizes are also essential, including a size 9 (65) for the finest fabrics, size 11 (75) or size 14 (90) for medium-weight cottons, and a size 18 (110) for heavy brocades or velvets.

A stitch guide is a magnetic device that can be attached to the machine bed or plate and will help you to maintain even seam widths.

Tape measure

A tape measure made from flexible synthetic or fiberglass material is essential, so that measurements can't be distorted by tearing or stretching of the tape. Make sure your tape measure is in good condition and with ends that are not damaged or frayed. A metal tape or ruler is also necessary for measuring window dimensions and for drawing the straight long edges required when making bonded blinds. A T-square is also very useful for ruling straight lines, as is a set of French curves for curved lines.

Tailor's chalk

Chalk should be used to mark fabric; after sewing, the chalk can easily be removed with a stiff brush. Air or water-soluble pens and pencils are a good alternative.

Most of the equipment is already in your home

Stitch Guide

Basting (fig. 1)

This is a row of larger-than-usual running stitches which are used to temporarily join fabrics together. Start with a knot, then take even stitches along the seam line. This can also be done with a sewing machine.

Gathering (figs. 2 and 3)

A running stitch is used to pull up excess width. Knot the thread end securely or take a small back stitch to begin. It is best to have two rows of stitches, $1/8"$-$1/4"$ (3mm-6mm) apart, either side of the seam line. Two rows gives more even gathering and gives a little insurance in case one thread breaks while you are pulling up the threads. Pull up the threads carefully until you achieve the desired length. Secure the gathering by knotting the two threads together or with several back stitches.

Overcasting (fig. 4)

This is a method for finishing a raw edge or loosely joining two pieces of fabric. Make small diagonal stitches, keeping the tension loose.

Blanket stitch (fig. 5)

This is another stitch commonly used to finish raw edges. As its name implies, it was the usual way of finishing the edges of blankets. It is now more commonly used for embroidery. Pass the needle from the front through to the back, about $1/4"$ (6mm) from the edge. Keeping the thread close to the fabric under the point of the needle, pull the needle through, forming a loop on the fabric edge.

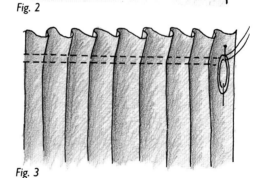

Fig. 1

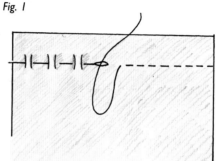

Fig. 2

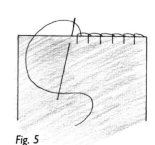

Fig. 3

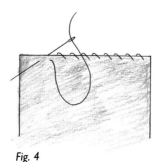

Fig. 4

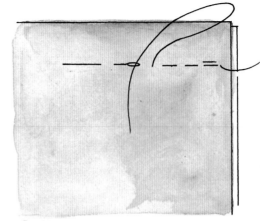

Fig. 5

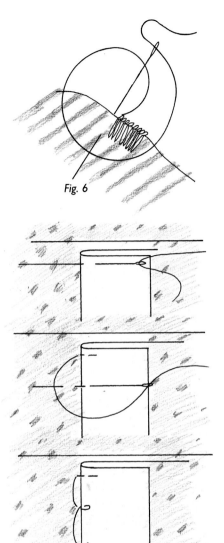

Fig. 6

Fig. 7

Buttonhole stitch (fig. 6)

This stitch is similar to blanket stitch but is worked from the back to the front with the stitches lying very close together. Pass the thread under the needle before pulling the stitch through.

Lock stitch (fig. 7)

This stitch is often used to secure a lining to an outer fabric where the stitching should not be visible, such as on the sides of curtains. Pin the two fabrics together with the lining on top, right side up. Fold back the lining and work loose blanket stitches, joining the folded edge to the fabric beneath. Make sure the stitches are big and loose so that the fabric falls without puckers.

Slipstitch (fig. 8)

This is a most useful stitch for all types of handsewing, particularly when openings in seams need to be closed or for finishing corners. Working on the right side of your work, take a small stitch in the fold on one edge of fabric and then through the fold on the opposite edge. Pull up the stitches to bring the edges together taking care to not pull the thread too tightly.

Hemstitch (fig. 9)

Small diagonal stitches catch the fabric to the hem. Pick up only a few threads at a time so they are not too visible on the right side. Try to keep the stitching even, without pulling the fabric.

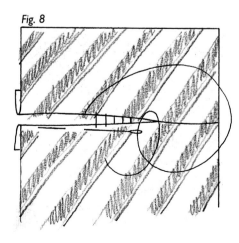

Fig. 8

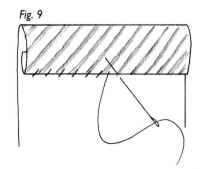

Fig. 9

Ladder stitch (figs. 1 and 2)

This stitch is useful for joining two patterned fabrics where the pattern must be matched perfectly on both sides. Press the seam allowance under on one side. Place the folded edge over the raw edge of the other piece of fabric until the patterns match exactly, then pin the top piece in place. Taking small stitches, pass the needle along the inside of the fold so the stitches lie on the lower fabric close to the fold.

Seams

❖

Flat seam (figs. 3 and 4)

Place two fabrics with right sides together. Stitch the seam with the required seam allowance. Trim the seam if necessary, then press it open.

Flat fell seam (figs. 3 to 5)

Place two fabrics with right sides together. Stitch a $^1/_2$" (1.2cm) seam. Trim the seam allowance on one side back to $^1/_4$" (6mm), then press the seam open. Press the raw edge on the longer side over then fold it again, covering and enclosing the seam allowances. Stitch in place close to the folded edge.

French seam (figs. 6 to 9)

Place fabrics together with the wrong sides facing. Stitch a $^1/_2$" (1.2cm) seam. Trim the seam allowance back to $^1/_4$" (6mm). Fold the fabrics along the seam line so that the right sides are facing. Stitch a seam, $^3/_8$" (1cm) from the folded edge, enclosing the raw edges of the first seam as you sew. Press the seam to one side.

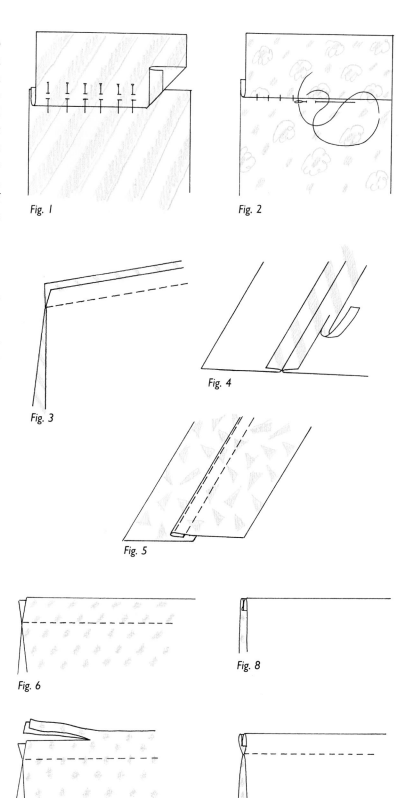

Fig. 1

Fig. 2

Fig. 3

Fig. 4

Fig. 5

Fig. 6

Fig. 7

Fig. 8

Fig. 9

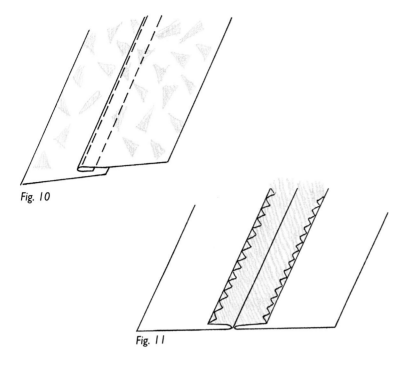

Fig. 10

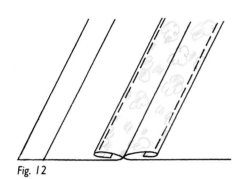

Fig. 11

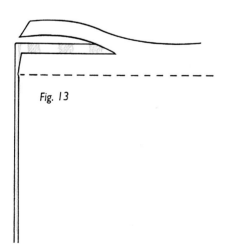

Fig. 12

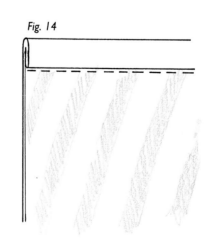

Fig. 13

Fig. 14

Lapped seam (fig. 10)

Press $\frac{5}{8}$" (1.5cm) under on one edge of one fabric. Pin it on to the right side of the second piece of fabric, $\frac{3}{8}$" (1cm) from the raw edge. On the right side, machine-stitch along the fold. Pin and stitch again $\frac{1}{4}$" (6mm) away.

Zigzag finishing (fig. 11)

This stitch is most often used to finish raw edges on seams. Select the stitch width and length that best suits your fabric.

Edgestitch finishing (fig. 12)

Stitch a flat seam and press the seam allowances open. Turn under $\frac{1}{8}$" (3mm) on both raw edges and stitch close to the folded edge, keeping the main fabric free.

Self-bound seams (figs. 13 to 14)

This seam is similar to a flat fell seam except that it is not stitched flat. With the right sides of the fabrics together, stitch a flat seam. Trim the seam allowance on one side to half its original width. Fold the other seam allowance over it. Fold the raw edge under and slipstitch in place at the seam line.

Curtains

UNLINED CURTAINS

TIE-ON CURTAINS

LINED CURTAINS

CAFE CURTAINS

SHIRRED CURTAIN PANEL

DECORATOR SCARF

CURTAIN TRIMS

SWAGS AND JABOTS

TIEBACKS

VALANCES

Curtains

BY CHOOSING THE CORRECT WINDOW TREATMENT, YOU CAN CONTROL THE
LEVEL OF LIGHT ADMITTED, CREATE VARYING LEVELS OF PRIVACY, REDUCE
NOISE AND, TO A CERTAIN EXTENT, BLOCK OUT HEAT AND COLD.

Over the years, architectural styles have been the major factor in determining the types of windows found in a home. Additions and alterations to a home at different architectural periods will usually result in a variety of windows that are rarely uniform in size or shape. This allows plenty of scope for variation in window treatments.

The basic functions of a window are to allow light and air to flow through the house and to keep cold and rain out.

While it is often costly or too difficult to alter the shape or position of a window, the choice and style of your window treatment can transform the look and feel of a room.

Window shapes

Before deciding how to dress a window, it is a good idea to understand the basic window types and how their shape affects the choice of window treatment.

Double-hung windows
In this type of window, two sashes move up and down to open and close the window. It is usually the easiest style to decorate and one of the most common in modern homes; more elaborate versions are found in many Georgian period homes. Many different window treatments can be used to complement the double-hung window, including Austrian and Roman shades.

Picture windows
This style of window is also found in many modern homes where an extensive window is used to frame an outside

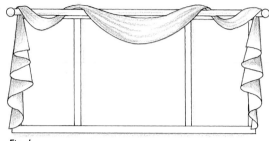

Fig. 1

view, hence the term "picture window". It is often a combination of a large fixed center window with double-hung windows at the sides for ventilation (fig. 1). Due to the size of picture windows, there are many opportunities for window decoration. Large scale prints and patterns become much easier to work with on a window of this size. Linings are an important feature when decorating picture windows – remember the lining can be seen quite clearly from the outside.

Ranch, clerestory or strip windows
This type of window is often found in

modern homes with high ceilings, or in split-level homes, as it allows plenty of light into a living area while maximizing wall space. Consider a plain window treatment, using small-scale prints or solids.

Corner windows
To maximize light, two windows may meet in a corner, leaving only a small amount of space between them. Even though you may feel limited in your choices when it comes to dressing these windows, you may be surprised to find there are a number of practical and decorative options available (fig. 2).

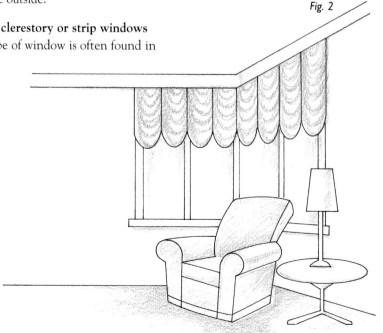

Fig. 2

Bay windows

A bay window has three or more windows set at an angle to each other to form an inside alcove. This style of window can be dressed up with individual decorative treatments for each window, or played down by adopting a uniform style for all the windows (fig. 3).

Dormer windows

A dormer window is deeply recessed, often providing an area for a window seat. These windows are a feature of attics and of upper floor extensions to existing homes. Dormer windows usually require special window treatments, and decorative valances can often be used to define a dormer window.

French doors

This elegant window style can take several forms, the most common consisting of a pair of inward or outward opening doors, often flanked by vertical windows. This style is often best treated as an individual window, allowing for a number of options (fig. 4).

Sliding doors

Many modern homes have sliding doors, allowing maximum light filtration and easy access to a garden or courtyard. They require special attention when it comes to choosing coverings that maintain their function as doors but also provide night-time privacy and warmth (fig. 5).

A creative curtain treatment for an unusual window

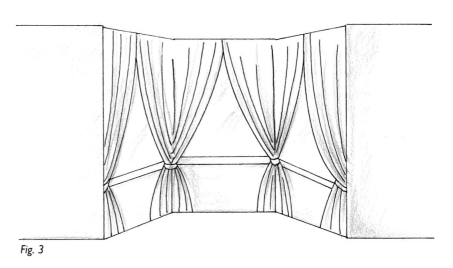

Fig. 3

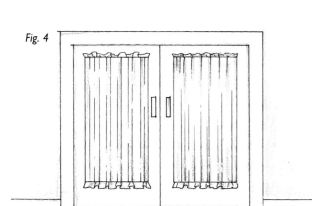

Fig. 4

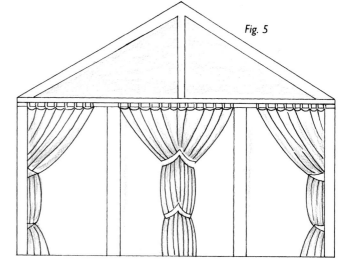

Fig. 5

Rods & poles

More than ever, the variety of hardware available to hang, drape and support window treatments is extensive and interesting. From the simple conduit or rod we now have ornate and decorative poles, fashioned from wood, cast iron and brass which add a decorator's touch to your windows.

Choosing the right rod or pole is crucial. Never underestimate the importance of the hardware that you use to mount your curtains. Don't fall into the trap of investing time and money in making a wonderfully sumptuous curtain from expensive fabrics and trims only to find that the flimsy pole you have purchased will not support the weight of the curtains.

The quality of the hardware you purchase will ultimately determine how your curtain will hang, just as your selection of heading tape will define how it drapes. Remember to match

hooks, gliders and finials (the decorative pieces at the ends of the pole that stop the curtains from sliding off) to the style of the curtain heading tape you have chosen.

Beautiful curtains must sit squarely on accurately positioned fittings. Use a retractable fiberglass or metal tape measure and carefully measure the window dimensions, frame size and the distance from the top of the window frame to the ceiling, from the bottom of the window frame to the floor and from the sides of the window frame to the corners of adjacent walls. These measurements are essential when planning special effects; for example, if you wish to create an impression of height on a shallow window, you can do this by hanging long curtains from poles or rods raised well above the natural top of the window or even suspended from the ceiling.

Your choice of curtain poles or tracks will be based on the shape and function of your window, the effect you

want to create, and your budget. If you are adding a valance, select a simple rod and a simple heading style for your curtain because both will be covered by the valance.

If you live in a rented home or apartment, opt for poles which are usually less expensive, easier to install, and highly portable. Special extendable poles will allow you to change the length of the pole to suit different windows as needed.

Unless curtains are frequently drawn, poles work best for heavy drapes which frame a window, or for lightweight privacy curtains. More sophisticated poles may be fitted with draw-cords and decorative finials. Prices will vary according to the style you choose.

Rods range from simple, straight or curved styles to pricier, composite products which can support both curtains and valances. These may have extension brackets to vary the distance between the curtains, the walls and the valance. Multiple rod systems are usually used when two or more window treatments are combined over a single window frame. A combination of a sheer shade, a curtain and a valance is an example of a window treatment requiring a multiple-rod system.

Always anchor poles or rods firmly with strong brackets screwed to wooden battens, or attached with wall plugs.

If possible, avoid hanging new curtains on old rods or poles. Choose fittings appropriate to the shape and style of your curtains. Heavy curtains may require special reinforcement, especially if they will be frequently opened and closed.

Purchased kits should contain everything you will need, including extra supporting brackets that are spaced at intervals between the usual end and center brackets.

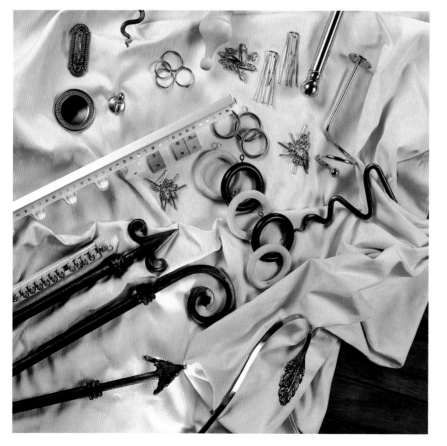

A selection of curtain rods, poles and hardware

Choose fittings that frame your windows beautifully and do their job reliably. Make sure the rod you choose allows heavy curtains to completely retract to maximize light. For recessed windows, select flexible or curved tracks which fit the shape of modern bay windows hung with one continuous curtain or three separate ones. Traditional bay windows in three sections separated by wide corner frames can use a single rod or three separate curtain poles. Instead of finials (end-stops), fit the last hook to a wall-mounted ring-fitting to hide the ends of the rod and to avoid ugly gaps between curtains and walls. Never hang curtains straight across the face of a recessed window; this will darken the room and detract from the charm of a traditional bay or dormer window.

Curtain headings

❖

The finished style of a curtain or blind will depend on your choice of heading tape. Different heading tapes cause the curtain to fall or drape in various ways. You can choose neat pleats for a formal look, soft gathers for a romantic style, or a curtain shirred into a flurry of folds for volume and definition.

The choice of tape will also determine how the curtain is to be connected to the rod and what hardware, such as hooks, will be needed. Here we show you how finished heading styles are achieved with certain types of tape as well as which poles and hardware will combine to produce the look you are aiming for. Embellishments such as covered buttons, tabs and bows can then be added to create your own style.

Gathered heading

Simple gathered headings can be achieved with a standard shirring tape, which gathers the fabric and is generally used where a valance is included in the window-dressing plan. Allow at least one and a half times the length of the rod in fabric width. The actual width will depend on the type of fabric and the effect you want to create. Experiment with a swatch of fabric before purchasing the entire amount. A simple hook connects the curtain tape to the rod or ring.

Rod pocket

This is another way of achieving a simple gathered curtain but without tape or hooks. Although the method of construction is simple, the inclusion of bindings and trims will make the final result quite sophisticated. Allow twice the length of the rod for the width of your fabric.

A rod pocket curtain

Pencil-pleated heading

This very popular heading style forms a continuous line of even pencil pleats. The advantage of this style of curtain is that it can be adjusted – either stretched or condensed – if your measurements are not one-hundred-percent accurate. Pencil-pleating tape is suitable for most fabric weights and for either rods or poles. For best coverage, you will need fabric from two to two and a half times the width of the rod (figs. 1 and 2).

Triple-pleated heading

This formal style of heading is most commonly used on solid fabrics or where a tailored look is desired. Allow twice the length of the rod in fabric width to achieve this style (figs. 3 and 4).

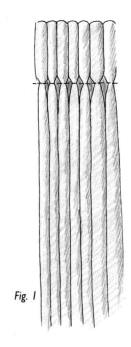

Fig. 1

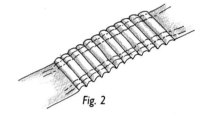

Fig. 2

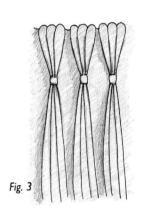

Fig. 3

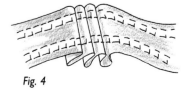

Fig. 4

Cartridge-pleated heading

Ideal for heavier weight fabrics such as velvets or brocades, cartridge-pleating tape draws the fabric into evenly spaced ruched cartridge pleats. To ensure that the two curtains match in the center of the rod, it is important to check the spacing of the pleats. You will need from two to two and a half times the rod length in fabric width (figs. 1 and 2).

Box-pleated heading

When this tape is pulled up, the fabric pulls into evenly spaced box pleats, again ideal for heavier fabrics and, like cartridge-pleating, it is necessary to ensure that the pleats are matched across both curtains. To be successful, box-pleating tape requires two and a half times the rod length in fabric width (figs. 3 and 4).

How much tape?

To determine the amount of heading tape required for your curtains, use the same method as for calculating fabric widths for the style of tape you are using. Allow an additional 4" (10cm) for turning under the ends.

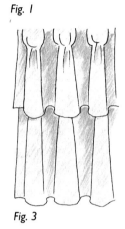

Fig. 1

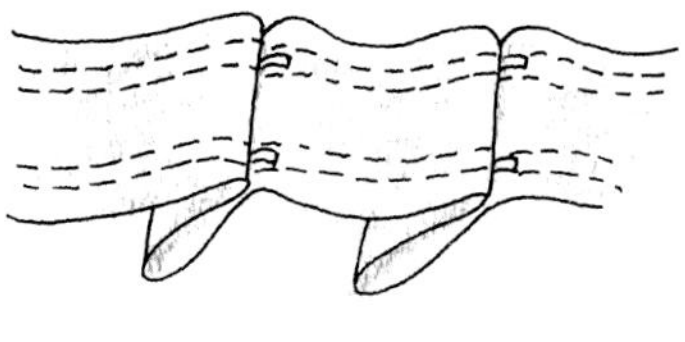

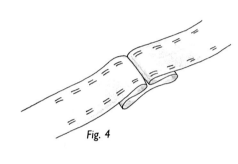

Fig. 2

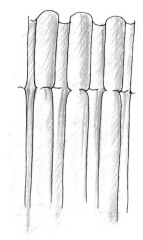

Fig. 3

Fig. 4

Measuring

❖

Measuring your windows for curtains is a simple process. To measure accurately you will need a metal ruler, and notepaper and a pen to take down the measurements. To ensure that accurate figures are recorded, it is better if there are two people to measure for curtains.

If you are installing new rods or poles, do not measure for your curtains before the rods or poles are in place. Rods should extend up to 12" (30cm) beyond the sides of the window to allow for the curtains to be drawn back.

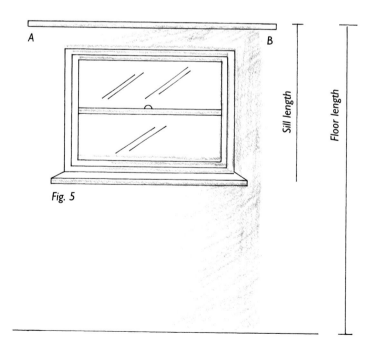

A   B   Sill length   Floor length

Fig. 5

The width

Measure the exact length of the rod or pole between the two points where the curtain will drape (A and B) – do not measure the window (fig. 5).

If the rod or pole has overlaps or returns, measure from the edge of the return to the end of the overlap on both the right- and left-hand sides.

The length

The length of your curtains is a matter of personal preference. However, in the majority of cases there are three obvious lengths to choose from: sill length; below sill length; or floor length (fig. 5).

Curtains should finish approximately $3/8$" (1cm) above the sill or 1" (2.5cm) from the floor. The length should be measured from the top of the curtain rod or, if using a pole with rings, from the underside of the ring (fig. 6).

A solid fabric needs no pattern matching

Fig. 6

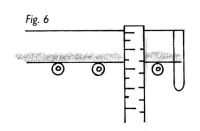

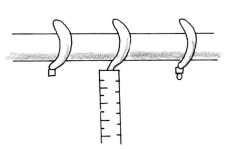

Fabric requirements

❖

After deciding which rod or pole type to use and the style of your curtains, it is now time to calculate the amount of fabric you will require to complete the project.

First determine the pattern repeat (see page 17). The supplier's tag attached to the roll of fabric should state the size of the repeat. If not, the assistant in the soft furnishings department should be able to help you determine the repeat.

Always check your calculations twice and feel free to show them to a soft furnishings expert where you purchase your fabric. They will be very happy to give you their professional advice. Remember to give them the length and style of your pole or rod, as well as the curtain length required, to ensure they have all the necessary information.

If you are still unsure about your measurements, it is always best to buy an extra yard or meter of fabric which

could get you out of a jam. If the fabric is not used for the curtain, it can always be made into a pillow or a trim, or used for coordinating tiebacks.

Solid (unpatterned) fabric

Where you have a solid fabric with no patterns to match, calculations are easy to make following the steps below.

To calculate the total length of fabric required when there is no pattern match, use the following measurements:

1 Total width = finished width + side hem allowance + any joining seam allowance + allowance for fullness

2 Number of fabric widths required = total width/fabric width (always round this figure up to the next whole number; for example, six and a half = seven)

3 Fabric cut length = finished length + hem allowance + top heading allowance + 1" (2.5cm) for squaring or ravelling ends

4 Total fabric required = cut length x the number of fabric widths

Patterned fabric

Correct pattern match will ensure that the finished design running across your window is uniform.

The calculation method is the same for steps 1 and 2 as for unpatterned fabrics; however, in step 3, determining the cut length is a little different. To do this, see how many times the pattern is repeated down a width so that each width can be cut and matched accurately. Again, always purchase that extra yard or meter of fabric to get you out of trouble if required.

To calculate the total fabric required for a patterned fabric, use the following measurements:

1 Total width = finished width + side hem allowances + any joining seam allowances + allowance for fullness

2 Number of fabric widths required = total width/fabric width (always round this figure up to the next whole number; for example, six and a half = seven)

3 Number of repeats required for each cut length = cut length/pattern repeat length (round this figure up if the answer is a fraction)

4 Adjusted cut length = the pattern repeat x number of repeats required for each cut length + allowances for hem and heading

5 Total fabric required = adjusted cut length x number of widths required

Linings

❖

Linings add substantially to the luxurious appearance necessary for good window treatments. They also provide a fuller look for maintaining soft drapability as well as protecting fabric from the elements.

When you are selecting a fabric, consider the function it will perform. If your home fronts on to a major thoroughfare, you will want to ensure that noise is eliminated or lessened. A heavy woven fabric will act as an insulator and, given the extra volume of lining fabric, the noise will be even further reduced.

As with fabrics, there are a number of lining options to be considered:
• Does your fabric need to be lined?
• Does your window face early morning or afternoon sun?
• Is the curtain purely decorative?

Unlined pattern fabrics or sheers can provide interesting illusionary effects when light is filtered through them, giving a dappled warm feeling to a room. However, linings add many benefits to a finished curtain. Firstly, linings add a more luxurious

Linings can be attached at the curtain heading

look to a good window treatment, help to provide better draping qualities, and maintain a fuller pleated look. A lined curtain gives uniformity to the exterior appearance of a home while allowing a variety of decorative choices such as patterns, weaves and color variation to be used inside. While sunlight and air pollution have varying effects on the color of a fabric, a lining will help to combat these elements, helping to keep the inside of your home warmer during the cooler months, cooler during the summer, and your fabric looking fresher for much longer. The extra fabric will absorb some of the noise of your teenager's stereo; no doubt an added bonus for your neighbors.

There are two major types of linings:

tightly woven one-hundred-per-cent cotton lining, which comes in a variety of neutral tonings and in the same widths as your fabric; and a lining with a coating made from particles of aluminum, which may be flocked to give it good draping properties. In addition there are block-out linings which consist of layers of coatings with a layer of grey aluminum particles sandwiched in between for light diffusion. These linings are excellent for bedrooms, especially for shiftworkers needing to sleep at odd hours; for windows that face the afternoon sun; in nurseries; or in commercial applications, such as hotels, where complete sun block-out may be required throughout the day.

As well as loose linings, some fabrics come with their own coating flocked directly on to the back of the fabric. The bonus is that you only need to handle one layer of fabric while sewing, but the curtain will still have the drape, handling and insulating qualities of one with a lining.

Linings can be attached in a number of ways. One way to attach a loose lining to a curtain is with a lining tape known as pocket tape. The tape splits in half, with one half sewn to the lining and the other half, which contains small pockets, sewn to the curtain fabric. Hooks are passed through both tapes, fastening the lining to the curtain. This arrangement also means that drapes and linings can be easily separated for cleaning.

Another popular method for attaching linings is to sew the curtain and lining fabrics edge to edge. Here heading and side hems are sewn together as for a bag, and the bottom hems are treated separately. This is an ideal method to add weights into lining and hems for the ultimate professional look.

Pattern matching & joining panels

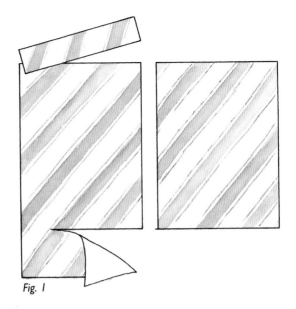

Fig. 1

To match patterns

1 Cut the first fabric length from the the fabric, with the beginning of a pattern repeat at the top edge, and lay it flat on a table (fig. 1). Mark the pattern repeat with two pins or tailors chalk and fold under the selvages.

2 Before cutting the second length of fabric, find the beginning of the next pattern repeat and measure the required length from this point, allowing for any necessary seam allowance above this point.

3 Fold in the selvages and baste the two pieces together so that the repeats are matching. Continue in this way, adding as many lengths as you require.

4 Trim the top and bottom edges even when all the lengths are joined.

Joining panels

Ideally, fabric panels should be joined in such a way that the stitching is as unobtrusive as possible.

1 Place the two panels together with right sides facing. Stitch them together with a $^5/_8$" (1.5cm) seam and press the seam flat (fig. 2).

2 Trim the seam allowance on one side back to $^1/_8$" (3mm) and turn in $^1/_8$" (3mm) on the raw edge of the other seam allowance (figs. 3 and 4).

3 Press the folded edge over to the seam line on the other fabric piece, enclosing the raw edges. Slipstitch the folded edge over the previous stitching (fig. 5).

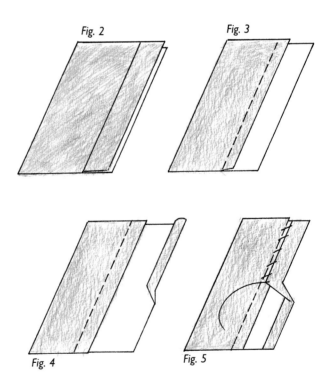

Fig. 2

Fig. 3

Fig. 4

Fig. 5

Scale & proportion

❖

Less-than-ideal room or window proportions can be improved through the use of visual effects. While this particularly applies to paints and wallpaper, you can also contribute greatly by choosing the right fabric and style for your window treatments.

A narrow window can be made to look wider by extending the curtain rod or pole for 12"-24" (30cm-61cm) on each side (fig. 1). To diminish the size of a too-large window, pull the curtains back to the sides of the sill in a graceful drape and secure them with interesting tiebacks or bows (fig. 2). To avoid covering a wall-mounted heater or air conditioner, either stop the curtains at the lower sill length or permanently fix drapes to either side of the window, adding a pull-down shade for privacy (fig. 3).

Window heights can appear to be increased or decreased with the addition of a valance. To add height to a too-short window, mount the valance 6" (15cm) above the top window frame, making sure the depth of the valance covers the frame and the heading tape on the curtains. Deep valances will also diminish the height of a too-tall window when fixed snugly onto the window frame (fig. 4).

Fig. 1

Fig. 2

Fig. 3

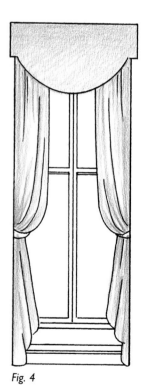

Fig. 4

The valance has been fixed higher than usual to give the appearance of a taller window

Unlined Curtains

THE SIMPLEST OF ALL CURTAINS ARE THE ROD POCKET AND
SHIRRING TAPE UNLINED CURTAINS.

Rod pocket curtain

Before you begin Fabrics with a back coating are not suited to this style of curtain, because over time the coating can stick to the metal rod due to the effects of heat and moisture, sometimes causing it to peel away.

Measuring

To calculate the total width of fabric, double the length of your rod and add ⅝" (1.5cm) for each joining seam and 1" (2.5cm) for each side hem. If your curtain will consist of two panels opening at the center, divide the total width by two. Determine the length of the curtain by measuring from 1" (2.5 cm) above the top of the rod (or the point you wish your heading to commence) to the point where your curtain will finish. Add an additional 4¾" (12cm) for the bottom hem and 4" (10cm) for the heading and casing. Calculate the amount of fabric you will need, following the guide on page 41 and taking into account any additional fabric required for pattern matching (see page 42).

following the guide on page 41 ... (see page 42).

MATERIALS
sufficient fabric
matching sewing machine thread
sufficient 4¾" (12cm)-wide contrasting bias-cut fabric to bind the edges of your curtain
pins
scissors
tape measure
sewing machine

Method

1 Cut the number of lengths needed for the total width. Trim the selvages. Pin, then stitch the lengths together with a flat fell seam. Press.

2 Press ⅜" (1cm) under on one long edge of each curtain panel (the edge that will be the outer edge of the curtain), then press another ⅝" (1.5cm) under. Pin and stitch the side hem. Press the hem.

3 Press in ⅜" (1cm) under on both sides of the bias-cut fabric. Fold the bias strip in half with wrong sides together and pressed edges even. Press.

4 Pin the folded bias strip over the remaining raw side edge of each curtain panel (the inner edge of the curtain).

A rod pocket curtain is quick and easy to make

Turn the raw edges under at each end of the binding. Pin, then stitch through both sides of the bias strip.

5 Measure the diameter of your rod. Press ³/₈" (1cm) to the wrong side at the top edge of the curtain, then another 3¹/₂" (9cm). Stitch along the folded edge. This line of stitching will fall underneath the rod.

6 Stitch a second line of stitching the diameter of the rod plus ³/₈" (1cm) above the previous stitching to form the casing. Slip the rod into the casing and adjust the gathers evenly. Hang the curtain and leave it for a day or two before you hem it.

7 Once your curtain is in position, determine how long you want it to be. Remember, if the curtain is to be pulled or tied back on each side, allow extra length. Mark the hem position while the curtain is hanging. Machine-stitch the hem, or slipstitch it in place. Either way, it is a good idea to take the curtain down and press the hem first, before sewing it.

Distribute the gathers evenly

❖

Shirring tape curtain

Before you begin Laces, voiles and sheers are ideal fabrics for use with shirring tape. Shirring tape is not recommended for heavier fabrics where the more durable pencil-pleating tape would be a better choice and will achieve a similar look.

Shirring tape is suitable for unlined curtains or small windows where there is not much fabric to add bulk and weight to the curtain. However, a loose cotton lining can be added and coated fabrics can also be used.

Measuring

To determine the total width of fabric needed, measure the length of your rod. Multiply by two or, for greater fullness, by two and a half, to give the total width, then add ⁵/₈" (1.5cm) for each joining seam and 1" (2.5cm) for each side seam. If your curtain will consist of two panels opening at the centre, divide the total width by two. To determine the length of the curtain, measure from the top of the rod to the point where you wish your curtain to finish, then add 4³/₄" (12cm) for the bottom hem and an additional 2³/₄" (7cm) for the curtain heading.

Calculate the amount of fabric you will need following the guide on page 41 and taking into account any additional fabric required for pattern matching (see page 42).

You will need the same length of tape as the total fabric width plus 4" (10cm) for turning under.

MATERIALS
sufficient fabric
matching sewing machine thread
sufficient shirring tape and appropriate hooks
pins
scissors
tape measure
sewing machine

Fig. 1

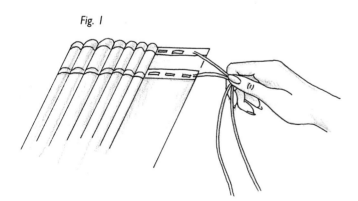

Fig. 2

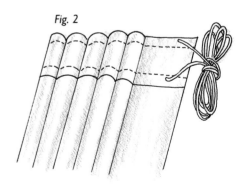

Method

1 Cut the number of lengths required to achieve the total width of your curtain. Trim the selvages. Pin, then stitch the lengths together with a flat fell seam. Press the seams.

2 Press $^3/_8$" (1cm), then another $^5/_8$" (1.5cm) under on the outside edges of the curtain. Pin and stitch the side hems. Press.

3 Press $^3/_4$" (2cm) then 2" (5cm) to the wrong side at the top edge. Position the shirring tape on the wrong side of the fabric, 1" (2.5cm) from the folded edge. Pin the tape in place, folding the raw ends of the tape under. Stitch the tape in place. Knot the cords together at one end of the tape. Pull up the tape from the other end, forming folds (fig. 1).

4 Hang the curtains in place. Adjust the width and the amount of gathering, then tie off the cords (fig. 2). You can also cut off any excess cord to avoid unnecessary bulk.

5 If the curtain has a loose weave, allow it to hang for a day or two before hemming, then mark the hem position. Take the curtain down. Press $^3/_4$" (2cm), then the remaining hem to the wrong side. Stitch the hem in place and press.

Above right: The lace Austrian shade is made in exactly the same way as the Austrian shade on page 84

Far right: A close-up of the shirring tape

Right: Detail of the pencil pleated tape used for the valance

Tie-on Curtains

TIE-ON CURTAINS ARE IDEAL IF YOU HAVE DECORATIVE POLES WHICH YOU WANT
TO FEATURE AS PART OF THE OVERALL EFFECT OF YOUR WINDOW SETTING.

Before you begin

This window treatment has the curtain bound on the sides and the top edge with a coordinating fabric. Again, the combination of color, print and texture will determine the final effect. The ties were made from a second coordinating fabric.

Measuring

To calculate the total width of fabric you will need, measure the length of your rod. Multiply by two and a half and add $5/8$" (1.5cm) for each joining seam and 1" (2.5cm) for each side seam. If your curtain will consist of two panels opening at the centre, divide the total width by two. Determine the length of the curtain by measuring from 1" (2.5cm) above the top of the rod (or the point where you wish your heading to start) to the point where you wish the curtain to finish. Add $4^{3}/4$" (12cm) for the bottom hem and another 4" (10cm) for the curtain heading.

MATERIALS
sufficient fabric
two contrasting fabrics for the borders and the ties
matching sewing machine thread
sufficient shirring tape
plastic or metal rings, one for every 4" (10cm) of tape used
tailor's chalk
pins
tape measure
scissors
sewing machine

Method

1 Cut the number of lengths required to achieve the total width of the curtain. Trim the selvages. Pin, then stitch the lengths together with a flat fell seam. Press.

2 Cut two 9" (23cm)-wide strips, each the same length as the panel. Press $3/8$" (1cm) to the wrong side on both raw edges of the strips. Press the binding in

Make the ties from matching or contrasting fabric, or use ribbon

half with the wrong sides together. Pin the binding over the raw edges of the curtains, sandwiching the curtain between the folded edges of the binding. Stitch through all thicknesses.

3 Cut a strip 4" (10cm) wide and bind the top edge of the curtain in the same manner, turning the raw edges under at each end.

4 Pin the shirring tape to the top of the wrong side of the curtain, 3" (7.5cm) from the top. Stitch in place around all edges.

5 Cut bias strips, 4" x $8^{1}/2$" (10cm x 22cm) for ties. Fold each length in half with the right sides together and matching raw edges. Stitch the long side and one end closed with a $3/8$" (1cm) seam. Turn the tie right side out and press. Slipstitch the remaining end closed.

6 Fold the ties in half and pin them, evenly spaced, across the back of the curtain, approximately $3/8$" (1cm) from the top of the heading tape (fig. 1).

7 Pull up the heading tape to the desired width and secure the cords.

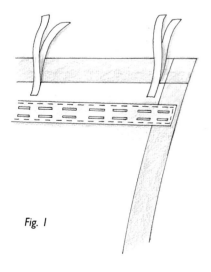

Fig. 1

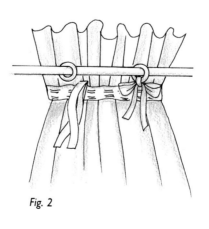

Fig. 2

Attach the curtain to the rings by tying the ties into bows (fig. 2).

8 Once the curtain is hung, determine the final length. If the curtain is to be pulled back to the sides, add extra length to allow for this. Mark the hemline with tailor's chalk or pins, then remove the curtain. Press ³/₄" (2cm) to the wrong side, then the remaining hem. Stitch in place close to the fold by hand or machine. Slipstitch the ends of the hem together.

Tie-on curtains have a delightfully informal look

Lined Curtains

CURTAINS CAN EITHER HAVE A LOOSE LINING, ATTACHED AT THE
HEADING, OR A DETACHABLE LINING.

Pinch-pleated curtain with loose lining

Before you begin Usually, no valance is required with this heading as it is an attractive finish in its own right. Often found in living or formal dining rooms, pinch-pleated curtains can be used wherever you are looking for a neat, tailored finish. Loose linings are the perfect partner.

The method for loose linings is somewhat different to detachable linings in that the lining is fixed in place before the heading tape is applied. Fabrics with an insulated backing or thermal coating provide an alternative to loose linings, create less bulk and also shorten your sewing time.

To make a fabric-covered rod, glue matching fabric around a wooden pole with craft glue. Add a pair of color-matched finials to complete the picture. With a little imagination, a piece of dowel can be converted into this delightful feature.

There are two types of pinch-pleating tapes: one has cords that are pulled up to form neat pinch pleats, the other has a series of slots to hold pronged hooks which form the pleat.

Measuring

To determine the total width of fabric you need, measure the length of your rod. Multiply by two and a half to give the final width, then add ⁵/₈" (1.5cm) for each joining seam and 1" (2.5cm)

Lined, pinch-pleated curtains have a generous appearance

for each side seam. If your curtain will consist of two or more panels, divide the total width by two or the appropriate number. To determine the length of the curtain, measure from the top of the rod to the point where you wish your curtain to finish. Add an additional 4³/₄" (12cm) for the lower hem and an additional 2³/₄" (7cm) for the heading. Calculate the amount of fabric you will need, following the

guide on page 41, and taking into account any additional fabric required for pattern matching (see page 42).

The same amount of fabric will be required for the lining, except that you will not need to allow any extra fabric for pattern matching.

You will need the same length of tape as the total fabric width plus 4" (10cm) for returns.

Top: Hang the curtain with
color-matched rings

Above: Pinch-pleating tape draws up
the lining and the fabric together

MATERIALS
sufficient fabric and lining
matching sewing machine thread
pinch-pleating tape and appropriate hooks
tape measure
pins
scissors
sewing machine

Method

1 Cut the number of lengths needed to achieve the total width of your curtain. Remember to cut an even number of lengths for both panels. Trim the selvages. Pin, then stitch the lengths together with a flat fell seam. Press. Cut and join the lining pieces in the same manner.

2 Press a double hem on the lower edge of the lining so that it is 4" (10cm) shorter than the finished length of the curtain.

3 Center the lining on the wrong side of the curtain fabric. Pin the two layers together and from now on treat them as a single layer. Press ³/₈" (1cm), then ⁵/₈" (1.5cm) to the wrong side on the sides of the curtain and lining. Pin and stitch the side hems. Hem the top edge in the same manner.

4 Do not stitch the bottom hem of the curtain until the final hem adjustment is made.

5 Pin the tape to the top edge of the fabric, on top of the lining, folding the raw end under. Stitch along both edges of the tape.

6 If the tape is the one that pleats, knot the cords together at one end of the tape and pull the cords up, forming the pleats. If the tape is the slotted type, insert the pronged hooks. Both styles of tape will result in the same effect.

7 Hang the curtains in place. If the curtain is a loose-weave fabric, allow it to hang for a day or two then mark the correct length, before hemming. Remove the curtain. Press ³/₄" (2cm) to the wrong side at the lower edge, then the remaining hem width. Stitch the hem by hand or machine. Press.

Pencil-pleated curtain with detachable lining

Before you begin Quite often, where pencil-pleating tape is used the heading will ultimately be covered by a valance.

Pencil-pleating tape has three positional placings where hooks can be inserted to adjust the length of the curtains, if necessary.

Detachable linings provide the body and protection your curtain needs and, most importantly, detachable linings are quick and easy to remove for cleaning. They can be incorporated quite simply into most curtain treatments.

Measuring
To determine the amount of fabric needed, measure the length of your rod. Multiply by two or, for greater fullness, by two and a half, to give the total width, then add ⁵/₈" (1.5cm) for each joining seam and 1" (2.5cm) for each side seam. If your curtain has two panels opening at the center, divide the total width by two. To determine the length of the curtain, measure from the top of the rod to the point where you wish your curtain to finish. Add an additional 4³/₄" (12cm) for the lower hem and an additional 2³/₈" (6cm) for the heading. Calculate the amount of fabric you will need, following the guide on page 41 and taking into account any additional fabric required for pattern matching (see page 42).

The same amount of fabric will be required for the lining except that you will not need the allowance for pattern matching.

You will need the same length of tape as the total fabric width plus 4" (10cm) for returns.

MATERIALS
sufficient fabric and lining
matching sewing machine thread
pencil-pleating tape and appropriate hooks
small hooks for attaching the lining
pins
scissors
tape measure
sewing machine

Method

Curtain

1 Cut the number of lengths needed for the total width of your curtain. Remember to cut an even number of panels for both sides if your curtains open in the center. Trim the selvages. Pin, then stitch the lengths together with a flat fell seam. Press.

2 Press ³/₈" (1cm), then ⁵/₈" (1.5cm) to the wrong side at the sides of the curtain. Pin and stitch the side hems. Press.

3 Press 1" (2.5cm) to the wrong side on the top edge. Pin the tape into place along the top edge, covering the raw fabric edge and folding the raw edges of the tape under at each end. Stitch the tape in place. Knot the cords together at one end of the tape. Do not pull up the tape until the lining is attached.

Detachable lining

1 Cut and join the lining lengths the same as for the curtain. Make the side hems in the same manner.

2 Turn the raw edge on the top of the lining to the wrong side and attach the lining heading tape in the same manner as the curtain. Pull up the tapes on both the curtain and the lining. Tie off the ends but do not cut them.

3 Attach the lining to the bottom row of the pencil-pleating tape with the small hooks. Make any adjustment to the length of the tape on the curtain or lining.

4 Hang the curtain and lining on the rod. Allow the curtain to hang for a day or two before hemming. Mark the curtain hem. Remove the curtain and pin up both hems, making the lining hem 1" (2.5cm) shorter than the curtain hem. Press ³/₄" (2cm) to the wrong side, then the remaining hem for both the curtain and lining. Stitch both hems. Press the hems.

Above and left: This pencil-pleated curtain has a detachable lining

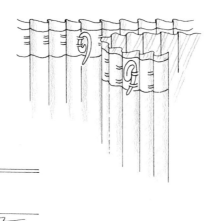

Figs. 1 and 2: The two main types of tape for detachable linings

Café Curtains

THIS SIMPLE METHOD OF WINDOW DRESSING WILL AFFORD PRIVACY AND AT THE SAME
TIME ALLOW PLENTY OF LIGHT TO ENTER THE ROOM.

Before you begin

Café curtains can be casual or formal, soft and feminine or dramatically contemporary, depending on the fabric you choose. Solid fabrics can be stenciled, appliquéd or trimmed with braid.

The style of café curtains has remained the same over the years, but with the increasing sophistication of decorative fabrics – such as chintzes, fine laces and linens – and the creative use of embellishment the café curtain has come of age.

Placement of rods

Before you begin making your café curtains, consider your window frame and then decide where to place your rods. Do you need total privacy or would you like to allow light to shine through and to be able to see out? Consider whether you want your curtains to overlap each other, giving an undulating effect down the window. You can create space between your curtains and highlight your rods by finishing the upper curtain $^3/_8$" (1cm) above the lower rod. This is particularly successful when working with special headings, such as a scalloped heading.

Windows with café curtains look better if the window is divided equally into halves, thirds or quarters.

If you have more than one vertical tier of curtains and privacy is paramount, overlap the lower edge of the upper curtain over the lower curtain about 3" (7.5cm). In this case, install the top rod then measure from the top of the rod (or from the bottom of the rings, if rings are to be used) to the finished length of the bottom curtain.

Divide this length by the number of tiers of curtains you are planning. If you plan a double tier, divide that length by two and mark this position on the window frame. Measure from this mark for 3" (7.5cm). This is the position for the second rod. If you are planning three tiers, divide the length into thirds. Mark the point for each rod 3" (7.5cm) up from the two lower markings.

If privacy is important, but you want to highlight decorative details, such as scallops, follow this method for mounting the rods to give you a perfect fit. Mount the top rod with a ring on it.

Rings are essential for scalloped curtains so measure the distance from the bottom of the rings to the finished length of the bottom tier. Divide this length by two or three, depending on the number of tiers. These are the positions of the bottom of your second and third rows of rings. Place the second rod at a suitable height above the second point (depending on the size of the rings) and position the third rod (if there is one) in the same way.

When a certain amount of privacy is desired, but you would still like to be able to look out over the bottom curtain, install spaced or graduated café curtains. Mount the top rod to the top of the window frame. Measure how long you would like the decorative valance to be by measuring from this rod. Measure from the bottom point of the decorative valance to the point where you wish the bottom curtain to finish. Divide this measurement in half and fix the second rod at that point for the best proportioned effect.

Hardware for café curtains

Hardware for café curtains need not be expensive. Covered wire casings with small hooks at either end can be used to mount café curtains on to your window frames. They remain hidden under the fabric folds of the finished curtain.

As with regular straight curtains, it is best to install the rods or wires before hanging the curtains.

Above left: This café curtain makes clever use of the fabric pattern

Left: A rod pocket heading is perfect for café curtains

Basic café curtains

Before you begin

To calculate the total width of fabric, measure the length of your rod or wire. Double the length and add ⁵⁄₈" (1.5cm) for each joining seam and 2" (5cm) for each side hem. For a two panel curtain, opening at the center, divide the total width by two. Determine the length by measuring from the bottom of the rings to the point where you wish the curtain to finish. (See page 53 for more on rod placement.) To this measurement add 6" (15cm) for the bottom hem and 2" (5cm) for the top hem.

This café curtain is hung with rings on café curtain wire

MATERIALS
sufficient fabric
café curtain wire and hooks or a rod
rings or hooks [you will need one for every 4" (10cm) of curtain width]
matching sewing machine thread
tailor's chalk
pins
scissors
tape measure
sewing machine

Method

1 Cut the number of lengths needed to make the correct width. Trim the selvages. Make sure you cut an even number of lengths for each side of the curtain if it is to open in the middle. Pin and stitch the lengths together with a flat fell seam. Press.

2 Press 3" (7.5cm) to the wrong side twice along the lower edge. Pin and stitch the bottom hem in place by hand or machine (fig. 1).

3 Press 1" (2.5cm) to the wrong side twice on the sides. Stitch the side hems (fig. 2).

4 Measure the finished length of the curtain from the bottom hemline to the top. With tailor's chalk, mark a dotted line along the right side of the fabric at this top point. Mark another dotted line 2" (5cm) above the first line. Trim any excess fabric above the second line (fig. 3).

5 Press 1" (2.5cm) to the wrong side on the top, then fold again so that the curtain will finish on the top dotted line. Stitch the hem in place and press.

6 Mark 4" (10cm) intervals along the top of the curtain. Handsew a ring at each marking.

Scalloped café curtains

Before you begin Scalloped café curtains are a stylish way to dress a window. Unlike other curtain styles they require less fullness – only one and a half times the rod length instead of the usual twice.

For a feminine touch, add decorative bows for attaching the curtain, rather than the traditional rings, or try sewing a number of shells or buttons to the top of your curtain for a fresh summer look. Sew eyelets into the tab headings and then twine a length of colored cord through the eyelets and over the rod for a country look.

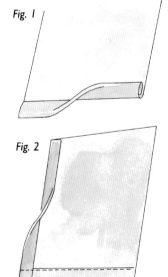

Fig. 1

Fig. 2

Fig. 3

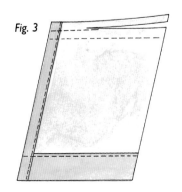

Measuring
To work out how much fabric you will need, follow the instructions for the basic café curtains, adding 4" (10cm) for the heading and another 6" (15cm) for the bottom hem. Allow 1" (2.5cm) for each side hem. If you need to join panels to achieve the desired width, add 3/8" (1.5cm) for both sides of the joining seams. If your curtain is to consist of two panels opening at the center, divide the total width by two.

MATERIALS
sufficient fabric
one hoop ring for every 4" (10cm) of curtain width and one for each end
glass or cup
firm plastic or cardboard for template
pencil
tailor's chalk or disappearing marker
matching sewing machine thread
pins
tape measure
scissors
sewing machine

Method

1 Cut the number of lengths required to achieve the total width of your curtain. If your curtain is to open in the middle, make sure you have an even number of lengths in both panels. Trim the selvages. Pin and stitch the lengths together with a flat fell seam. Press.

2 Press 3" (7.5cm) to the wrong side twice at the bottom edge. Pin and stitch the bottom hem in place by hand or by machine.

3 Press 3/8" (1cm) to the wrong side on the sides, then another 5/8" (1.5cm). Stitch the side hems.

4 Make a template or pattern for the scalloped edge, using a glass or cup. Our glass had a 4" (10cm) diameter and we allowed 3/4" (2cm) between each scallop. It is easier if you make a paper pattern with five or six scallops, rather than trying to use the cup for each scallop. You may need to make

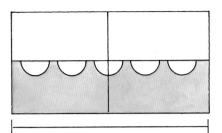

Fig. 4

a slight adjustment if you do not have room for a complete scallop at each end (fig. 4).

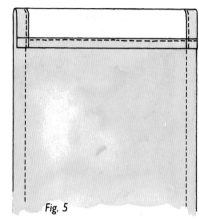

Fig. 5

5 Press 1/4" (6mm) to the wrong side twice at the top edge. Stitch in place.
6 With right sides together, fold the top of the curtain over 3 1/2" (9cm) and press. Pin the fold in place and slipstitch the sides together (fig. 5).
7 Pin the template on the fold line of scallops along the fold. Trace around the scallops with the tailor's chalk or disappearing marker. Remove the template (fig. 6).

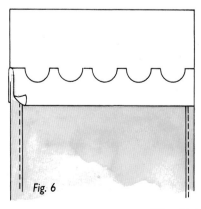

Fig. 6

Graceful scallops decorate this café curtain. Team it with a ruffled valance gathered onto a pole for a more formal look

8 Stitch along the marked lines. Cut out the scallops, $^1/_4$" (6mm) beyond the stitching. Trim and clip the seam allowance to just above the stitching line (fig. 1).

9 Turn the curtain right side out and press carefully. Take care to push out the corners at the top of each scallop. Slipstitch the side and lower edges of the scalloped panel to the curtain.

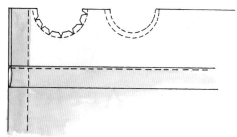

Fig. 1

10 Handsew rings to the top edge at each peak and each end. If desired, make ties or cut ribbons and sew them to the top of the curtain in pairs (fig. 2). Allow 12" (30cm) for each ribbon.

Fig. 2

Shirred Curtain Panel

Before you begin Shirred panel curtains are stretched between two rods or curtain wires. In such an arrangement, the lower rod or wire keeps the fabric from catching when the window or door is opened and closed. Sash curtains such as these are ideal for French doors and casement windows. The headings can be varied, but the easiest of all is the rod pocket style shown here.

Measuring

To calculate the total width of fabric you will need, measure the length of the rod or wire. Double the length for gathering and add 5/8" (1.5cm) for each joining seam and 1" (2.5cm) for each side seam. If your curtain will be two panels opening at the center, divide the width by two and then add the hem allowances. The only additional measurement you will need is for the depth of the curtain. Allow for the circumference of the rod plus 5" (13cm) for top and bottom hems.

MATERIALS
sufficient fabric

two café curtain wires or rods, and attachments

matching sewing machine threads

tailor's chalk

pins

scissors

tape measure

sewing machine

Method

1 Cut the number of lengths needed for the total width. Trim the selvages. If your curtains are to open in the middle, make sure you have an even number of lengths in each panel. Join the lengths together with a flat fell seam. Press.

Left: A shirred curtain panel is ideal for French doors

2 Press 1/2" (1.2cm) to the wrong side twice on the raw side edges. Stitch the side hems.

3 Press 1¼" (3cm) to the wrong side twice on the lower raw edge. Stitch close to the first fold. Check for an accurate fit by measuring from the top of the bottom pocket to the bottom of the top pocket. Mark this point across the curtain width with tailor's chalk. Trim the fabric 2½" (6cm) above this line. Make a double hem as for the bottom pocket, pressing 1¼" (3cm) to the wrong side each time. Stitch along the marked line.

4 Insert a rod or wire into each pocket (fig. 3). Adjust the gathers evenly.

Fig. 3

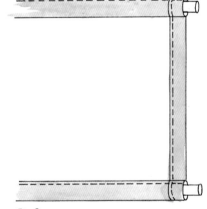

Right: This rod pocket café curtain and valance is made exactly the same way as the one above, without the lower rod pocket, and with the addition of headings

Decorator Scarf

A DECORATOR SCARF IS MADE FROM TWO LENGTHS OF COORDINATING FABRICS THAT ARE DRAPED AROUND A CURTAIN ROD TO GIVE A FORMAL LOOK.

Before you begin Simple to make, the scarf can be trimmed with tassels, braid or piping to add a little formality. If the contrast of the fabrics is dramatic enough, no embellishment is necessary. We used two coordinating fabrics with a decorative fringe trim.

Measuring

To calculate the amount of fabric you will need, use the following formula: The width of the window plus twice the desired side length plus 1¹/₈yds. (1m) draping allowance for every 2¹/₄yds. (2m) of pole length. You will need fabric about 24" (61cm) wide. For this reason, 48" (122cm) or 60" (152cm) wide fabric is ideal because you can cut down the center of the fabric.

MATERIALS
sufficient main fabric and the same amount of coordinating fabric
sufficient decorative fringe
matching sewing machine thread
pins
scissors
tape measure
sewing machine

A decorator scarf gives a very elegant look to a formal dining room

Method

1 Cut the fabric down the center, lengthwise, to make two pieces. Join them with a flat fell seam to achieve the correct length. Repeat this step for the coordinating fabric.

2 Place the main fabric and the coordinating fabric with right sides together. Cut both ends to form diagonals, taking care to cut the diagonals in opposite directions.

3 Remove the coordinating fabric. Pin the fringe down one long side of the scarf, with ³/₄" (2cm) overhang at both ends. Pin on the right side of the main fabric with the straight edge of the fringe matching the raw edge of the fabric. Baste. Repeat for both short ends.

4 Place the coordinating fabric on top of the main fabric with the right sides together and matching the raw edges. With the zipper foot on your sewing machine and starting halfway along the untrimmed side, stitch around the scarf through all thicknesses leaving a 12" (30cm) opening for turning. Keep stitching as close to the fringe as possible. Snip into the corners to make points at the corners of the scarf. Trim the excess fringe. Turn the scarf right side out, taking care to turn the corners out neatly. Press. Slipstitch the opening closed.

5 Drape the scarf around the pole and around the finials, leaving even amounts of fabric to fall from both ends of the pole.

Curtain Trims

THE BASIC CURTAIN STYLES WE HAVE SEEN
CAN ALL BE EMBELLISHED TO ADD YOUR OWN PERSONAL TOUCH.

The inside edge of a straight curtain can often be made a feature. With a little imagination, you can give a very professional finish to your curtains using ruffles, piping and braids. These are just a few of the ways you can individualize your window dressings.

Ruffles Attach a self-fabric ruffle or a contrast ruffle, using a coordinating chintz or a smaller print fabric, to the inner edges of your curtains. (See the section on ruffles on pages 23 and 24.)

Double ruffles Usually the outer ruffle is the same as the curtain with the inner ruffle being solid or contrasting with the main fabric (fig. 1).

Piping and ruffles In this case, the piping is usually made in a coordinating color that you wish to highlight. The ruffle could be in the curtain fabric or in another more dramatic solid color. (See the section on ruffles on pages 23 and 24 and the one on piping on page 21.)

Flat trim This trimming is usually made from a contrasting fabric, but you can achieve a very interesting effect by cutting a bias strip of the main curtain fabric and using that as the trim. The trim width can be varied according to your personal preference (fig. 2). (See the section on making and attaching bias strips on pages 20 to 21.)

Inset trim An elegant row of braiding can be stitched directly on to the curtain, 1¹/₄"-2" (3cm-5cm) in from the edge of the curtain (fig. 3).

Other decorative embellishments, such as braids and cords, can also be added to the inner edge of your curtain. Check the display at your local soft furnishings speciality store. You will be amazed at the variety of colors, styles and finishes to choose from. Some of these trims can be very costly but often only a small amount can give a special touch to a plain curtain in an inexpensive fabric. Well worth the cost!

When you are planning to add these extra touches to your curtains or drapes, purchase a sample piece of the braid or make a short length of ruffle and pin it into position to see if you are happy with the effect before you purchase the whole amount. As well as these relatively simple solutions, you can add a touch of drama to your curtains with a row of tassels, such as on the decorator scarf on page 58.

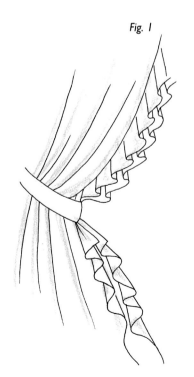

Fig. 1

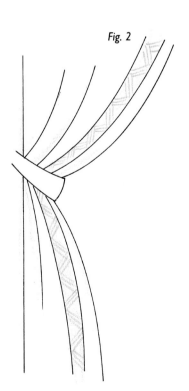

Fig. 2

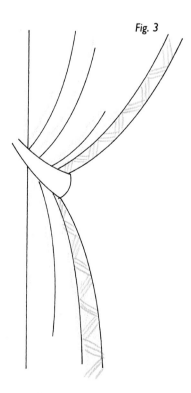

Fig. 3

Swags and Jabots

THIS WINDOW TREATMENT IS STYLISH YET SIMPLE.

Before you begin

Two shaped side curtains are caught back to reveal the contrasting fabric beneath and a swag is draped across the top of a pole or stapled into position on a board.

This type of treatment is also known as a dress curtain because when hung it is not adjustable; the curtains cannot be opened or closed. However, with the addition of a second pole underneath the swag, curtains could be drawn back and forth. Alternatively, you can hang a sheer curtain or shade, if you want more privacy.

Measuring

To calculate the total width of fabric and lining for the swag, measure the length of your pole. This style of curtain looks best when two panels are drawn back to each side, so if you use the length of the pole for the width of each panel this will give you a generous allowance for gathering. If you need to join lengths to achieve the required width, add 5/8" (1.5cm) for each joining seam allowance.

To determine the length needed for the jabots, measure from the top of the pole to where you want the curtain to finish, allowing for the drape to each side and adding 4 3/4" (12cm) for the lower hem and 4" (10cm) for the heading.

MATERIALS
two contrasting fabrics (main fabric and lining) plus fabric for the swag

contrasting or same fabric bias binding

matching sewing machine thread

paper to make pattern

pencil

steel ruler

tape measure

staple gun and staples

mounting board

pins

scissors

sewing machine

Method

Swag

1 Measure the width of the window to be covered and add half this length again. Measure the depth of the swag by holding a fabric tape measure at one end of the top of the mounting board, draping it to the desired length and bringing the tape back up to the other end of the top of the pole. Allow an extra 2" (5cm) for stapling along the top edge.

2 Cut a rectangle twice the depth of the final depth plus 2 1/2" (6cm). Fold the rectangle in half widthwise, placing the fold at the bottom, and draw the shorter edges up on each side, forming soft folds as you go.

3 Baste along the top edge to hold the folds in place (fig. 1). Pull up the basting until the swag fits the mounting board. Secure the stitches.

4 Press the raw edges to the wrong side at the top and staple the swag to the center of the mounting board.

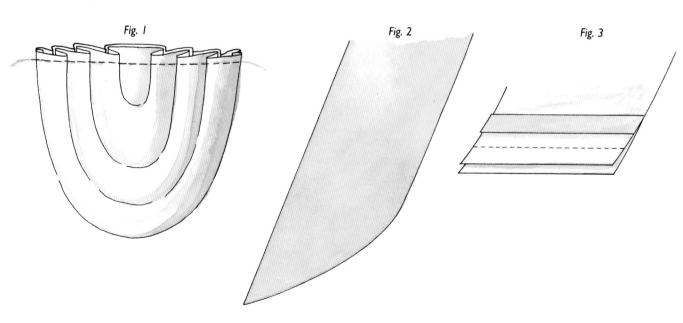

Fig. 1   Fig. 2   Fig. 3

NOTE: Several swags may be used across a wide window, overlapping the edges of each swag as you work along the board. Hanging curtains from a rod or pole mounted under the board will allow the curtains to be opened and closed.

Jabots

1 To make a paper pattern for the jabots, draw the shape, marking a gentle curved line on the inner edge (for the right-hand side) starting just above windowsill height down to the left-hand side to the point where you wish the tail to end on the left-hand side (fig. 2).

2 Using the pattern, cut out a right- and a left-hand side tail reversing the pattern for the opposite side, reversing the pattern for the opposite side. Repeat for the lining.

3 With the wrong sides together and using a ⁵/₈" (1.5cm) seam allowance, stitch one main fabric and one lining piece together along the straight and curved long edges.

4 At the top raw edge, press ³/₈" (1cm) to the wrong side.

5 Bind the curved edge and then the straight edges around the curtain tails with purchased or fabric bias binding (fig. 3). If you wish to make a dramatic statement with this binding, make it quite wide, but if you wish it to be more unobtrusive, make the binding narrower. (See pages 20 to 21 for how to make and apply bias binding.)

6 Staple the top edge of the tails to the top of the mounting board, over the ends of the swag.

Above: A pretty floral is the perfect choice for this swag and jabot arrangement

Left: For a more dramatic effect, choose strongly contrasting color and fabric, as for this draped scarf

Tiebacks

TIEBACKS ARE BOTH PRACTICAL AND DECORATIVE, ADDING A FINISHING
TOUCH TO YOUR WINDOW TREATMENT. THE RIGHT TIEBACK CAN ADD
LIFE AND COLOR TO A PLAIN WINDOW TREATMENT.

Tiebacks offer a great opportunity for creative use of braids, ribbons and tassels. Solid fabric tiebacks can be stenciled with motifs which are echoed on the walls. Tiebacks can be imaginative and even a little outrageous. In the right setting, a tieback trimmed with a collection of colored glass beads or appliquéd with felt motifs will add a feeling of fun. For a more festive effect, wind some fine wire around holly, or dried or silk flowers, then attach the garland to a standard tieback.

Braid and tassel tiebacks are very expensive, but with a little imagination you can make your own from the selection of braids and trims at your haberdashery shop. The drape of a loose-knotted tieback is a very pleasing complement to a swag.

The size of the tieback should be considered; the larger the tieback, the greater the impact it will have. It is also important to keep in mind the weight of the curtain the tieback will be holding back. If your curtain is heavy, line your fabric tiebacks with interfacing for extra support.

Remember to allow enough fabric in the body of your tieback to hold the drape in place without bunching up the drape fabric or creasing it too much.

A tieback is generally attached to a hook at windowsill height on each side of the window. The length of the loop which attaches it will vary according to the size of the hook. When the hook is small, the loop need only be about 4" (10cm) long. If the loop has to pass over a fitting with an ornate heading, the loop will need to be somewhat longer.

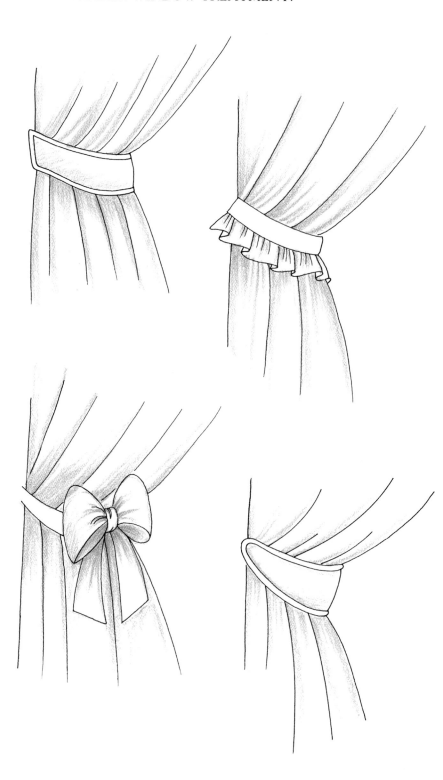

Shaped piped tieback

Before you begin

This is the basic method for making a lined tieback. Braids, piping and other accessories can be added.

Use fusible interfacing to give the tieback stability and support, especially for larger tiebacks or where there is a lot of fabric weight to be supported.

The finished size of this tieback is 4¼" x 23" (11cm x 59cm). Adjust the length or width to suit your own drape and window.

MATERIALS

¼ yd. (.25m) fabric

¼ yd. (.25m) fusible interfacing

sufficient contrasting piping to bind all the edges of the tieback

sufficient 2⅜" (6cm)-wide bias strip for two loops plus ⅝" (1.5cm) on each loop for returns

matching sewing machine thread

pins

template cardboard

felt tip marker

tailor's chalk

scissors

turning hook or knitting needle

sewing machine

iron

Method

1 Draw the shape of the tieback in the desired size on the cardboard with the marker, following the illustration (fig. 1).

2 Using the template, cut out two fabric pieces and one interfacing piece for each tieback. Cut two bias strips for the loops.

3 Following the manufacturer's instructions, fuse the interfacing to the wrong side of one fabric piece.

4 Pin the piping around the fabric piece without interfacing, with the right sides facing and the raw edges even. Clip the seam allowance of the piping to allow it to bend smoothly around the curve (fig. 2). Baste the piping in place.

5 Place the interfaced fabric on the piped fabric with the right sides together and the raw edges even. Pin, then baste. Clip the seam allowances at the curves.

6 Stitch through all thicknesses with the zipper foot on your sewing machine, stitching as close as possible to the piping and leaving a 4" (10cm) opening for turning. Trim the seam allowance. Turn the tieback right side out. Slipstitch the opening closed.

7 Fold the bias strips for the loops in half with wrong sides together. Stitch along the long side. Turn right side out. Fold each strip into a loop and slipstitch to each end of the tieback on the wrong side ¾" (2cm) in from the end.

The simplest of all lined tiebacks, this one is still very effective

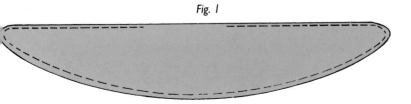

Fig. 1

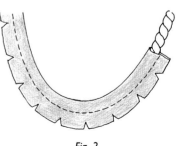

Fig. 2

Ruffled tieback

Before you begin To calculate how much fabric you will need for the ruffle, see the section on ruffles on pages 23 and 24. The finished size of this tieback is 4¼" x 23" (11cm x 59cm). Adjust the length or width to suit your own drape and window.

MATERIALS
¼ yd. (.25m) main fabric

¼ yd. (.25m) fusible interfacing

sufficient ruffle fabric for all the edges of the tieback, approximately 6" x 48" (15cm x 122cm) for each

four metal rings, ¾" (2cm) diameter

matching sewing machine thread

pins

template cardboard

felt tip marker

tailor's chalk

scissors

sewing machine

turning hook or knitting needle

Method

1 Draw the tieback at the size you need on to the cardboard with the marker, following the diagram (fig. 1).

2 Using the template, cut out two fabric pieces and one interfacing piece for each tieback.

3 Following the manufacturer's instructions, fuse the interfacing to the wrong side of one fabric piece.

4 Cut a ruffle strip. It should be at least twice the total measurement around the outside edge of the tieback. If you need to join pieces to achieve this length, add ⅝" (1.5cm) for each seam allowance. Press the ruffle strip in half lengthwise with the right sides together. With the right sides together, stitch the ends of the strip together to form a circle. Turn the ruffle right side out and press.

The ruffling on this tieback adds charming detail

5 Stitch two rows of gathering stitch, ¼" (6mm) and ⅜" (1cm) from the raw edge. Pull up the gathering to fit around the outer edge of the tieback. Pin the ruffle to the right side of the main fabric piece without the interfacing, with the raw edges even. Baste in place (fig. 2).

6 Pin the interfaced fabric piece over the ruffled piece with the right sides together. Baste. Stitch, leaving a 4" (10cm) opening on the longest edge for turning. Clip the seam allowances (fig. 3). Turn right side out. Press. Slipstitch the opening closed.

7 Slipstitch one metal ring to each end of the inside back of each tieback.

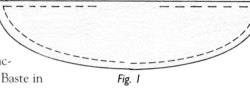

Fig. 1

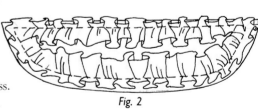

Fig. 2

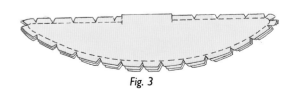

Fig. 3

Appliquéd tieback

Before you begin Fusible interfacing will give a tieback stability and support, especially a larger tieback or where the fabric drapes to be supported are heavy.

MATERIALS

$1/4$ yd. (.25m) main fabric
(solid color fabric)

$1/4$ yd. (.25m) fusible interfacing

8" (20cm) piece contrasting fabric
(curtain fabric)

fusible web

four metal rings

matching sewing machine thread

pins

template carboard

pencil

scissors

sewing machine

Method

1 Draw the shape of the tieback to the required size, using the cardboard and pencil. Cut out the shape to use for a template.

2 Using the template, cut out two main fabric pieces and one piece of interfacing for each tieback.

3 Make a second template $2^{1}/_{2}$" (6cm) smaller all around than the first template. Cut one piece each of the contrasting fabric and fusible web, for each tieback.

4 Fuse the interfacing to the wrong side of one main fabric piece. Pin the two main fabric pieces together with the right sides facing and the raw edges even. Stitch around the outside edge with a $^{5}/_{8}$" (1.5cm) seam, leaving an opening for turning. Clip the seam allowances at the curves and trim the seam. Turn the tieback right side out and slipstitch the opening closed.

5 Following the manufacturer's instructions, fuse the contrasting fabric piece to the center of the main tieback. There should be an even amount of the main fabric showing around the edges of the contrast fabric. Satin stitch around the contrasting piece covering the raw edges.

6 Slipstitch one metal ring to each end of each tieback.

The unusual edging effect has been achieved by appliquéing the curtain fabric to a tieback made in a contrasting fabric

Valances

VALANCES ARE ANOTHER WONDERFUL WAY TO FINISH OFF A WINDOW TREATMENT.

A valance can cover an unattractive curtain rod, add interest to a dull window, or alter the shape and proportion of a window to better suit a room. Whether you choose a simple ruffle or a padded and shaped valance, you will enjoy the decorative effect as well as the practical benefit.

Choosing the right shape and style of valance to complement your curtains and your room is a matter of assessing the proportions of your room and window and the total look you wish to achieve.

Ruffled piped valance

Before you begin This valance is attached to the window frame on a wall-mounted rod, without any additional hardware. Allow enough fabric for the returns (sides), so that the fabric covers the entire rod system.

Measuring

To calculate the amount of fabric needed, measure the rod and the returns and double this figure. If you need to join pieces to achieve this length, add $5/8$" (1.5cm) for each seam allowance and 1" (2.5cm) for each side hem.

Decide on the depth of the valance after considering the proportions of your window and the type of fabric you are using. If your fabric has a printed border, take advantage of this feature and incorporate it into your design.

The amount of pleating tape needed will be twice the length of the curtain rod plus 2" (5cm) for side hems.

MATERIALS
sufficient fabric
sufficient contrasting piping
sufficient pleating tape
matching sewing machine thread
hooks or rings, one for each pleat or every 4" (10cm) of tape
pins
tailor's chalk
tape measure
scissors
sewing machine

Method

1 Cut and stitch the fabric widths together with a flat fell seam to achieve the length required. Press $1/4$" (6mm), then $3/4$" (2cm) to the wrong side on both sides. Stitch the side hems. Press 1" (2.5cm) to the wrong side on the top edge.

2 Pin the tape in place along the top edge on the wrong side of the fabric,

A ruffled valance is the perfect addition to a nursery curtain

covering the raw edge. At one end, fold under the raw edge of the tape and knot the cords together.

3 Stitch the tape in place with two rows of stitching, one at the top of the tape and one at the bottom. Do not pull up the tape.

4 Place the piping along the bottom edge of the right side of the valance fabric, raw edges matching. Using the zipper foot on your sewing machine, stitch as close to the piping cord as possible.

5 Cut the ruffle strip, 3" (7.5cm) wide, joining the length if necessary. With right sides together, fold the ruffle in half, lengthwise. Stitch across the ends and trim the seam allowance before turning the ruffle right side out.

6 Stitch two rows of gathering, one $^1/_4$" (6mm) and the other $^3/_8$" (1cm) from the raw edge, catching both layers of fabric. Pull up the gathering to fit the bottom edge of the valance.

7 Pin the gathered ruffle over the piping, with right sides together and the raw edges even. Stitch along the previous stitch line, with the zipper foot of your sewing machine. Trim the seam allowances if necessary. Press.

8 Insert the hooks or rings in the tape. Draw up the cords to fit the rod, tie off the cords and trim the excess.

If the valance is hung on a separate rod, you can open and close the curtain beneath the valance for more privacy

---

Valance with jumbo piping

Before you begin This valance shape was cut from plywood, and the fabric and padding were applied over the wood. Follow the instructions for measuring and calculating fabric quantities given for the buckram valance on page 68.

MATERIALS

piece of 16mm thick plywood, the desired width and 12" (30cm) deep, for the front piece

two pieces of 16mm thick plywood, 6" (15cm) wide x 12" (30cm), for the side pieces

pencil

two L-brackets and screws

bullet-head nails and hammer

jigsaw

large sheet of paper for the pattern

felt tip marker

sufficient fabric

4" (10cm) wide bias strips for the piping

piping cord, size 10

two pieces of fabric, 6" x 12" (15cm x 30cm), to cover the inside of the box sides

sufficient batting

staple gun and staples

craft glue

spray adhesive

Method

1 Draw the shape of your valance on to the large sheet of paper, using the grid pattern method to enlarge the pattern to fit the size of your window.

Match a brightly coloured valance to a blind for an all-over effect

Draw a grid the same length as your mounting board and with even sized squares. Copy into the squares that part of the pattern which appears in the corresponding square of the grid pattern (fig. 1).

2 Draw the pattern on to the front piece of the valance. Using the jigsaw, cut out the shape.

3 Make up the box with the bullet-head nails, so that the sides are butted to the front.

4 Cut out the batting and the fabric slightly larger than the shape of the box. Glue the batting to the sides and the front of the box. Trim any excess.

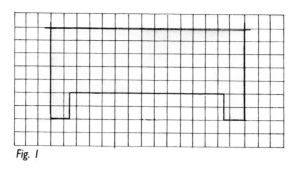

Fig. 1

5 Spray adhesive onto the back of the fabric and glue it over the batting. Trim the fabric, leaving a 2" (5cm) allowance extending on all sides.

6 Staple or tack the excess fabric to the inside of the box, pulling the fabric quite tight over the batting. Trim any

excess fabric bulk.

7 Press ³/₈" (1cm) under around the raw edges of the contrasting fabric pieces for the side panel linings. Glue the folded edges in place inside the box.

8 Fold the bias tape over the piping cord. With the zipper foot on the sewing machine, baste the cord in place.

9 Glue or staple the piping to the inside edge of the front of the valance box. Cover the staples with a length of masking tape, if desired.

10 Attach the box to the wall with L-brackets.

Buckram valance

Before you begin This buckram valance is fixed to a mounting board made from particle board or plywood (depending on the weight of the valance). The valance is fixed to the mounting board with Velcro® tape, allowing it to be easily removed for cleaning.

The valance is most effective when it is padded and machine-quilted in any one of a number of quilting patterns.

As for all treatments, the mounting board for a buckram valance should be installed first. You will need a piece of board 16mm thick x 6" (15cm) deep x the width of the window frame plus an extra 2" (5cm) on each side of the window frame. You will need two right-angled brackets to mount the board on the wall (fig. 2).

Simplicity is the key to quilting. If you are working with a large print, use a simple quilting pattern; if working with a solid fabric, use a more elaborate quilting design. Outline quilting some of the elements of a fabric print is very effective.

Measuring

Measure the required width and depth of your valance. To calculate the width, add the front width B plus the side returns A plus 2" (5cm) on each side. The finished depth of a valance should be approximately 12"-16" (30cm-40cm). Add 1" (2.5cm) to the length for turning hems.

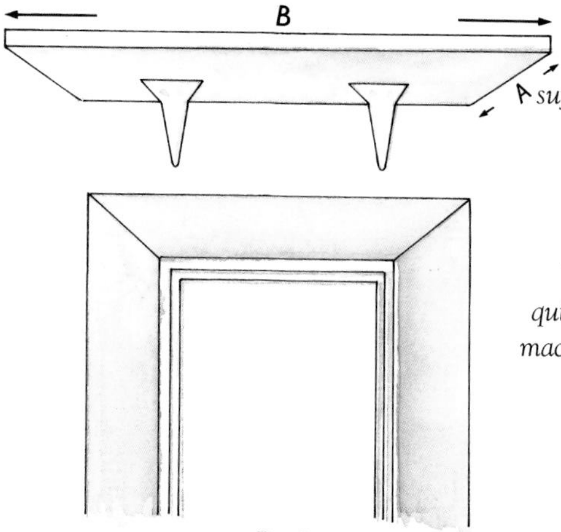

Fig. 2

Another advantage of the buckram valance is that the fabric can be turned sideways, so that no seams in the fabric are necessary. In some cases, the print on the fabric makes this impossible. Turn your fabric sideways to see if it will work.

MATERIALS
mounting board
screws
electric drill
two right-angled brackets
sufficient fabric and an equal amount of hi-loft batting
cotton lining
tailor's chalk
matching sewing machine thread
quilting pattern template (your sewing machine may have a program for special quilting patterns)
sewing machine
tape measure
scissors
Velcro®
fabric glue or staples and a staple gun

The simple checked fabric makes a charming statement in this country-style valance

Method

1 Screw the corner brackets securely to the wall. The board can be painted or some of the valance fabric glued or stapled over it, if desired. Place the mounting board on top of the brackets and secure in place.

2 Cut the fabric, batting and lining to the desired size. For a 12" (30cm) finished depth, you will need to quilt up 16" (40cm) of fabric and you will need to add 4" (10cm) to the length. Place them sandwiched together with the lining, face down, the batting and the fabric on top, right side up. Baste the layers together securely, around all the edges and at 4" (10cm) intervals across the width of the fabric.

3 Transfer the quilting design to the fabric and quilt it by hand or machine.

4 Cut the quilted fabric to the length for the valance plus 3/8" (1cm) on each end for turning.

5 Turn in 3/8" (1cm) on the short sides and 1" (2.5cm) on the bottom edge.

Stitch the returns in place.

6 Attach the hook side of the Velcro® tape to the front edge of the mounting board with glue or staples. Stitch the loop side of the Velcro® tape to the top edge of the wrong side of the valance along both the top and bottom edges of the Velcro® and the length of the valance. If necessary, press the valance before attaching it to the mounting board with the Velcro® tape.

Draped rectangular valance

Before you begin

Determine the depth of your valance; ours measured approximately 12" (30cm) finished. To this measurement, add ⁵/₈" (1.5cm) for the lower hem and 2" (5cm) to the top for stapling to the mounting board. Cut the width of the valance 1¹/₈yd. (1m) wider than the width of the window, for an 18" (46cm) length on either side. Add 1¹/₄" (3cm) for hems. Cut the entire length in one piece so there are no visible seams. If you are making two or three valances, cut the fabric through the width.

MATERIALS

sufficient main fabric for valance and bias strips

sufficient contrasting fabric

scissors

matching sewing machine thread

tape measure

sewing machine

pins

staples and staple gun, or thumb tacks

16 mm thick mounting board cut to the width of your window and 6" (15cm) deep

two L-brackets

screws

electric drill or screwdriver

Method

1 Decide on the position of the valance and attach the mounting board.
2 Cut the main fabric and the contrasting fabric in two strips to the required length and width. Place the two fabrics with right sides together and the raw edges even. Stitch down one long side, then turn right side out. Press the fabric so that all the raw edges are even.
3 Make sufficient continuous 2³/₈" (6cm)-wide bias binding, joining the length with flat seams. (See pages 20 to 21 for making continuous bias binding.)
4 Press the bias binding in half with the wrong sides together. Pin and stitch

A simple draped valance lined with a contrasting fabric can bring a color scheme together

a length of the bias binding over the long raw edge, then bind the two short ends, folding under the raw ends.

5 Center the valance on the mounting board, ensuring that equal lengths drape down each side. Staple or thumb tack the top of the valance to the board 2" (5cm) in from the front edge. At the corners, drape the valance into three soft folds and secure with staples or tacks.

Rod pocket valances are the easiest to construct and hang

Rod pocket valance

Before you begin To calculate the total width of fabric you will need for the valance, measure the length of your rod and double to allow for gathering. Add ⅝" (1.5cm) for each joining seam and 1" (2.5cm) for each side hem. Add 4" (10cm) to the length for the casing and 3" (7.5cm) for the lower hem. The length should suit the size of the window. This one is approximately 15¾" (40cm) long.

MATERIALS
sufficient fabric
matching sewing machine thread
pins
scissors
tape measure
sewing machine

Method

1 Cut the number of lengths needed for the total width of the valance. Trim the selvages. Pin, then stitch the lengths together with a flat fell seam.

2 Press ⅜" (1cm), then ⅝" (1.5cm) to the wrong side on the side edges. Pin and stitch the side hems.

3 Measure the diameter of your rod. Press ⅜" (1cm) to the wrong side at the top edge of the valance, then another 3½" (9cm). Stitch along the folded edge; this line of stitching will fall underneath the rod. Stitch a second line of stitching the diameter of the rod plus ⅜" (1cm) above the stitched row to form the casing.

4 Turn in and press 1" (2.5cm) on the lower edge, then another 2" (5cm). Pin and stitch the hem in place.

5 Slip the rod into the casing and adjust the gathering.

Shades

BONDED ROLLER SHADES
ROMAN SHADES
AUSTRIAN SHADES
TIE-UP SHADES

Shades

USED ALONE OR COMBINED WITH A VALANCE OR CURTAIN, SHADES ARE
ONE OF THE MOST ENERGY-EFFICIENT WINDOW TREATMENTS.

A shade will reflect the sun during the summer and help to stop the heat inside your home escaping during the winter months.

A shade also increases privacy, particularly if it is backed with a stiffened or lined fabric. Where privacy is not required, the shade can be purely decorative, made from lace or a lightweight fabric.

Shades add affordable style to a room and their easy application and relatively low cost mean that seasonal changes become possible.

There are various types and styles of shades, so finding one to suit your decor is not difficult. For example, the classic lines of roller and Roman shades fit well in a contemporary setting. Both shades use approximately the same amount of fabric and both must be perfectly "square" in order to hang straight in the window. When lowered, both shades appear to be flat to the window, but a roller shade virtually disappears when raised, while a Roman shade falls into pleated folds, creating a geometric look.

Festoons or Austrian shades, on the other hand, feature folds of fabric that can be used to filter the flow of light. These two types of shades have lines of shirring tape sewn vertically, evenly spaced, across the reverse side of the shade. Thin cords running through the tapes to the top of the shade allow it to be pulled up to form elegant swags or scallops. Austrian shades differ from festoon shades in that there is an additional row of tape at the top of the Austrian shade and the cords are pulled through it to one side in order to raise and lower the shade.

Shades can be simple or very ornate, depending on your choice of trims and finishing treatments. A stenciled motif on a plain roller shade gives it a touch of country charm, while a single ornate tassel as the draw cord adds a classic touch to the same roller shade. Ruffles are a great way to trim any swagged or gathered shade.

Shades can be a very practical way to cover your windows. They don't take up a lot of room and are ideal for windows where the covering should only be sill length, such as above a sink or basin, above a desk or in a playroom – or any place where there is a working area below the window.

With so many ideas to choose from, take the time to consider them all before making a decision.

Equipment

❖

Before making your own shades it is a good idea to make a small drawing of the finished shade. On the drawing, note all the dimensions, including the base hem, eyelet spaces, and the size and depth of the mounting board. This small drawing does not need to be a masterpiece, but as long as all the correct measurements are there, it will serve as a handy reference for checking your work as you go.

You will need an adequate working area – large enough to spread your fabric out flat. If the shade is allowed to hang over the edge of a table while you are working on it, it may stretch, distorting your final measurements.

As shades need to be as square as possible, always use a metal ruler and a T-square when marking the pattern.

A dressmaker's cutting board is invaluable for marking the position of pleats, tapes, tucks rings or slats and will allow you to pin and secure fabric with ease.

Tacky craft fabric glue will allow you to make many short cuts when constructing shades. Trims, tapes and facings can all be glued into position, sometimes avoiding the need for sewing. Glue will also keep raw edges from fraying and will hold knots secure.

Fusible web is another practical product which will save a lot of time and effort. When placed between two layers of fabric, the web fuses and bonds the fabrics when heat is applied, usually with an iron. Fusible web can be purchased by the yard (meter) and cut to any shape or size, or as a tape. It can be used for hemming; for attaching appliqués, trims and braids; and as a interfacing for support. Fusible web will be one of your most valuable aids when making roller shades.

Shirring tapes are sold by the yard (meter) in a variety of styles and can be purchased from your local fabric store.

Choose shades to work with your window style, as well as to be an accent for other window treatments

Measuring for shades

❖

Accurate measurements are essential when making shades. Even a small discrepancy can interfere with the smooth running action of the shade or allow light to filter through.

Windows often look the same size at a glance but often are not; a window frame can even vary in size from the top to the bottom of the window. It is critical that each window is measured separately and carefully.

For roller shades, first mark the positions where the brackets are to be installed. Note that the mounting position of the bracket foot is not the point from which you take the measurements. It may be best not to mount the brackets at this stage, because you will not know the diameter of the roller until the shade is complete. If this is the case, use the measuring point as your guide.

Mounting shades

There are three ways to mount roller shades: inside the recess (A to B), outside the recess (C to D) and from the ceiling. Shades on tracks are mounted above the window frame.

Shades hung inside the recess give a tighter fit, allowing less light to escape. If you are going to hang your shades inside the recess, measure the width and length of the recess. It is a good idea to take measurements at various points inside the recess to ensure that dimensions do not vary significantly.

If the shade is to be mounted outside the recess, you are less likely to be troubled by variations in the window measurement and can compensate more easily for any variations that do exist. When taking your measurements, add at least 3" (7.5cm) on each side to the width of the recess and 4" (10cm) to the length above and below the recess.

When a shade is to be hung from ceiling brackets, it should overlap the window frame by at least 1" (2.5cm) on all sides to avoid gaps.

As a general rule, add 12" (30cm) to the measured length of your window frame to allow for the roll-over so that the shade will not tear when the roller is pulled down. If your roller shade has a decorative finish added to the bottom, allow 15¾" (40cm) for the roll-over.

Selecting fabrics

Just as for curtains, there are many beautiful fabrics to choose from for making shades, but the appearance of the fabric is not the only consideration. For roller shades, the construction of the fabric is also important. A tightly woven cotton is ideal for a bonded shade because it will hang smoothly and roll up evenly. Cotton fabrics are usually fused to a layer of backing for extra stiffness, but there are also

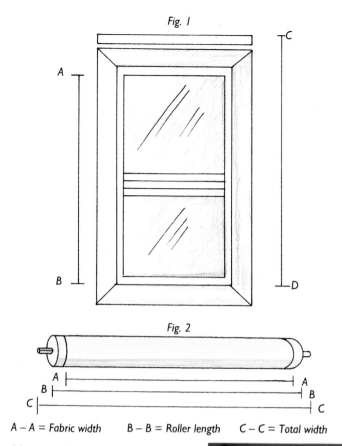

Fig. I

Fig. 2

A – A = Fabric width   B – B = Roller length   C – C = Total width

fabrics, such as heavyweight chintz, that can be used without lining.

Roman shades can be made from any tightly constructed cotton fabric, but they are especially suited to heavier woven fabrics, such as Indian cottons or jacquards, particularly if the shade is to be unlined.

Austrian and festoon shades are commonly used to filter light rather than to block it out altogether. Because they are often purely decorative, the range of suitable fabrics is much more extensive. Laces, light voiles, fine cottons and silks are used for soft, romantic effects; cotton chintz, cotton sateens and polyviscose give a crisper, more sophisticated look. Heavy fabrics are not suitable for Austrian and festoon shades because the weight of the fabric may cause the shade to droop if the tapes and rings are not strong enough to accommodate the weight. Choose a fabric that drapes and gathers well.

The soft effect of lace works well for an Austrian shade. For privacy, add a curtain which can be drawn over the shade

Trimming

❖

A simple shade can become a work of art with the addition of a braid or trim detail. Contrasting colors on a solid shade will create an interesting focal point; exotic braids will add interesting textures, and ruffles add a touch of elegance.

It is important to consider the structure of your shade, when selecting a trim. The simplicity and clean lines of a Roman shade should be maintained with simple trimming. A deep border around three sides or a thick braid added only to the bottom hem will give a neat finish. Austrian and festoon shades, on the other hand, suit a more fussy style with lace trims, tassels and bobbles emphasizing the elegant curved lines.

Bonded shades lend themselves to interesting shaping on the bottom edge, highlighted with contrasting or coordinating flat braids. Add an elegant tassel for the shade pull, a covered ring or, for a more casual look, a braided length of contrast fabric can be wound into a knot and a ring sewn behind it.

You can even change the look of an existing roller shade with a little imagination and some clever trimming.

Cut the bottom off of the shade, leaving a raw edge (fig. 3). Draw the outline for the new shape on to the shade and cut it out (fig. 4). Glue an attractive braid to follow the cut shape, then bind the raw edge with bias binding, or finish with seam sealant (fig. 5). Add a new tassel or ring to pull the shade up and down.

A decorative valance, made with contrasting fabrics, covers a shade beautifully when not in use

Fig. 3

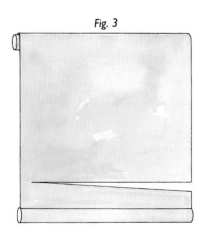

Fig. 4

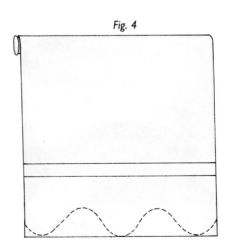

Fig. 5

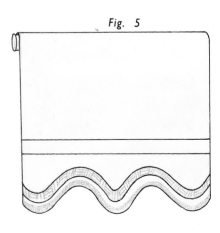

Bonded Roller Shades

Before you begin A roller shade kit can be purchased from specialist soft furnishing stores and from major hardware stores. The kits contain a roller which encases the winding mechanism or spring (figs. 1 and 2). It has a square pin on one end and a round pin and cap on the other end. Once you have established the finished width of the shade, you can cut the roller down to size and fit the round cap.

Also included in the kit is a wooden or plastic slat which is inserted at the base of the shade for added stability. If your design requires a second slat, have one cut to the size you need. A cord pull, ring or tassel can be attached to this slat. All kits come with instructions and sometimes diagrams. Always read the complete instructions before you begin.

The slotted bracket for the square pin should be fitted to the left-hand side of the window and the round bracket to the right-hand side for a conventional roll. In a conventional roll, the fabric comes off the back of the roller, making the shade fit closely to the window (fig. 3). Reverse roll shades are mounted with the winding mechanism (the square pin end) to the right-hand side. The shade fabric rolls off the front of the shade so that the shade sits slightly out from the window sill, avoiding any handles or locks (fig. 4).

When measuring the positions for the brackets and rollers, measure from tip to tip.

The fabric is fixed to the roller with staples, heavy duty glue or tacks.

Stiffened shade

Before you begin Decide where your shade is to be mounted – inside or outside the recess or on the ceiling. For an inside or ceiling-mounted shade, measure the recess and add 1" (2.5cm) on each side for the side hems and 4" (10cm) for the bottom hem. If the shade is to be mounted outside, add 3" (7.5cm) to each side and the bottom. If you need to join widths, add ⅝" (1.5cm) for each joining seam. In all cases allow an additional 12"-14" (30cm-35cm) for the roll-over (the fabric can be trimmed more exactly later to fit the roller and window).

MATERIALS
roller shade kit and second slat
sufficient main fabric
8" (20cm) of contrasting fabric the same width as the shade
bias strips of the main fabric for binding the contrast panel and covering the ring
fabric scrap for the pull tab
large wooden ring
spray fabric stiffener
staples and staple gun, tacks or woodworking glue
scissors
T-square
metal ruler
FrayCheck® to prevent fraying (optional)
dressmaker's cutting board
sheet of paper as wide as the shade to draw a grid on
tailor's chalk
matching sewing machine thread
sewing machine

Method

1 Cut the main fabric to the calculated width. If you need to join fabric

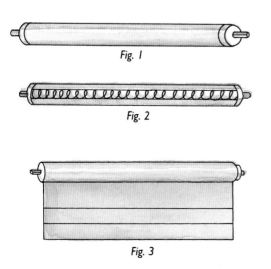

Fig. 1

Fig. 2

Fig. 3

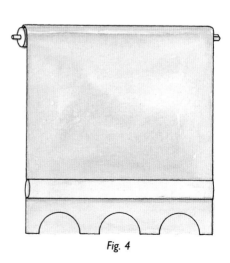

Fig. 4

A simple shape, bias bound, is a striking finish on a roller shade

widths, take care to match the pattern carefully, allowing for the ⅝" (1cm) overlap. Use a flat fell seam for joining.

2 Press 1" (2.5cm) to the wrong side on each side edge. Apply fabric glue to the raw edges to prevent fraying. Stitch the side hems in place.

3 Apply fabric glue to the bottom edge to prevent fraying. On the wrong side of the fabric, mark a line 3⅛" (8cm) above the bottom edge with tailor's chalk and a metal ruler. Lightly spray the area below the mark with fabric stiffener, then fold the bottom edge up to meet this line to form a casing. Press and stitch the casing in place.

4 On the sheet of paper, draw up a 2" (5cm) square grid, using the metal ruler and T-square. On the grid, draw the pattern for the lower edge of the contrast panel. Cut the contrast panel 6¾" (17cm) x the width of the shade. Place the pattern on the bottom edge of the contrast panel and cut out the shape.

5 Spray the wrong side of the contrasting panel with fabric stiffener and allow to dry. Stitch the side hems as for the main fabric.

6 Make up sufficient bias binding for the bottom edge of the contrasting panel. (See pages 20 to 21 for how to make and apply bias binding.) Bind the lower edge of the contrasting panel with the bias binding, folding in the raw edges and pleating and folding fabric at the corners and curves.

7 Press the fabric, then spray fabric stiffener on the rest of the shade. Spray again, if necessary.

8 With tailor's chalk and a metal ruler, mark a line 7" (18cm) up from the bottom of the casing on the back of the shade. Draw another line 3⅛" (8cm) above this line. Fold the fabric so that the lines are matching on the wrong side. Stitch along the line, forming a casing.

9 Cover the wooden ring with a bias strip of the main fabric. For the pull, cut a scrap of the main fabric 4" (10cm) wide. Fold the strip in half with right sides together and raw edges even. Stitch down the long side then turn the strip right side out and press. Fold

the strip around the covered ring, so that the raw ends are matching. Pin and baste the raw ends to the center of the top edge of the contrasting panel.

10 Place the contrasting panel on the shade with the side edges and the bottom corners matching, slipping the contrasting panel under the upper casing. Stitch the top edge of the panel to the shade under the casing, catching the pull strip into the seam.

11 Trim the wooden slats ¾" (2cm) shorter than the finished width of the shade. Insert the slats into the casings and stitch over the ends of the casings to hold the slats in place.

12 Depending on whether you want a conventional or reverse roll, place the roller on the front or back of the fabric. Fold the top edge of the shade over and place the folded edge on the marked line. Staple, tack or glue in place.

13 Wind the shade by hand to ensure that the winding mechanism is at the right tension. Screw the mounting brackets to the window frame.

Install the shade on the mounting brackets, then pull up the shade to check the tension again. If it is not correct, remove the shade and wind the roller up by hand again.

❖

Lined shade

Before you begin Decide where your shade is to be mounted – inside or outside the recess or on the ceiling. For an inside or ceiling-mounted shade, measure the recess and add 2" (5cm) on each side and the bottom. If the shade is to be mounted outside, add 3" (7.5cm) on each side and on the bottom. If you need to join widths add ⅝" (1.5cm) on both sides for each joining seam. In all cases allow an additional 12"-14" (30cm-35cm) for roll-over (the fabric can be trimmed later to exactly fit the roller and window) and an additional 4"-6" (10cm-15cm) for the bottom hem if you are shaping the bottom of your shade.

MATERIALS
roller shade kit
sufficient fabric and the same amount of fusible web and backing fabric (if the web is not wide enough to cover your fabric, use two lengths with a ⅜" (1cm) overlap)
staples and staple gun, tacks or heavy-duty glue
scissors
T-square
metal ruler
FrayCheck® to prevent fraying (optional)
dressmaker's cutting board
tailor's chalk
2⅜" (6cm) diameter metal ring
contrasting fabric, 16" (40cm) x the width of the shade plus 2" (5cm) for hems and the same quantity of fusible interfacing
contrasting piping
narrow bias binding for the ring pull
matching sewing machine thread
sewing machine

Method

1 Cut the fabric to the width needed. If you need to join fabric widths, take care to match the pattern carefully, allowing for the ⅜" (1cm) overlap. Use a flat seam to join the fabric lengths.

2 Cut the fusible web and backing fabric the same size as the front. Join lengths of the backing fabric as for the main fabric, if necessary.

3 Lay the front fabric face down on the work area with the lining on top, right side facing up. Sandwich the web between.

4 Following manufacturer's instructions press firmly, working from the center to the outer edges. Allow the fabrics to cool completely before continuing.

5 With tailor's chalk, mark a line 24" (61cm) from the lower edge on the right side of the main fabric.

6 Fuse the interfacing to the wrong side of the contrasting panel. With right sides together and raw edges even, apply the piping to the top and bottom edges of the contrasting fabric panel.

7 Place the contrasting panel on the right side of the main fabric piece with the right sides together and the piping stitching line at the top of the contrasting panel matching the chalk line. Pin and stitch the contrasting panel to the main fabric along this line. Press the panel down.

8 For the ring pull, fold a length of bias binding in half and stitch down one long side. Thread the metal ring on to the pull and make a knot, leaving the bias binding tails free.

9 Press the lower raw edge to the wrong side on the contrasting panel. Baste the tails of the ring pull in place under the center point of the pressed edge. Topstitch the bottom edge of the panel in place on the main fabric, stitching along the piping stitching line and catching the ring pull into the seam. Topstitch along the top piping stitching line in the same way.

10 Press 1" (2.5cm) to the wrong side on each side edge, then another 1" (2.5cm). Stitch the side hems in place.

11 Press ⅝" (1.5cm) to the wrong side on the bottom of the shade, then another 3¼" (8.5cm). Stitch close to both folds, forming a casing.

12 Trim the wooden slat ¾" (2cm) shorter than the width of the shade. Slip the slat into the casing and stitch over the ends of the casing to hold in place.

13 Depending on whether you want a conventional or reverse roll, place the roller on the front or back of the fabric. Place the folded edge of the fabric on the marked line and staple, tack or glue in place.

14 Wind up the shade by hand to ensure that the winding mechanism is at the right tension. Install the mounting brackets on the window frame. Install the shade on the mounting brackets, then pull up the shade to check the tension again. If it is not correct, remove and re-wind the roller.

Right: Use contrasting fabrics and colored piping for highlights
Below: This color scheme and fabric will delight a young child

Roman Shades

A ROMAN SHADE IS FIXED TO A MOUNTING BOARD AT THE TOP OF
THE WINDOW FRAME. WHEN RAISED, IT FOLDS INTO SOFT HORIZONTAL DRAPES.
WHEN IT IS LOWERED, IT LIES FLAT AGAINST THE WINDOW FRAME.

Before you begin

The way a Roman shade is mounted will influence the measurements you take. Roman shades can be mounted inside the window recess or mounted above the window frame.

You will need a mounting board 16mm thick x 2" (5cm) deep x the length required for mounting the shade. The board can be painted or covered in fabric if you wish. (See mounting instructions on page 76.)

Right-angled brackets are used to support the board and screw-in eye hooks are spaced evenly at approximately 12" (30cm) intervals along the bottom of the board (fig. 1).

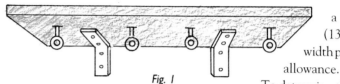

Fig. 1

Measuring

For the amount of fabric and lining required, use the following calculations:

Total width = measured width + 2" (5cm) + ⅝" (1.5cm) seam allowance on both sides of any joining seam if lengths need to be joined

Total length = measured length + 3" (7.5cm)

For the facing, from the main fabric cut a piece of fabric 5" (13cm) x the finished width plus 3⅛" (8cm) hem allowance.

To determine the amount of cord needed add 8" (20cm) to the finished length of the shade and multiply by the required number of vertical draw cords, placing one cord every 12" (30cm) across the width of the shade. Alternatively, purchase pre-threaded ring tape for Roman shades.

MATERIALS

mounting board

2" (5cm) thick wooden slat, the same width as the shade

right-angled brackets and screws

screw-in eye hooks
(see Before you begin)

sufficient main fabric and an equal amount of cotton lining

strip of main fabric for the facing

matching sewing machine thread

fusible web (optional)

30 to 40 rings

metal ruler

tailor's chalk

staples and staple gun, tacks or heavy-duty glue

thin nylon or cotton cord

brass cleat

decorative toggle

tape measure

pins

scissors

dressmaker's cutting board

sewing machine

Roman shades give a neatly tailored finish

Method

1 Cut the required number of lengths, joining them with flat fell seams for the total width if needed. Press.

2 Lay the fabric right side down on the cutting board and check that it is square. Press ¼" (6mm) to the wrong side on the side edges, then another ¾" (2cm).

3 Trim the lining fabric to the same size as the pressed shade fabric. Lay the lining fabric on top of the shade fabric and slip the side edges of the lining under the pressed side hems of the shade fabric. Pin the side hems in place over the lining.

4 Pin the facing strip to the bottom edge of the main fabric, with the right sides together and raw edges even. Note that the facing extends 1" (2.5cm) on each side of the shade. Stitch together with a ⅜" (1cm) seam. Press the facing strip to the wrong side of the shade. Press the 1" (2.5cm) ends under on each side. Insert a layer of fusible web between the layers and press the extensions in place, or sew them in place if desired (fig. 2).

5 Press the top raw edge of the facing strip to the wrong side, then stitch a 3" (7.5cm) hem. Stitch again 1" (2.5cm) down from the previous stitching to form a casing.

6 Place the shade on the work surface with the wrong side up. To determine the tape positions on the back of the shade, use the metal ruler and tailor's chalk to mark the width every 12" (30cm), rounding up or down to the nearest whole number to give you the same positions as the screw-in eye hooks on the mounting board. Mark every 4" (10cm) from the top to the bottom of the shade for the folds. Mark the folds with a warm iron as guidelines to ensure they remain straight.

7 Cut one tape for each side hem and one each for every marked vertical line across the width of the shade. Make sure the position of the bottom ring on the tape is close to the casing (fig. 3). Pin the tapes to the shade, pinning

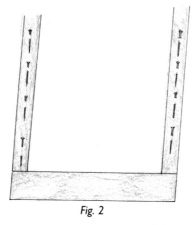

Fig. 2

along the center of the tapes. Make sure all the tapes are perfectly straight, then stitch in place.

8 Secure the cords at the bottom ring or tape position with a sturdy knot. Thread the cords up through the tapes or rings to the top of the tape or to the highest ring position, allowing an extra 2" (5cm) at the top. These top positions should all line up across the shade.

9 Take the tapes up to the top raw edge, placing the last ring 3" (7.5cm) from the top. On the top edge, press ¼" (6mm) to the wrong side, then another ¾" (2cm), treating the main fabric and the lining as a single layer. Stitch the top hem in place.

10 Attach the shade to the mounting board with tacks, staples or glue.

11 Insert the slat into the casing and slipstitch the ends of the casing closed (fig. 4).

12 Thread the cords from the top of the shade, through each of the eye hooks and over to one side, each time taking the cord across the top edge through each eye hook as it appears and down the edge of the shade. Knot the cords together at the top. Pull up the shade to check that it works smoothly and make any adjustments necessary before knotting the cords together lower down the shade (fig. 5).

13 Screw the cleat into the window frame. Pass the cord ends through the toggle and knot them together. Trim the ends close to the knot and pull the knob down to cover the knot. Wind the cord around the cleat to fix the height of the shade.

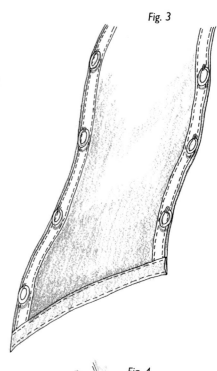

Fig. 3

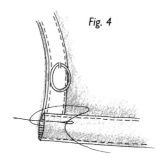

Fig. 4

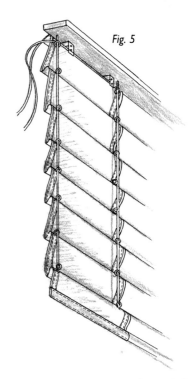

Fig. 5

Austrian Shades

THE IMPACT OF AN AUSTRIAN SHADE DEPENDS A GREAT DEAL ON THE FABRIC
AND ITS SETTING. EVEN THE SIMPLEST FABRICS, SUCH AS VOILE OR
MUSLIN, CAN LOOK VERY STYLISH MADE UP THIS WAY.

Before you begin

These shades are the easiest to make, because accurate measurements are not so important.

Austrian shades should be very full and luxurious – do not skimp on fabric.

There are two types of tape available for Austrian shades. and both have rings through which the draw cords are threaded. One type of tape has thin cords on either side which are pulled up to gather the shade. The other type doesn't have gathering cords. Decide whether you want a gathered or flat effect up the corded lines and this will tell you which tape to choose. Tape and cord quantities are the same for both.

The distance the vertical tapes are placed apart will determine the draping effect you achieve. Placing the tapes approximately 12" (30cm) apart will result in small scallops; placing them further apart will produce swag-like scallops. You will need at least three tapes, each one as long as your shade.

MATERIALS
*fabric piece, twice the width x twice the
length of the window*

*ruffle strips 4" (10cm) wide and length
twice the width of the shade*

sufficient piping

*shirring tape, the same length as
the fabric width*

brass cleat

sufficient Austrian shade tape

cord for each tape

matching sewing machine thread

sewing machine

*An otherwise uninteresting bathroom
window becomes a feature with the addition
of a ruffled Austrian shade*

Method

1 Cut the fabric to the required size. If necessary join pieces to achieve the correct width, with flat fell seams.
2 Press ¼" (6mm) to the wrong side, then another ¾" (2cm) on the sides of the shade. Stitch the side hems in place.
3 Mark the tape positions on the wrong side of the fabric. Fold the fabric along these lines and press lightly. Use the pressed creases as a guideline.
4 Join the ruffle strips together to make the desired length. Press ¼" (6mm), then another ⅜" (1cm) to the wrong side on one long edge and the sides of the ruffle. Gather the long raw edge to fit the lower edge of the shade. Pin the piping to the lower edge of the shade with right sides together and raw edges even. Pin the ruffle to the shade with the right sides facing and raw edges even. Baste. With a zipper foot, stitch the ruffle in place through all thicknesses, catching the piping in the seam.
5 Press ¾" (2cm) to the wrong side on the upper edge. Stitch the shirring tape along the top edge ⅜" (1cm) from the top (fig. 1).

6 Stitch the lengths of Austrian shade tape along the pressed guidelines, starting slightly above the ruffle and finishing slightly below the top. Make sure the rings are even just above the ruffle on each tape (fig. 2).

7 Mount the Austrian shade rod. Attach the shade to the rod with appropriate hooks.

8 If you are using tape which draws up, draw up the gathering cords on the tape and secure them when the shade is gathered to fit. Secure the cord in the bottom ring on each tape and then thread the cords up through the rings on each tape. Thread all the cords through the brass cleat in the window frame.

A combination of an Austrian shade with a curtain and valance is a great opportunity for creative use of fabric. The ruffle on the Austrian shade has been cut across the fabric to make the best use of the stripes

Fig. 1

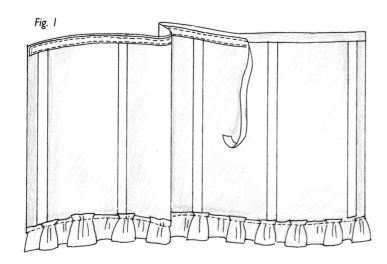

Fig. 2

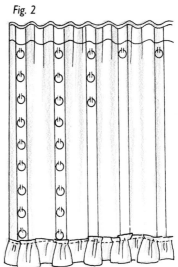

Tie-up Shades

FOR A LIVING AREA WHERE YOU NEED TO BALANCE A CERTAIN DEGREE OF
PRIVACY WHILE ALLOWING THE WARMTH OF THE SUN AND DAYLIGHT TO
ENTER, THIS SIMPLE TIE-UP SHADE COULD BE THE ANSWER.

Charming tie-up shades can be combined with simple matching curtains for a total window treatment

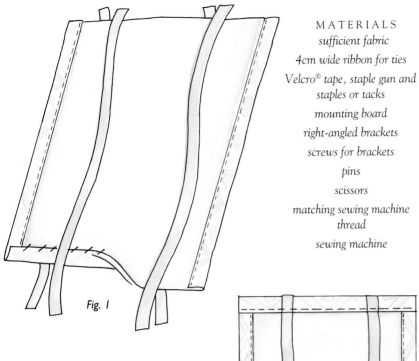

Fig. 1

MATERIALS
sufficient fabric
4cm wide ribbon for ties
Velcro® tape, staple gun and
staples or tacks
mounting board
right-angled brackets
screws for brackets
pins
scissors
matching sewing machine
thread
sewing machine

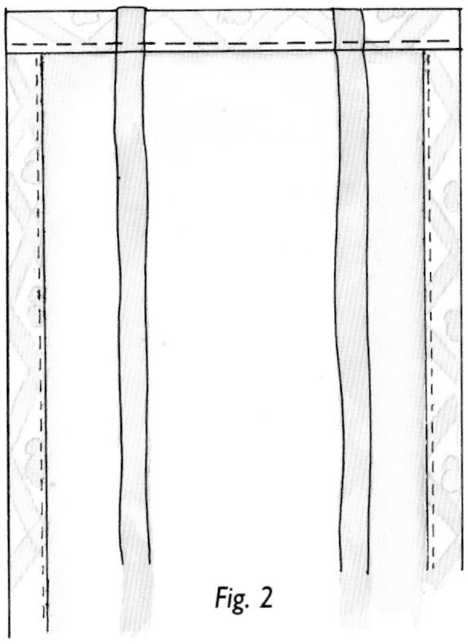

one tie on the wrong side of the fabric along the guideline and pin in position. On the front of the shade, pin another tie in the same position (fig. 1). Pin all the layers together down the middle of the tie. Baste through all thicknesses. Stitch down each side of the tie, beginning at the top and ending between one-third and halfway down the shade. The further down the shade you sew the ties, the lower the height the shade can be drawn up will be.

5 Press 2" (5cm) to the wrong side along the top edge, turning in the ends of the ties at the same time. Press another 2" (5cm) under and stitch the hem in place (fig. 2).

6 Sew the hook side of the Velcro® tape to the back across the width of the top hem. Attach the loop side to the mounting board with glue or staples. Alternatively, staple or tack the shade directly to the top of the mounting board (fig. 3).

Before you begin

Designed for lightweight unlined fabric, this shade is held up with fabric ties or contrasting ribbon or braid. It is not designed to be raised and lowered frequently and is only suitable for a relatively narrow window.

You will need two ties for each shade. Decide where you wish the ties to be placed. In our shade, they line up neatly with the window frames.

This shade is mounted on a board (approximately 16 mm thick x 2" (5cm) deep x the width of the shade) which is attached to the wall with right-angled brackets. The board may be painted or covered in fabric if desired.

Measuring

The fabric is the width and length of the window plus 2" (5cm) for each side hem, 2" (5cm) for the bottom hem and 4" (10cm) for the top hem.

Fig. 2

Method

1 Press ⅜" (1cm) to the wrong side on the sides of the shade, then another 1½" (4cm). Stitch the side hems.

2 Repeat for the bottom hem.

3 Mark the position of each tie on both the right and wrong sides of the shade.

4 Cut each ribbon tie the length of the shade plus 12" (30cm) for the bows. Lay

Fig. 3

Pillows

PIPED PILLOWS
HEIRLOOM PILLOWS
STENCILED PILLOWS
BOLSTERS
CHAIR CUSHIONS
ROUND BUTTONED PILLOWS

Pillows

A SIMPLE PILLOW HAS THE POTENTIAL TO PULL A DECORATIVE SCHEME TOGETHER THROUGH ITS COLOR, PRINT, STYLE AND EMBELLISHMENTS.

Versatile pillows will transform a tired corner into a focal point of the room, give your chair or sofa a new look, or make a hard chair inviting and comfortable. As well as adding finishing touches, large pillows can provide valuable extra seating.

Choosing the style of your pillows is a matter of personal taste combined with consideration for their intended use. This balance will determine whether you are trying to achieve a crisp, neatly defined look with straight piping or single lengths of braid, or a totally feminine look with ruffles and lace. Your choice of trims will give your pillow unique character. Experiment with some of the ideas shown in this chapter, mixing and matching them for different effects.

Pillows can also help you highlight the attractive features of a room or camouflage the ones you would rather forget. Round pillows scattered on your high-backed sofa will de-emphasize the harshness of high ceilings and soften the line of tall pieces of furniture. On the other hand, irregular or asymmetrically shaped pillows in an array of colors will draw the eye to a particular object, taking the attention away from other less pleasing aspects of a room.

Mix and match pillow styles, fabric and trims to maximize their impact

Fabrics and fillings

The selection of fabric for pillows will depend upon their end use. Durable fabrics are required for floor pillows and loose covers; lace and delicate broderie anglaise should be used only for purely decorative pillows; while general furnishing fabrics are ideal for all types of scatter pillows.

For the dining and kitchen areas use easy-care fabrics that can be thrown into the washing machine. Fabrics that are in constant use, such as in the family room, can be treated with a stain-repellent sprays, such as Scotchgard®. These products need to be reapplied after each wash. Upholstery-weight fabrics are often pre-treated with a similar product, offering immediate protection.

The strength of the fabric should also be considered. A dress-weight fabric would not be recommended for anything but decorative pillows that are placed on a bed and removed at night. Heavy cottons and tightly woven fabrics are ideal for floor pillows and loose seating covers. Soft furnishing fabrics are ideal for pillows because they are wide and therefore more economical. Natural fabrics, such as cottons and linens, and man-made fabrics, such as polyester, acrylic and acetate, have beneficial properties. Natural fabrics are easy to clean but can shrink and become distorted; synthetic fibers are more likely to attract dirt but less likely to lose their shape when cleaned. A blended fabric, such as a poly cotton, which is a combination of polyester and cotton, possesses qualities from both groups, being easy to clean and less likely to lose its shape.

Polyester fiberfil is fully washable, inexpensive and easy to work with, giving a final product that is soft and pliable. It is available loose, or in a pillow form.

Use feather or down fillings only with tightly woven fabrics; fabrics which are loosely woven will allow the feathers or down to migrate through. (Fine cotton or chintz is ideal for casings for down or feather fillings.) Foam chips are less expensive than feathers or down, but are lumpy and will crumble over time. Foam blocks can be cut to any shape or size.

Trimming pillows

❖

Pillows can be embellished in numerous ways. Apart from the basic decorative ruffles and piping you can also use ribbon, braid, beading, patchwork, appliqué and stenciling – to add a special finish.

In this section, you will find many trimming methods described in detail. Use them alone or combined to create pillows with a unique touch.

Continuous corded piping

To make corded piping, begin by making a length of continuous bias binding. You can, of course, use purchased bias binding or, for that matter, purchased piping, but when you want to use the same fabric or match a particular color, the following simple method will make it easy:

1 Cut a piece of fabric. Mark the bias strips as shown, the diameter of the cord, plus ¾" (2cm) seam allowance apart (fig. 1).
2 Fold the fabric with the right sides together, so that points A and B are matching. Note that one strip width extends at each side. Stitch together with a ¼" (6mm) seam and press the seam open (fig. 2).
3 Cut along the marked lines to make one continuous strip of bias fabric.
4 Fold this strip in half with the wrong sides together, enclosing the piping cord. With the zipper foot on your machine, secure the cord inside the bias fabric by stitching close to the cord through all thicknesses.
5 With the right sides of the piping and the fabric together and raw edges even, pin the piping around the edge of the pillow front, clipping the piping seam allowances at the corners to allow the piping to curve more easily.
6 Cut ¾" (2cm) of the piping cord out of one end of the piping to lessen the bulk at the overlap. Overlap the ends of the piping. Stitch as close to the piping cord as possible, using the zipper foot on your sewing machine.

Using purchased trims

To save time and still create a truly beautiful pillow, invest in one of the many trims that are available from retail outlets. Heavy braids and trims beautifully complement heavier fabrics, such as tapestries and jacquards.

Braids can also be sewn by hand to the outside of a finished pillow. Undo 2" (5cm) in one of the side seams of the

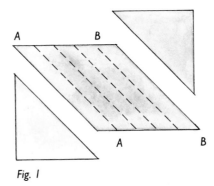

Fig. 1

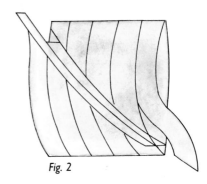

Fig. 2

pillow cover and poke one end of the braid into the opened seam section. Handsew the braid around the pillow, then poke the other end into the opening and slipstitch the opening closed.

How to make a double ruffle

1 Cut the ruffle double the desired finished width, plus ¾" (2cm) seam allowances, and twice the circumference of the pillow in length. For example, for a 4" (10cm) ruffle on a 16" (40cm) pillow, your ruffle strip will measure 8½" x 3½yds. (22cm x 3.2m). If necessary, join strips with a flat fell seam to achieve the length needed.

2 Join the short ends of the ruffle to form a loop using a flat fell seam.

3 Fold the ruffle strip in half, lengthwise with the wrong sides together and the raw edges even. Press. Gather the ruffle with two rows of gathering stitches in the seam allowance, either by hand or by machine.

4 To ensure that the ruffle is even all around, divide its length into quarters and mark with pins. Pull up the gathering to fit around the pillow front. Pin the ruffle around the right side of the pillow front with the right sides together and the raw edges even, placing a pin mark at each corner of the pillow front. Adjust the ruffle with your fingers placing a little extra gathering at each corner. Stitch in place along the line of gathering stitches (fig. 1).

5 Place the pillow back on the pillow front with the right sides together and the raw edges even. Baste through all thicknesses. Ensure that the ruffle is properly sandwiched between the front and back and stitch along the basting, leaving an opening for turning. Remove any visible basting stitches. Turn the pillow right side out.

How to make a two-color double ruffle

This clever method produces a ruffle which works on both sides and gives the appearance of having been bound.

1 Cut two ruffle strips, one 11" (28cm) wide and one 8½" (22cm) wide in a contrasting fabric. The length of both strips should be twice the circumference of the pillow cover plus 1¼" (3cm) for seams.

2 Place the two strips with right sides together along one long side. Stitch together ¾" (1cm) from the edge. Press the seam to one side. Join the short ends of the combined ruffle to make a loop.

3 Fold the ruffle in half, lengthwise, with wrong sides together and the raw edges even. Press.

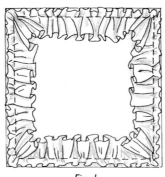

Fig. 1

4 Gather the raw edges of the ruffle with two rows of gathering stitches in the seam allowance. Divide the length of the ruffle into quarters and mark with pins. Draw up the ruffle to fit around the outside edge of the pillow front.

5 Pin the ruffle to the pillow front with the right sides together and the raw edges even, placing a pin mark at each corner. Adjust the ruffle with your fingers, placing a little extra gathering at each corner. Stitch in place along the line of gathering.

6 Place the pillow back on the pillow front with the right sides together and the raw edges even. Baste through all thicknesses. Ensure that the ruffle is properly sandwiched between the pillow front and back and stitch along the basting, leaving an opening for turning. Remove any visible basting stitches. Turn the pillow right side out.

Stenciling

Stenciling was one of the first methods of printing on fabric. Pure cotton is the best choice of fabric for stenciling. As the finish in some fabrics repels paint, wash your fabric thoroughly before beginning.

For stenciling, use a firm, clear plastic sheet or sheets purchased stencil cardboard or plastic. Choose fabric stenciling paint that is appropriate for the surface you are stenciling and a special stenciling brush. Experiment with the stencil first on scraps of fabric to test absorption and color strength. Don't judge a color until it is dry. When the paint is dry, heat-seal the colors by ironing on the back of the fabric or by using a very hot hairdryer on the paint surface. Check the manufacturer's instructions on the paint bottle.

Above left: A two-color double ruffle
Left: A double ruffle

Ruffled pillows have an old-world charm that is very appealing

If you are repeating a pattern, for example across the top of a sheet, measure out each position before you begin stenciling. Reposition the stencil accurately each time, using masking tape to hold the stencil in place while you are working. Be sure to keep the tape clear of the area to be stenciled.

Stencil brushes are thick, with an even end surface, because the best way of applying paint is by tapping the brush down in a pouncing motion on the space to be painted. Brush strokes can blur the outlines. Before applying the paint, remove any excess paint from the brush with a rag.

Appliqué

If your machine can zigzag, you can appliqué beautiful motifs very easily. Think of appliqué as a way of painting a picture with fabric.

Decide on your appliqué motif. Look for clear bunches of flowers or motifs that will be attractive as a feature.

You may find it easier to position the motif with fusible web. This way it will not slip while the edges are being sewn. If fusing, cut out your fabric around the general area of the motif, then following the manufacturer's instructions, fuse a piece of fusible web to the wrong side of the fabric. Cut out the detail of the motif, then fuse it in place.

When using this appliqué method, choose a sewing thread close to the background fabric color and always use a sharp machine needle.

Bows and ties make a very attractive closure on these striped pillows

Closures

A pillow cover needs to be easily removed for laundering. Zippers are the most common way to close pillow covers; however, Velcro®, buttons and ties are all suitable.

The placement of the closure can vary. A vent in the middle of the pillow back is often used when the pillow will not be turned over. A side vent opening can be concealed in a side seam so that the pillow can be reversible.

Decorative additions, such as buttons and bows, provide interest as well as a functional method for closing.

The instructions given here describe the basic steps in making a back vent closure, as well as other closure methods. They can all be incorporated into the pillow cover patterns in this chapter. Choose the one that best suits your decor, fabric, and style of pillow.

Back vent closure

This easy method that uses a fabric overlap as its only means of closure is the most simple; the only drawback being that if the insert is too full, the vent can spread open if it is not stitched closed.

1 Cut the pillow cover front to the finished size plus ⅝" (1.5cm) seam allowance all around. Cut a pillow cover back the same size, adding 4" (10cm) to two opposite sides to form a rectangle. Cut the rectangle in half crosswise; the cut edges will be the center back edges.

2 Press ⅝" (1.5cm) to the wrong side twice along the center back edges and stitch the hems in place.

3 Place the backs over the front so the hemmed edges overlap to form the back vent. Baste the edges of the backs together.

4 Complete the pillow cover following the instructions for the desired cover.

5 When the pillow cover is right side out, remove any visible basting, place the pillow form in the cover and slipstitch the vent closed.

Velcro® closure

1 Cut the pillow cover front to the finished size plus ⅝" (1.5cm) seam allowances all around. Cut the back the same size, adding 4" (10cm) to two opposite sides to form a rectangle. Cut the rectangle in half crosswise; the cut edges will be the center back edges.

2 Press ⅝" (1.5cm) to the wrong side twice along the center back edges and stitch the hems in place.

3 Pin one half of the Velcro® strip to the right side of one half of the pillow cover back over the stitched hem. Pin the other half of the Velcro® strip to the wrong side of the remaining half over the stitched hem. Test the closure to ensure the pillow back will close in a perfect square before stitching the Velcro® in place.

4 Complete assembly of the pillow

cover following the instructions for the desired pillow cover.

Buttons

1 Cut the pillow cover front to the finished size plus ⅝" (1.5cm) seam allowances all around. Cut the back to the same size, adding 4" (10cm) to two opposite sides to form a rectangle. Cut the rectangle in half crosswise; the cut edges will be the center back edges.
2 Press ⅝" (1.5cm) to the wrong side twice along the center back edges and stitch the hems in place.
3 Mark the positions for the buttons and buttonholes on the two stitched hems with a disappearing marker.
4 Stitch buttonholes to the top half of the opening and sew the buttons to the right side of the bottom half. Test the closure.
5 Complete the pillow cover following the instructions for the desired pillow cover.

Bows or ties

In addition to your main fabric, you will need approximately 2½" x 8" (6.6cm x 20cm) of fabric for each tie. These can be cut on the bias or the straight grain.
1 Decide how many pairs of ties you need and cut out the required pieces.
2 For each tie, fold the fabric strip in half lengthwise with right sides together and raw edges even. Stitch along the long side and across one end. Turn the tie right side out and press.
3 Cut out a pillow cover front and back with a ⅝" (1.5cm) seam allowance all around. Pin the raw ends of the ties to the right side of the back and front, so that the raw ends of the ties and the pillow cover are even. Make sure the pairs of ties are matching in position.
4 Cut two pieces of facing fabric, each 2" (5cm) wide by the width of the pillow. Place one facing piece on each side of the pillow cover over the ties with the right sides together and raw edges matching along the opening edge. Stitch along the opening edges

turn the facing to the wrong side. Press.
5 Complete the pillow cover following the instructions for the desired pillow cover.

Inserting a zipper

❖

Zippers are the most commonly used closure for pillow covers. Always use a good quality zipper.

Inserting a centered zipper

1 Measure and mark on the opening the length of the zipper teeth plus ¼" (6mm). Baste the zipper seam closed and press the seam open.
2 Open the zipper and place it face down on the seam allowance with the zipper teeth along the seam line. Baste the zipper in place along one side of the zipper tape. Close the zipper and baste the other side in place.
3 Turn the fabric right side up. Using the zipper foot on your sewing machine and starting at the top of the zipper, stitch down one side, across the bottom of the zipper, back to the top and across the top. Remove the basting stitches.

Inserting a lapped zipper in a piped seam

1 Press the seam allowance of the opening to the wrong side along the seam line.
2 With the piped pieces together, pull back the top seam allowance to expose the piping seam allowance.
3 Open the zipper, lay it face down over the seam allowance with the zipper teeth resting on the top of the piping. Baste along the zipper tape close to the zipper teeth. Check that the zipper will open and close smoothly, before stitching it in place. Remove the basting stitches.

Inserting an offset zipper

1 With the zipper open, position it over the opening so that the zipper teeth are centred over the right-hand seam allowance. Baste one side of the

Top: The centered zipper
Center: The offset zipper
Above: The zipper in the side seam

tape into position ¼" (6mm) from the zipper teeth.
2 Close the zipper and baste the other side of the zipper to the other seam allowance.
3 Turn the fabric right side up and topstitch the zipper in place through all the layers of fabric, using the zipper foot on your sewing machine and stitching close to the ends of the zipper. Remove the basting.

Piped Pillows

Basic piped pillow

MATERIALS

15" (38cm) square of fabric for the pillow cover front

two pieces of fabric, each 8½" x 15" (22cm x 38cm), for the pillow cover backs

15" (38cm) square pillow form

12" (30cm) zipper

2yds. (1.8m) of corded piping (see how to make and apply piping on page 91)

matching sewing machine thread

scissors

pins

tape measure

sewing machine

Method

1 Place the two long edges of the backs with right sides together and raw edges even. Stitch a 2" (5cm) seam at each end, leaving an opening in the center for the zipper. Insert the zipper (see page 95). Open the zipper for turning the pillow cover right side out.

2 With right sides together and raw edges even, pin the piping around the edge of the pillow cover front, clipping the piping seam allowances at the corners so it will curve gently. Cut ¾" (2cm) of the piping cord out of one end of the piping to lessen the bulk at the overlap. Overlap the piping ends. Stitch the piping in place using the zipper foot on your sewing machine and stitching as close as possible to the piping.

3 Pin and baste the pillow back and front with the right sides together and raw edges even. Stitch around all sides, stitching along the piping stitching line. Trim the seams and clip the corners.

4 Turn the pillow cover right side out through the zipper opening. Remove any visible basting stitches. Press.

An interesting fabric, such as this one, needs only simple piping to make an attractive pillow

Contrasting ruffles and piping makes a strong decorative statement

Ruffled piped pillow

MATERIALS

15" (38cm) square of fabric for the pillow cover front

two pieces of fabric, each 8½" x 15" (22cm x 38cm), for the pillow cover backs

2yds. (1.8m) of contrasting piping

12" (30cm) zipper

3½yds. (3.2m) of two fabrics for the ruffle

15" (38cm) square pillow form

matching sewing machine thread

scissors

pins

tape measure

sewing machine

Method

1 Make two single ruffles as instructed on page 23, one ½" (1.2cm) wider than the other. Make the piping as instructed on page 91 or purchase ready-made piping.

2 With right sides of the fabric together and raw edges even, sew the piping and then the completed ruffles around the pillow cover front. If attaching the ruffles separately after the piping, sew along the piping stitching line.

3 Place the two long edges of the back with the right sides together and the raw edges even. Stitch a 2" (5cm) long seam at each end, leaving an opening in the center for the zipper. Insert the zipper (see page 95). Open the zipper for turning the pillow right side out.

4 Place the pillow cover back and front with the right sides together and raw edges even. Stitch around the outside edge along the piping stitching line. Trim the seams and clip the corners to reduce bulk. Turn the pillow cover right side out through the zipper opening and press.

Pillow with contrast band

MATERIALS

15" (38cm) square of fabric for the pillow cover front

two pieces of fabric, each 8½" x 15" (22cm x 38cm), for the pillow cover back

four strips of border fabric, each 2" x 13" (5cm x 33cm)

2yds. (1.8m) of contrasting corded piping (see how to make corded piping on page 91)

12" (30cm) zipper

15" (38cm) square pillow form

matching sewing machine thread

tape measure

scissors

pins

sewing machine

Method

1 Trim the short ends of the border strips to perfect diagonals (fig. 1). Join the strips with mitred corners to form a square to fit the pillow cover 1½" (4cm) in from the outside edge. Clip in ⅜" (1cm) on the inner corner seams. Press the seams open.

2 Press ⅜" (1cm) to the wrong side on the inside and outside edges of the square. Center and pin the square to the pillow cover front. Edgestitch into place (fig. 2). Press.

3 Attach the piping to the pillow cover front. Insert the zipper into the pillow

Simple trimmings, cleverly applied, make a plain pillow into a unique one

cover back (see page 95). Open the zipper.

4 Place the pillow cover front and back with the right sides together and the raw edges even. Stitch around the outside edge. Trim excess bulk from the corners and seams. Turn the pillow cover right side out through the zipper opening. Press.

Machine-appliquéd pillow

MATERIALS

fabric, featuring flowers, animals, borders or any free-standing motif that will lend itself to being cut out

12" (30cm) square of fabric for the pillow cover front

two pieces of fabric, each 6¾" x 12" (17cm x 30cm), for the pillow cover backs

fabric strip for the ruffle, 4¾" x 2⅝yds. (12cm x 2.4m)

10" (25cm) zipper

12" (30cm) square pillow form

fusible web

pins

scissors

matching sewing machine thread

sewing machine

warm iron

pressing cloth

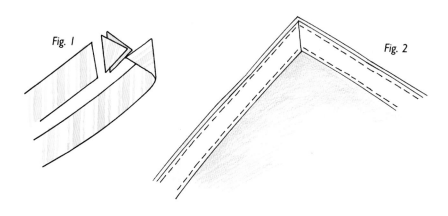

Fig. I

Fig. 2

Method

1 Cut out around the motif, leaving a ³/₄" (2cm) margin all around. Following the manufacturer's instructions, apply fusible web to the wrong side of the motif. Center the motif on the pillow front and fuse the motif in place, using a pressing cloth.

2 Set the sewing machine for satin stitch, and stitch around the motif, covering the raw edges.

3 Join the short ends of the ruffle strip. Press the strip in half crosswise with wrong sides together and raw edges even. Gather the raw edges together. Stitch the ruffle to the pillow front following the instructions on page 92.

4 Insert the zipper into the pillow cover back following the instructions on page 95. Open the zipper.

5 Place the pillow cover back on the front with the right sides together and the raw edges even. Stitch together through all thicknesses. Turn the pillow cover right side out through the zipper opening and press.

❖

Triangular pillow

Before you begin You can make a triangular insert for this pillow from muslin, following these instructions but omitting the zipper; or, simply stuff the pillow cover with polyester fiberfil.

MATERIALS

⅝yd. (.6m) of 54" (137cm)-wide fabric
3yds. (2.7m) of 2⅜" (6cm)-wide contrasting bias binding
3yds. (2.7m) of piping cord
matching sewing machine thread
12" (30cm) zipper
polyester fiberfil
scissors
pins
tape measure
sewing machine

This triangular pillow features bright contrasting piping

Method

1 Cut two equilateral triangles with each side measuring 16½" (42cm) including a ⅝" (1.5cm) seam allowance.

2 Make two lengths of piping, each 50" (130cm) long. (See page 91.)

3 Cut a piece of fabric for the boxing strip, 5" x 50" (13cm x 130cm) including seam allowances. If you need to join pieces, add ⅝" (1.5cm) for seam allowances on joining seams.

4 Pin the piping to the right side of the top and bottom pieces with the right sides together and raw edges even. Clip into the seam allowance of the piping to curve it around the corners. Cut out ¾" (2cm) of piping cord at one end. Overlap the ends as neatly as possible. Stitch in place.

5 To attach the boxing strip, pin and baste the ends of the strip together to form a loop. Check the fit. Make any necessary adjustments. Pin the boxing strip to the top with the right sides together and raw edges even. Stitch in place along the piping stitching line. Trim the seam allowance.

6 Stitch the boxing strip to the bottom in the same way, leaving a 12" (30cm) opening along one side for the zipper. Trim any excess bulk around the corners and at the seams.

7 Insert the zipper, and leave it open. Turn the pillow right side out through the open zipper and press.

8 Stuff the pillow firmly and evenly with the fiberfil, ensuring that the corners are well filled or make and insert a muslin pillow form if desired. Close the zipper.

Heirloom Pillows

MADE FROM SILK AND LACE, THESE PILLOWS USE BASIC PATCHWORK
TECHNIQUES AND HAND-APPLIQUE TO GIVE THEM A LOOK OF DISTINCTION
THAT WILL BECOME MORE CHARMING WITH AGE.

Lace patchwork pillow

MATERIALS
2¼yds. (2m) of 2" (5cm)-wide lace
⅓yd. (.3m) of 45" (115cm)-wide
natural-colored silk for the pillow front
two pieces of silk, each 8½ x 15" (22cm x
38cm), for the pillow cover backs
12" (30cm) zipper

15" (38cm) square pillow form
pins
needles
matching sewing machine thread
tape measure
sewing machine

Method

1 Cut two 4¾" (12cm)-wide strips the
width of the fabric. Stitch both sides of
the lace down the center of the fabric
strips, stitching close to the edge of the
lace. Press, then cut the strips into
sixteen 4¾" (12cm) squares.

2 Sew the squares together in four
rows of four squares each, alternating
the direction of the lace as shown. Sew
the four rows together to form the pillow front.

3 Complete the pillow as desired. We
have added a ruffle – you will need
extra fabric to do this.

*Lace, silk and appliqué give
these pillows a rich romantic
look (Make the Battenburg
lace pillow in the same way
as the ruffled pillow, adding
a lace edging instead of the
ruffle.)*

Hand-appliquéd pillow

Before you begin The traditional hand-appliqué method is ideal for delicate voile pillow-cases and lightweight cotton pillow covers, as well as chintz motifs that can be cut out and appliquéd onto softer colored backgrounds.

MATERIALS
pillow cover of your choice

tracing paper

pencil

fabric in a contrasting color or texture for the bow

dressmaker's marker

needle

pins

scissors

matching sewing thread

Method

1 Trace the bow motif, on tracing paper with a pencil. Cut out the appliqué patterns.

2 Pin the appliqué patterns to the right side of the pillow front and trace around them.

3 Cut out the bow appliqué from the contrasting fabric, adding ¼" (6mm) around each piece. Press the seam allowances to the back of each piece and baste in place. When working around curved edges, gather in the basting stitch slightly so that the edge will lie flat. Snip into corners and curves where necessary.

4 Pin the motif to the pillow front and baste in place. Working from the back, with small slipstitches stitch the motif in place. Remove the basting.

If you are making your own pillow cover, you can use the appliqué fabric for a ruffle or a bias trim

Stenciled Pillows

MATERIALS

purchased plastic stencil sheet

permanent fine marker

sharp craft knife or scalpel

bread board or cutting board

stencil brushes

fabric paints

masking tape

extra fabric for testing colors

15" (38cm) square of muslin for the
pillow cover front

two pieces of muslin, each 8½" x 15"
(22cm x 38cm), for the pillow cover back

muslin strip for the ruffle

checked cotton fabric strip for
the second ruffle

15" (38cm) square pillow form

matching sewing machine thread

pins

scissors

tape measure

sewing machine

Method

1 Place the stencil sheet over the motif and trace around the design with the marker. Cut the stencil out on the cutting board with the craft knife or scalpel. Remember to leave 'bridges' in the design that are not cut through.

2 Place the stencil on the pillow cover front. To stencil areas that will be the same color, cover all other areas with masking tape. Taking care to paint the elements in order (main color first, then details), start stenciling from the outside, gradually filling in the entire area until you have achieved the desired depth of color. Each time you finish stenciling a color, cover it with tape and uncover the next area to be painted. Allow each section to dry before beginning the next one, to avoid the colors bleeding. Allow all the paint to dry before sewing.

3 Make two double ruffles as instructed on page 92, one ½" (1.2cm) wider than the other.

4 Complete the pillow in the same way as the double ruffled pillow on page 92.

The stencil pattern below provides a basic outline – change any details you wish, to personalize the design.

For a fresh country look, stencil muslin pillows with farmyard motifs

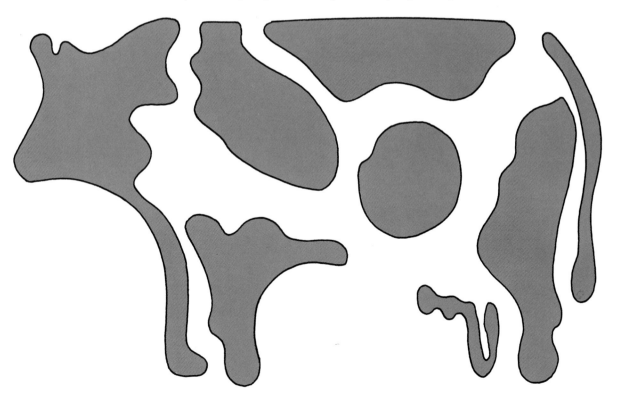

Bolsters

LARGE BOLSTERS ARE OFTEN USED AS NECK ROLLS ON A BED, WHILE SMALLER
VERSIONS CAN BE USED PURELY AS DECORATION FOR A WINDOW SEAT OR
TO COMPLEMENT OTHER PILLOWS ON A COUCH OR A BED.

Before you begin Like pillows, bolsters can also be uniquely embellished with embroidery and a variety of trims. There are two styles of bolsters: one with a gathered end and the other with a flat end. The materials required vary slightly for the two styles.

Gathered-end bolster

MATERIALS
sufficient fabric
bolster pad
two self-covering buttons and a 2" (5cm)
square of fabric for covering each button
matching sewing machine thread
scissors
pins
tailor's chalk
quilting thread
long needle
tape measure
sewing machine

Method

1 Cut a rectangle of fabric 1¼" (3cm) wider than the circumference of the bolster pad and 1¾" (4.5cm) longer than the length of the bolster pad.

2 Sew the long edges with right sides together with a ⅝" (1.5cm) seam. Press the seam open and turn the tube right side out.

3 Position the pad in the center of the fabric tube, so that equal amounts of fabric extend on each end. Mark the

Bolsters with simple gathered ends, are a charming addition to a traditional day bed

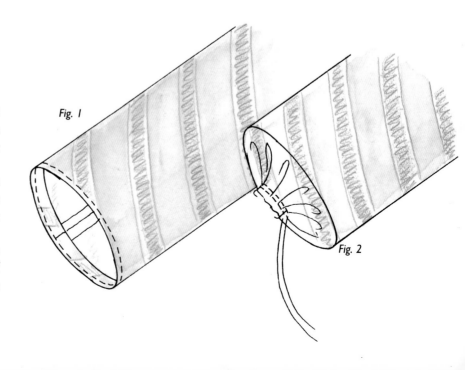

Fig. 1

Fig. 2

position of the pad with pins or chalk and remove the cover.

4 Press ⅝" (1.5cm) under on each end (fig. 1). Gather around the circumference of each end close to the folded edge. Replace the pad in the cover. Gather the fabric tightly at each end and secure (fig. 2).

5 Cut the button fabric ⅜" (1cm) larger than the circumference of the button. Gather around the circumference of the fabric, and draw it up around the button. Tie off the ends of the thread. Attach the buttons with quilting thread and the long needle to the center of each end, covering the gathering.

Bolsters can be quite simple or lavishly trimmed with piping and a tassel

---

Piped flat-end bolster

MATERIALS
sufficient fabric

twice the circumference of the ends of the bolster plus 1¼" (3cm) in contrasting corded piping (see how to make and attach corded piping on page 91)

bolster pad

10" (25cm) zipper

two decorative tassels

matching sewing machine thread

scissors

pins

tape measure

tailor's chalk

sewing machine

Method

1 Cut a rectangle of fabric 1¼" (3cm) longer than the bolster pad and 1¼" (3cm) wider than the circumference.

2 Cut two circles for the ends of the bolster, the same diameter as the pad plus 1¼" (3cm) seam allowances.

3 Pin the piping to the right side of the fabric on the short edges of the rectangle, matching raw edges. Clip into the seam allowance of the piping to allow it to curve.

4 Pin the long edges of the rectangle together with right sides together. With a ⅝" (1.5cm) seam allowance, stitch each end, leaving a 10" (25cm) opening in the center for the zipper. Baste the rest of the seam closed along the seam line.

5 Press the seam open. Remove the basting stitches and insert the zipper

(see page 95), following the instructions for a centered zipper (fig. 3). Open the zipper.

6 Cut notches into the seam allowances of the two circles. Baste the ends in place over the piping. With the zipper foot on your sewing machine, stitch the ends in place (fig. 4). Trim and clip the seam allowances. Turn the cover right side out through the zipper opening.

7 Stitch a decorative tassel in the center of each end. Insert the bolster pad and close the zipper.

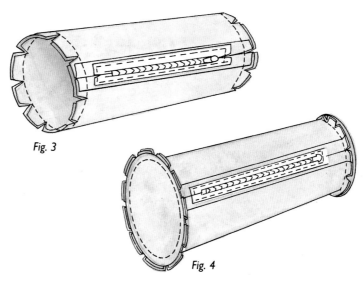

Fig. 3

Fig. 4

Chair Cushions

CHAIR CUSHIONS ARE AN EASY WAY TO ADD COMFORT AND STYLE TO
WOODEN CHAIRS. CHOOSE A WASHABLE FABRIC AND ONE THAT WILL
COMPLEMENT YOUR COLOR SCHEME.

The shape of these two cushions will vary according to the shape of your chair. Begin by making a pattern

Boxed chair cushions

MATERIALS
*two pieces of medium-weight fabric, each
18" x 20" (46cm x 51cm), for the seat
cushion cover, and two pieces
approximately 20" (51cm) square for the
back rest*

*20" (51cm) of 2½" (6cm)-wide fabric for
the boxing strip*

*5½yds. (5m) of contrasting piping (see
how to make and apply piping on page 91)*

polyester fiberfil

large sheets of paper

pencil

ten matching covered buttons

matching sewing machine thread

quilting thread

tailor's chalk

pins

scissors

sewing machine

Method

1 To make the pattern, trace the shape of the chair seat and the back rest on to the large sheets of paper. Using the paper pattern, cut two seat cushion pieces and two back rest pieces adding ⅝" (1.5cm) seam allowances.

2 Stitch the piping to the right side of each seat cushion piece, clipping the seam allowance of the piping at the corners. Stitch the piping to the right side of one back rest piece in the same manner as the seat.

3 Starting at the center back, pin the boxing strip around the edge of one cushion cover piece over the piping, with right sides together and the raw edges even. Stitch the center back seam of the boxing strip, then stitch the boxing strip to the cushion cover along the piping stitching line.

4 With right sides together, pin the remaining cushion cover piece to the boxing strip, then stitch in place along the piping stitching line, leaving an opening at the back for stuffing. Turn right side out and press. Stuff the cushion with fiberfil, distributing it evenly.

5 Fold in the seam allowance at the opening and slipstitch it to the piping.

6 For the back rest, place the front and back with right sides together and raw edges even. Stitch around the outside edge, leaving a 5" (15cm) opening at the bottom. Turn right side out and press.

7 Stuff loosely. With quilting thread, stitch three buttons on each side, roughly corresponding to where the chair arms begin, pulling the thread firmly through the button and the stuffing to the back of the back rest. Stitch four buttons to the seat cushion in the same manner.

Boxed chair cushions can be made to any size or shape to suit a variety of chair styles

Chair cushion with deep ruffle

Before you begin

You will need two fabric strips for the ruffles: one should be one and a half times the length of the back edge of the chair, the other one should be one and a half times the length of the three remaining sides of the chair, adding an extra 1¼" (3cm) to each piece for hems. Decide how wide you wish your ruffle to be and add ⅝" (1.5cm) for the top and bottom seam/hem allowances.

MATERIALS
two pieces of medium-weight fabric, each 18" x 20" (46cm x 51cm), for the cushion cover

polyester fiberfil

2¼yds. (2m) of 2½" (6cm)-wide fabric strips for ties

fabric strips for the ruffles

large sheet of paper

pencil

matching sewing machine thread

pins

scissors

tape measure

turning hook or knitting needle

sewing machine

Method

1 To make the pattern, trace the shape of the chair seat on to the large sheet of paper. Using the paper pattern, cut two cushion cover pieces, adding ⅝" (1.5cm) seam allowances.

2 To make the ruffle, press ¼" (6mm) to the wrong side twice on the sides and ends of the two ruffle strips. Stitch the hem. Gather the top edge of each strip.

3 Baste the shorter ruffle to the back edge of the cushion cover front with the right sides together and matching raw edges, starting 1" (2.5cm) in from both back corners. Baste the longer ruffle around the front and side edges of the cushion cover front with right sides facing and matching raw edges, starting 1" (2.5cm) in from both back corners.

4 Cut the tie strips into four equal lengths. Fold each length in half with the right sides together and raw edges even. Stitch along the long side and across one short end. Turn the ties right side out with the turning hook or knitting needle and press. Pin the ties at the four corners with the raw edges matching. Baste.

5 Place the cushion cover back and front with right sides together and raw edges even, and with the ruffle in between. Stitch around the outside edge in the ruffle basting line, leaving an opening at the center back. Turn the cushion cover right side out and press.

6 Stuff the cushion evenly. Slipstitch the opening closed.

Above and below: Make a ruffled chair cushion in a washable fabric to coordinate with your decor

Piped chair cushion

MATERIALS

two pieces of medium-weight fabric, each
18" x 20" (46cm x 51cm), for the
cushion cover

polyester fiberfil

1⅝yds. (1.5m) of corded piping (see
how to make and apply corded piping on
page 91)

2¼yds. (2m) of 5½" (14cm)-wide fabric
strips for ties

large sheet of paper

pencil

matching sewing machine thread

pins

scissors

tape measure

turning hook or knitting needle

tailor's chalk

sewing machine

A cushion adds comfort as well as charm to a wooden chair

Method

1 To make the pattern, trace the shape of the chair seat on to the large sheet of paper. Using the paper pattern, cut two cushion cover pieces.

2 Stitch the corded piping to the right side of one cushion piece.

3 Cut the tie strips into four equal lengths. Fold each length in half with right sides together and the raw edges even. Stitch along the long side and across one short end. Turn the ties right side out with the turning hook or knitting needle and press. Place the ties on the right side of the front cushion cover, with the raw edges matching. Baste in place.

4 Place the cushion cover back and front together with the right sides together and raw edges even. Stitch around the outside edge along the piping stitching line, leaving an opening for turning at the center back. Turn right side out and press.

5 Mark and stitch around four small squares evenly spaced in the center of the cushion (fig. 1). Stuff the cushion with fiberfil, distributing the stuffing evenly. Slipstitch the opening closed.

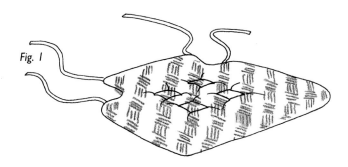

Fig. 1

Round Buttoned Pillow

MATERIALS

1⅛yds. (1m) of 45" (115cm)-wide fabric

2¾yds. (2.4m) of corded piping (see how
to make corded piping on page 91)

two buttons

matching sewing machine thread

quilting thread

long needle

polyester fiberfil

pins

tape measure

scissors

sewing machine

large sheets of paper

pencil

string

push pin

dressmaker's cutting board

Method

1 To make a paper pattern for the circles, cut a square of paper larger than the area of your pillow, then fold the paper into quarters, with the folded center of the paper at the upper left corner. With the push pin, pin one end of the piece of string to the folded corner, pushing the pin into a cutting board. Tie the pencil to the other end of the string at a distance equal to the desired radius of the circle plus ⅝"

(1.5cm) seam allowance. (The radius is the distance from the center of a circle to its circumference.) In the pillow shown here, the radius is 8" (20cm). Draw the quarter of the circle on the paper and cut along the drawn line through all the thicknesses of paper. Unfold the paper for the circle pattern (figs. 1 and 2).

2 Pin the circle pattern to two layers of fabric and cut out.

3 Sew the piping to the right sides of the front and back of the pillow cover with right sides together and raw edges even, clipping into the seam allowance of the piping so it will curve.

4 Cut a strip of fabric 4" x 50" (10cm x 130cm), for the boxing strip. If it is necessary to join fabric for the boxing strip, ensure that all pieces are cut in the with the grain running in the same direction on the fabric. Join the pieces into a loop with flat fell seams to fit the circumference of the pillows and trim any excess fabric. Press the seam open.

5 With the right sides together, pin one edge of the boxing strip to the pillow cover front, sandwiching the piping in between, and stitch into place through all thicknesses. Trim any excess fabric and clip into the curve all the way around. Press the seam open.

6 Pin and stitch the other edge of the

boxing strip to the back of the pillow cover leaving an opening for turning. Trim the seam and press open.

7 Turn the pillow cover right side out. Insert the fiberfil and slipstitch the opening closed.

8 Cut out fabric for covering the buttons ⅜" (1cm) larger than the circumference of the button. Gather around the edge of the fabric, draw up the fabric around the button and tie off the ends of the thread.

9 With the quilting thread and the long needle, attach one button to the pillow front and one button to the pillow back, drawing the needle through the pillow cover at least three times from button to button to ensure they are securely attached.

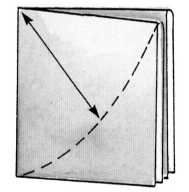

Fig. 1

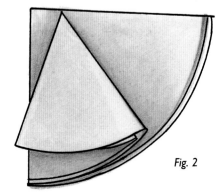

Fig. 2

A rich brocade works very well for this pillow style

Slip-covers

EDGE TREATMENTS

ARMCHAIR COVER

DROP-IN SEAT COVER

DIRECTOR'S CHAIR COVERS

TAILORED CHAIR COVER

RUFFLED CHAIR COVER

INSTANT SOFA COVER-UP

Slipcovers

IT IS USUALLY BEST TO LEAVE TRADITIONAL UPHOLSTERY TO THE PROFESSIONALS, BUT THERE ARE LOTS OF QUICK AND EASY FURNITURE-COVERING PROJECTS SUITABLE FOR THE ENTHUSIAST.

Wouldn't that old sofa that you bought at the last garage sale look great with a smart slipcover? A few lengths of fabric and a couple of weekends' work and hey presto, a new sofa! If only it were that easy. Traditional furniture upholstery can be a minefield of pitfalls for the amateur. Furnishing fabrics are expensive and mistakes can quickly swallow up your decorating budget. Even the simplest type of upholstery involves fixing a covering fabric over a tightly stretched muslin cover which itself covers padding and possibly springs. The variety of furniture shapes and styles is almost endless. Some furniture pieces have shapes which create particular problems and awkward corners to work around.

There are very simple cover projects – such as renewing dining-room chairs, or recovering pillows – that are perfect do-it-yourself projects. There are step-by-step instructions for these in the following pages. These projects are not 'upholstery' in the traditional sense – no repairs, new stuffing, web or springs are required. They do, however, provide decorative solutions to tired and worn-out chairs, or practical removable covers where laundering is required.

Choosing fabric

Choosing the right fabric for the job and the room is crucial to the success of the project, and the great variety of fabrics available can be daunting to the home decorator. The four natural fibers – cotton, wool, silk and linen – are widely used for covers. Cotton, which is mass-produced and generally economical, is a popular choice for slipcovers and pillows. Prewash all cottons to allow any shrinkage to take place before cutting out. Wool is very hard-wearing, flame-resistant, light, and relatively waterproof. It has been popular for furniture coverings from time to time. Silk is the glamour fabric, but because of its relatively high cost, it is usually reserved for trimming, pillows or luxury pieces. Linen is one of the oldest domestic fibers and because of its long-wearing qualities has always been a popular choice for loose covers – especially in high-traffic areas. Many synthetic fibers are also available and these are often blended with natural fibers. This reduces fabric cost and takes advantage of the good wearing and washing qualities of polyester and viscose fabrics.

Color and pattern

The choice of color and pattern for a particular loose cover or upholstery project will be determined by a number of factors. Are you re-covering an entire suite or will your slipcover have to fit in with existing pieces? Is your room big enough to cope with a large splashy floral or will your print be overwhelmed by other objects in the room? Do you need to warm up a room with yellows, pinks and reds or do you need to cool it down with blue? Remember that colors can be affected by the light in a room, both natural and artificial. Working with a story board of the total room color and pattern concept will be a big help. Before buying fabric, it is a good idea to take home a large sample piece. Drape it over your sofa or chair and leave it there for a day or two so you can judge the effect of the light in the room and how you think it will fit in with the curtains, wallpaper and other colors and patterns in the room. Generally, the larger your room the more you can get away with. There are exceptions, of course, but as a rule of thumb, it will help you avoid decorating disasters.

Matching patterns, where fabric pieces join can be a nightmare. If you are not experienced, or endowed with endless patience, you are probably best to stick to solids or all-over small prints which do not need matching. Stripes need careful matching but provide their own easy-to-follow guidelines. Floral bouquets or medallion patterns are more difficult because the motif has to be centered on seat cushions and backs, often wasting a lot of fabric. Checks are the hardest of all, having to be matched in all directions at once.

Before you buy, it's a good idea to check whether the fabric you like will present pattern-matching problems. Lay two lengths side by side as though they were joined, then move one slightly up or down. Now stand back and see the difference. You can do the same test if patterns are to meet end-to-end.

Trimming

Piping and trims add a professional finishing touch to your coverings. They also define the line of a piece of furniture and give strength to areas, such as the arms, that receive constant hard wear. When selecting a suitable color for piping or trims, it is usual to highlight one of the colors found in your fabric. If you use one of the colors from the main color palette of your fabric the piping will blend in rather than create a decorative highlight.

There are different sizes of piping cord available, and they are measured by the diameter of the cord. The size you should select is determined by the fabric to which it will be attached. As a general rule, a thick fabric requires a thin cord and a thin or fine fabric will require a thicker cord to give the fabric body. Thick piping on covers is often called welting.

On page 21 you will see how to make piping for cushions. The same method can be applied to upholstery piping. Lengths of bias fabric are joined with 1/4" (6mm) seams, or you can cut continuous bias (see page 20). Lay the piping cord on the wrong side of the fabric. To join the ends of the piping cord, butt the ends together and bind them neatly with heavy embroidery thread. Fold the fabric in half, enclosing the cord. Stitch close to the cord, using the zipper foot on your sewing machine.

Edge Treatments

CHOOSING THE RIGHT EDGE TREATMENT TO FINISH YOUR
SLIPCOVERS IS A MATTER OF PERSONAL TASTE AND STYLE.

Before you begin A ruffled edge creates a look of country cottage comfort, informal yet inviting; knife pleats ensure a tailored look; soft scalloped edges are harmonious and feminine; while a flush edge gives a neat and simple finish. Concealed edges show the clean lines of the chair or suite, enhancing the natural characteristics of the fabric. Braids can be used to cover seam lines and can be secured with upholstery tacks.

A staple gun is a handy tool for securing fabrics to a wooden base. The staples can subsequently be covered with flat braids.

Concealed bottom edge

Before you begin This method will give you a fitted tailored look with four separate strips (one for each side of the base) that are secured underneath the chair with ties.

You will need four 4¾" (12cm)-wide strips: two that are the same length as the width of the chair base and two that are the same length as the depth of the chair base. Add 2" (5cm) to the length of each strip for the side hems and 1" (2.5cm) for the bottom hem.

MATERIALS
four fabric strips, the same as the body fabric of the chair cover

sewing machine with a needle suitable for sewing through several layers of fabric

narrow piping cord

large safety pin

pins

scissors

tape measure

Method

1 Pin the strips to the bottom edges of the chair cover. Trim away the excess fabric around the chair legs or casters, leaving at least a 1" (2.5cm) seam allowance. Remove the strips. Press ¼" (6mm) under on the side edges, then another ¾" (2cm). Machine-stitch the side hems in place.

2 Hem the bottom edges of the strips in the same manner, forming a casing by stitching close to both folds. Stitch the strips to the chair cover.

3 Using the safety pin, thread the cord loosely through the casing. Fit the cover over the chair. Turn the chair on its side, pull up the cord and tie the two ends of the cord in a bow or knot (fig. 5).

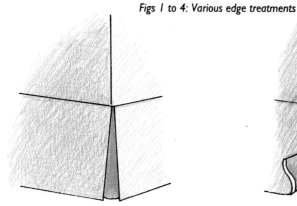

Figs 1 to 4: Various edge treatments

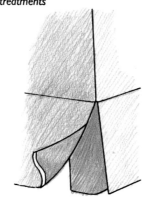

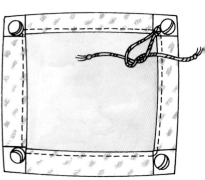

Fig. 5

Ruffled valance

Before you begin

Measure around the bottom edge of the chair cover. For ruffles, you will need twice this measurement plus ⅝" (1.5cm) for each seam allowance on any joining seams. The depth of the valance will be determined by the style of the chair. Make any necessary adjustments. Add 1" (2.5cm) for the hem and another ⅝" (1.5cm) for the gathering and top seam allowance.

MATERIALS
fabric, the same as the body
fabric of the cover

sewing machine with a needle suitable for
sewing through several layers of fabric

matching sewing machine thread

quilting thread for gathering
the ruffle (optional)

pins

scissors

tape measure

Method

1 Cut as many strips of the required depth to achieve the total length, following the grainline of the fabric and matching any pattern. Join the strips together with flat fell seams.

2 Hem the bottom edge and the short ends by machine or by hand; the latter method is preferable if a light fabric is being used, so that the stitches are not obvious.

3 Gather along the top edge and pull up the gathers to fit the bottom of the chair cover. With the right sides together, pin and baste the ruffle to the bottom edge of the chair cover, allowing extra fullness at the corners. Place the cover on the chair and make any adjustments before machine-stitching the valance into place, placing the opening at the back leg, where the chair cover is also open.

Box-pleated valance

Before you begin

The valance must begin and end at the back leg where the chair cover is also open. The pleats should be evenly arranged, preferably with a pleat at each corner, one at the center front and one at the center back. Making a paper pattern like those here is a good idea (figs. 6 and 7).

Measure around the bottom edge of the cover. You will need three times this measurement plus ⅝" (1.5cm) for each seam allowance on any joining seams. Determine the height of the pleat to suit your chair, adding 1" (2.5cm) for the hem and another ⅝" (1.5cm) for the top seam allowance.

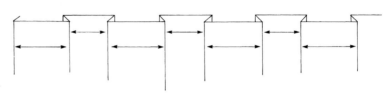

Fig. 7: Measure around the bottom of the chair and determine the width of each pleat

MATERIALS
fabric, the same as the body fabric
of the chair cover

sewing machine with a needle suitable for
sewing through several layers of fabric

matching sewing machine thread

stiff cardboard, the width of your pleat by
the depth of the box-pleated edge

tailor's chalk

pins

scissors

pencil

steel ruler

Method

1 Cut as many strips as necessary of the required size to achieve the total length, following the grainline of the fabric. Join the strips together with flat fell seams.

2 Hem the bottom edge and the two short ends.

3 Cut a cardboard template for the pleats, the width of your pleat, about 8" (20cm) x the height of the pleat. Moving the template along the length of the fabric, mark the pleats with tailor's chalk, marking both the top and bottom edges.

4 Fold and pin the pleats. Press the pleats carefully, then baste them in place. Machine-stitch across the top to secure the pleats. Remove the basting.

5 To attach the valance, begin at the back leg where the cover is open and pin the valance to the bottom edge of the chair cover, with right sides together and raw edges even; stitch.

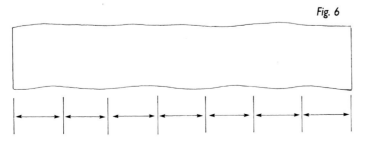

Fig. 6

Easy Chair Cover

GIVE AN OLD EASY CHAIR A TOTALLY FRESH
LOOK WITH A FEW YARDS OF NEW FABRIC AND
A LITTLE INGENUITY!

Before you begin Easy covering is all about revamping furniture with minimum fuss and expense. If the frame of your chair is solid, but the fabric is shabby, this type of re-covering is an ideal solution for the home stitcher. However, if your chair has stretched or torn web, or the odd spring is poking through, you will have to consider using a professional upholsterer.

The instructions given here are for re-covering an easy chair, but you can cover a sofa or couch the same way.

Measuring

Measuring and making a pattern for a chair or couch slipcover is an exacting process. When you are making a large investment in fabric, it is essential that you buy the correct quantity. Remember, it is a good form of insurance to buy an extra ½yd. (.5m) of fabric. If it is not needed for the cover, it can be converted into a beautiful throw pillow to complement your slipcover. Time is your best friend when measuring for slipcovers – avoid working in a hurry and always check all measurements. It is often wise when making a slipcover to make a muslin pattern or mock-up first so that any problems appear or so adjustments can be made at this preliminary stage rather than with your expensive fabric.

Make a sketch or drawing of the piece you are covering, with the measurements for each plane of the chair marked on it (fig. 1). On this same piece of paper keep a running list of all measurements. This list should include measurements for: inside back, seat, inside arms, outside arms, front border,

Fig. I

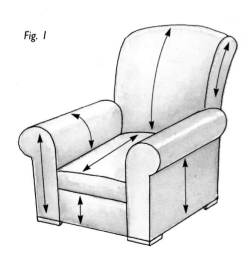

Fig. 2

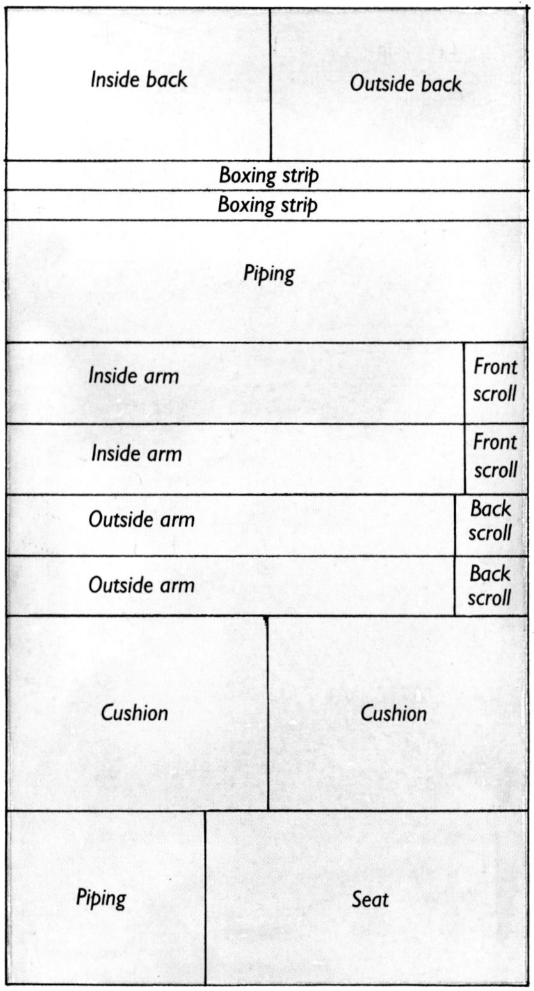

Inside back		Outside back	
Boxing strip			
Boxing strip			
Piping			
Inside arm			Front scroll
Inside arm			Front scroll
Outside arm			Back scroll
Outside arm			Back scroll
Cushion		Cushion	
Piping		Seat	

front scrolls, back scrolls, outside back, cushion boxing strips, borders and piping. Always write the measurements with the length of the fabric first, followed by the width. The drawing and the list will prove a handy cross-check system for all your measurement requirements.

Consider the style of the furniture piece as well as the pattern and weave of the fabric. When working with a patterned fabric, the pattern on the arms of the chair should run in line with the center back, which should in turn be in line with the seat. When working with a fabric that has a raised pile, the pile must always run down the chair. Always take measurements on the widest point of each section and allow 1" (2.5cm) for each seam allowance. Add an additional 4" (10cm) for the tuck-in, the part of the fabric that runs between the seat and the inside back and helps to keep the cover in place.

If the chair has a removable cushion, remember to take the cushion out so that you can measure the cover that sits underneath it. You will also need to decide how you wish to finish the bottom edge of your slipcovers. On pages 116 to 117 you will see a number of options. Allow extra fabric for whichever of these options you choose.

Also, remember to allow fabric for piping. Approximately 7yds. (6.5m) of piping can be made from 10" (25cm) of 48" (122cm)-wide fabric. It is a good idea to allow extra fabric for covers for arm rests or head rests, which will help to protect your chairs from soiling.

When cutting out your pattern, work with rectangles of fabric that are a little larger than you need. They can be trimmed to shape and size as needed.

Linens and cottons should always be cut with pinking shears in order to minimize fraying.

Pattern layout (fig. 2)
To calculate your fabric requirements, draw up a scaled pattern with each separate pattern piece drawn in, with

Contrasting piping is a feature of this charming floral easy chair slipcover

its correct position in relation to the grain and pattern of the fabric. Where pieces are required that are larger than the width of the fabric, for example on the inside back – try to get the best possible pattern placement. If this is impossible, join two pieces together with a piped seam to disguise the imperfect match.

MATERIALS
sufficient muslin, approximately 9yds. (8m) for an easy chair
upholstery weight fabric, the same quantity as the muslin, allowing extra for pattern matching [2yds-5½yds. (2m-5m) additional fabric]
upholstery pins or upholstery tape
tailor's chalk or masking tape for marking pieces
quilting thread
matching sewing machine thread
upholstery needle
Velcro® tape or hook-and-eye tape
felt tip marker
sewing machine with a suitable upholstery-gauge needle
sufficient bias-cut fabric strips (the width of the strips will be determined by the diameter of the cord used)
sufficient piping cord

Method

1 Cut rectangles from the muslin for each piece marked on your pattern layout. With the marker, mark the location of each pattern piece on the muslin.

2 Working with one piece at a time, pin or tape each muslin piece to the corresponding area on the chair. Mark the final shape on each piece. Remove the muslin pieces and add a 1" (2.5cm) seam allowance all around. Place each piece back in position to check the fit.

3 Pin all the pieces together.

4 Sewing pieces together in the right order will help to ensure that the finished pattern can be easily worked. Baste together with quilting thread in the following order:

- the outer back piece to the inside back;
- the inside back to the seat;
- the seat to the lower front panel;
- the seat to the arms along the inside edge;
- the inside arm to the outside arm;
- the front of the arms between the inner and outer arms;
- the end of the arm pieces to the back and inside back, leaving an opening on one back seam approximately 14" (35cm) from the base to the back of the inside scroll; and
- the bottom edge treatment.

5 Slip the cover on the chair, wrong side facing out. On curved areas, such as the arms, it may be necessary to take out some fullness. Undo the basting stitches and make tiny gathers or pleats on the wrong side, taking up the slack. Make any darts as necessary. Stitch the basting back into place to ensure a perfect fit. Once you are satisfied with the fit of the pattern, remove it from the chair. Cut through all the basting stitches, making tailor's tacks. Mark all seam lines, gathering and the darts.

6 Lay the fabric on the floor with the right side facing up. Place the muslin pattern pieces (right side up) on top of the fabric, checking that the grain is running in the right direction. Mark and label the fabric pieces, marking the top and bottom of each piece. Once all the pieces are marked they can be cut out.

7 If you are going to use piping, make up a little extra. Apply the piping to the right side of all relevant pieces, with right sides together and raw edges even. (See page 21 for how to apply piping.)

8 Follow the same order for joining pieces as with the muslin pattern.

9 Stitch one half of the Velcro® tape to each side of the back opening (fig. 1). Zippers are not recommended because they are often not strong enough, but hooks and eyes, spaced evenly along the opening, can be used.

10 If you wish to add a box-pleated valance like the one pictured, follow the instructions on page 117, or, finish as desired.

Sewing corners

Shaping around curved backs or arms can be done in a number of ways:
- Hand-sew gathering stitches along the seam line on the curve. Pull up the gathering to fit and join the pieces together (fig. 2).
- Making small flat pleats is another way to achieve a smooth finish (fig. 3).
- If there is a lot of fullness to be taken out, darts are a good method to consider. Pin the darts as shown to ensure a good fit before you stitch (fig. 4).
- If your chair back has straight corners, join the pieces as shown in fig. 5.

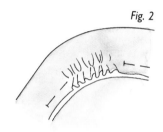

Fig. 2

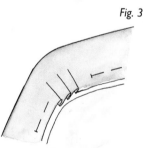

Fig. 3

Fig. 4

Fig. 5

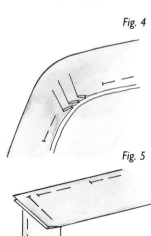

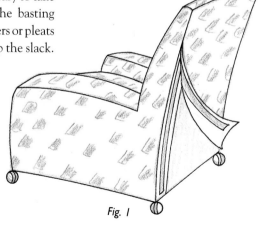

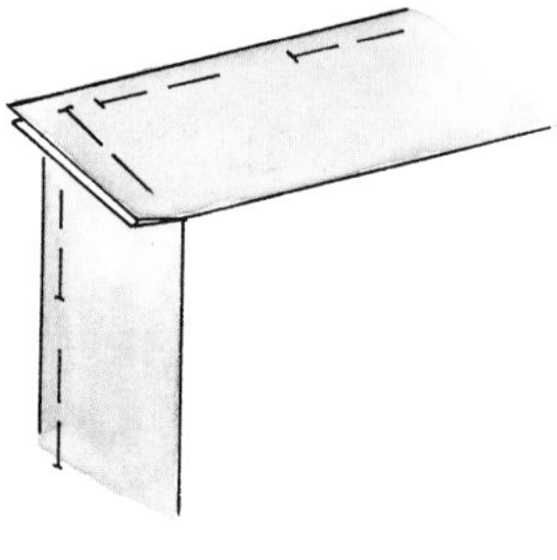

Fig. 1

Box seat cushion

Before you begin

Loose, box seat cushions are often found on sofas and couches. The method given here is a basic guide for covering a foam block cushion. The same method can be used for other fillings, such as down and feather or foam chips, but a tightly woven form from muslin or cotton should be made first to hold the filling in place.

For most upholstery-weight cushions, it is best to conceal the zipper in the side seam so that the cushion can be reversed to share the wear and tear.

Most couches and easy chairs have loose seat cushions

MATERIALS
fabric, the same as the main chair fabric
contrasting fabric for piping
piping cord
upholstery thread
upholstery needle
sewing machine with a needle suitable for sewing through several layers of fabric
12"-15" (30cm-38cm) metal zipper (depending on the size of the cushion)
tailor's chalk

Method

1 Cut two pieces of fabric large enough to cover the top and bottom of the cushion with 1" (2.5cm) seam allowances all around.

2 Measure the length of piping needed. Cut sufficient bias strips from the contrasting fabric to achieve that length and wide enough to wrap around the piping cord plus ⅜" (1cm) on each side for seam allowances. Join the lengths and make the piping as shown on page 91.

3 Pin the piping to the right side of the top and bottom panels with the raw edges even and right sides together. Cut a square from the seam allowance of the piping to allow it to curve around the corners (fig. 3). Where the two ends of the piping meet, cross them over as neatly as possible, pulling them into the seam allowances. Stitch.

4 For the boxing strip, cut four strips to the required length, adding 1" (2.5cm) seam allowance at each end. With right sides together, pin and baste all the short ends together to form a square (fig. 4). Check the fit, adjust, stitch and press the seams open.

5 Stitch the bottom panel to the boxing strip with right sides together and raw edges even, stitching along the piping stitching line.

6 Insert the zipper between one side and the top panel. (See page 26 for how to insert a zipper.) Open the zipper.

7 Pin and baste the top panel to the remaining three sides in the same manner as for the bottom panel. Try the cushion cover on the pad to check the fit, then stitch the seams. Turn the cover right side out through the open zipper. Press.

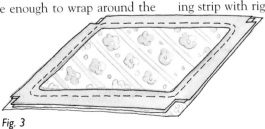

Fig. 3

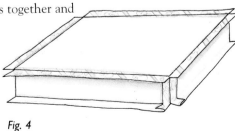

Fig. 4

Drop-in Seat Cover

VERY OFTEN THE SEAT PADDING ON DINING CHAIRS IS QUITE SOUND, ONLY NEEDING A NEW FABRIC COVER TO BE REBORN.

Before you begin Ensure that your chair frames and padding are in good condition. It does not make much sense to spend time and money recovering the seat of a chair that's on its last legs – literally!

Measuring

Measure the seat of your chair to establish how much fabric you will need for each seat (fig. 1). Don't forget to allow for the height of the cushioning. If you can, use the old cover as a pattern for the new one. The lining fabric only needs to be sufficient to cover the underside of the chair base.

MATERIALS
sufficient fabric and lining
staples and staple gun or upholstery tacks and a small hammer
braid for the perimeter of the chair seat plus 3" (7.5cm) for overlap and turns
craft glue

Method

1 Remove the old fabric and lining from your chair seat. Using the tip of a screwdriver or pliers, lift out any remaining tacks or staples.
2 Using the old cover or your measurements, cut out the new covers.
3 Place the new cover over the seat, folding in the corners and fastening the fabric underneath the seat with staples or upholstery tacks (fig. 2).
4 Press the edges of the lining piece under. Position it over the center of the underside, so that the previous stapling is covered. Staple or tack the lining in place at the edges (fig. 3).
5 Glue the braid over the staples or tacks, overlapping the ends and turning the upper raw end under.

A drop-in seat is very easy to re-cover

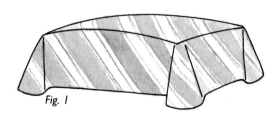

Fig. 1

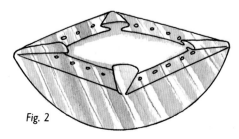

Fig. 2

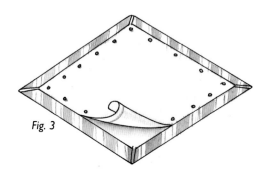

Fig. 3

Director's Chair Covers

DIRECTOR'S CHAIRS HAVE FOUND A PLACE IN MANY HOUSEHOLDS.
REASONABLY PRICED, COMFORTABLE AND EASY TO STORE, THEY
CAN UNDERGO ENDLESS TRANSFORMATIONS.

Director's chair 1

Before you begin

This is a great way to dress up a director's chair. Whether you choose a solid fabric or a bold print, these inexpensive chairs will take on a whole new look.

You may wish to re-cover your director's chairs to coordinate with the new tablecloth and napkins you have just made for summer, or you may wish to make a statement by stenciling a new seat and back panel for your chairs. Either way, your final project will be a work of art when you paint the woodwork in a coordinating color.

Measuring

Remove the existing covers from your chair and use them to estimate the amount of fabric you will need. Don't forget to add seam and hem allowances and extra fabric for wrapping around the frame and attaching the cover to the chair.

MATERIALS

sufficient fabric, such as lightweight canvas

sewing machine with a heavy-gauge needle suitable for sewing upholstery

upholstery tacks

matching sewing machine thread

tailor's chalk

scissors

pins

tape measure

Method

1 Using the old covers as your pattern, cut new back and seat covers for the chairs. To prevent fraying, finish the edges with a serger, zigzag stitching, or as desired. Mark the hems with tailor's chalk.

2 Pin the hems at the markings and check the fit before sewing. Make any necessary adjustments. Stitch the hems. Replace the covers on your chairs.

Crisp stripes are the perfect choice for a casual garden setting

Director's chair 2

Before you begin

Director's chairs vary in size so it is important that you measure your chair before you begin.

Starting at the front of your chair at ground level, measure the distance up to the seat, plus the depth of the seat up to the top of the chair back plus the distance from the top of the chair, then back to ground level. Record the measurement for the depth of the seat and the width of the back rest separately. Measure from the ground level up to and over each arm rest and down to the seat. Add ⅝" (1.5cm) seam allowances to all measurements. Sketch these elements on a sheet of paper and use the sketches as a guide only – you do not need to make a proper pattern. For this chair, our main pattern piece is 24" x 87" (61cm x 221.5cm); the arm pieces measured 20½" x 36" (51.5cm x 90cm).

MATERIALS
pencil and paper
approximately 3¼yds. (3m) of 48"
(120cm)-wide fabric
12" (30cm) of contrasting fabric for the ties
matching sewing machine thread
scissors
tape measure
pins
sewing machine

Method

1 Using your drawings as a guide, cut out the three pattern pieces. Cut four 6" (15cm)-wide ties, each 15" (38cm) long.

2 Do not remove the existing seat or back rest; the slipcover will slip over the top. Place the main pattern piece over the chair, wrong side up. Do the same with each arm piece. Pin the arm pieces to the main piece at the seat level and at the front leg. Pin the front and back of the main piece together

down to the arm level of the chair.

3 Return to the front of the chair and pin a dart across the top of each arm front at right angles to the front seam. This will ensure the drape over the arm sits straight.

4 Remove the slipcover and stitch all the seams. Trim excess seam allowances, if necessary.

5 Return the slipcover to the chair, wrong side out. Press ¼" (6mm), then another ⅜" (1cm) for the hem around the bottom edge and at the back leg openings.

6 Fold the strip for each tie in half with right sides together and raw edges even.

Sew one short end and along the long side. Turn right side out. Pin and baste the raw end of one tie to the hem on the side and back edges of each back opening. Remove the slipcover from the chair and stitch all the hems and seams, catching the ties. Turn the slipcover right side out and press.

Below: A bold check cotton slipcover gives new life to an old chair

Right: The painted chair frame and the combination of many coordinating fabrics give this setting a decorator's touch

Director's chair 3

Before you begin Applying two coats of high gloss enamel paint will give the frame an instant lift. Sand lightly between coats to give a satin-smooth finish.

If you are working with a heavy sateen or upholstery fabric, use a double thickness of fabric for extra strength. Fusible web between the layers of fabric will also add strength and keep the fabrics firmly in place.

Measuring

Measure from the top of the back rest down to the seat and along the seat to the front of the chair. This measurement plus hem allowances at both ends is the total length. Measure the width required and add sufficient to fold the fabric around the frame on both sides.

On a large sheet of paper, draw a rectangle to the length and width you have calculated. At one end of the rectangle mark the length of the back rest. At the other end, mark the depth of the seat. Add sufficient allowance for turnings.

Draw in the shape of the chair cover with a rectangle at one end for the back rest and one rectangle at the other end for the seat, connected by a curved back rest extension.

MATERIALS
large sheet of paper
pencil
ruler
high gloss enamel paint
paintbrush
sufficient fabric
fusible web
heavy-gauge sewing machine needle
matching sewing machine thread
pins
heavy duty staples and stapler
scissors
tape measure
sewing machine

Method

1 Remove the existing covers and paint the wooden frame.

2 Cut out the fabric (or fabrics) for the chair cover. If you are using two fabrics, fuse them together following the manufacturer's instructions. Stitch a double hem at each end of the fabric.

3 Make a narrow double hem along both sides of the fabric.

4 Place the cover on the chair, taking the turnings over to the wrong side, then attach the cover to the frame with a staple gun.

Tailored Chair Cover

IF YOU HAVE WOODEN DINING CHAIRS THAT ARE STILL SOLID BUT HAVE SEEN BETTER
DAYS, THIS SLIPCOVER PROJECT IS AN IDEAL REFURBISHING SOLUTION.

Before you begin This easy-cover project may be the perfect opportunity to convert six odd chairs into a matched set. This slipcover pattern is designed for chairs which are flat across the top of the back rest and do not have protruding knobs – all the lines and surfaces of the chair should be as straight as possible. Bowed backs and curved seats will not allow the fabric to hang properly. Choose your fabric carefully. You will need a medium-weight fabric that doesn't present too many problems with matching patterns on adjacent surfaces.

Choose a contrasting or complementary fabric for the lining as it will show at the joins, or, the slipcover can be lined with the main fabric for an all-over look.

For added comfort you can include a layer of batting or fusible fleece between the main fabric and the lining.

Measuring

You will need to take the measurements of your chair then draw those rectangles on to a sheet of paper. Mark each rectangle with its position and mark all the measurements on it. The drawings here are intended as a guide only.

• *Pattern piece 1* Measure the length from the seat up the chair back and down to the floor (allowing for the width of the chair frame at the top of the back rest) by the width of the chair (allowing for the width of the chair frame at the sides).

• *Pattern piece 2* Measure the depth of the seat plus the distance to the floor by the width of the chair.

• *Pattern piece 3* Measure the depth of the seat plus the width of the timber frame by the height of the seat from the floor. Cut two.

Once you have established these measurements you can calculate the amount of fabric required.

MATERIALS

sheet of paper

pencil

ruler

main fabric for chair
cover and ties

lining fabric

batting or fusible fleece in the same size
(optional)

matching sewing machine thread

pins

scissors

tape measure

sewing machine

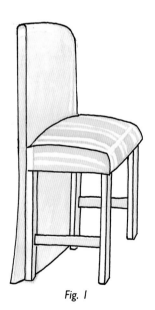

Fig. 1

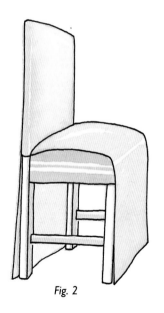

Fig. 2

Fig. 3

Method

1 Cut out the pattern pieces from the main and the lining fabric, adding ⅝" (1.5cm) for seam allowances. Take care to match and center any fabric pattern at this point.

2 On pattern piece 1, sew the sides together from the top of the chair back rest to the seat (fig. 1). Press.

3 Sew pattern piece 1 to pattern piece 2 at the seat back edge (fig. 2). Attach a pattern piece 3 at each side (fig. 3). Press.

4 Make eight 12" (30cm) long ties out of scraps of the cover fabric. Pin one end of each tie, with raw edges together, on the right side of the fabric front and back edges, just below seat height.

5 Make the lining the same as for the cover. Add batting or fleece if desired. Place the lining and the cover with right sides together and raw edges even. Sew around the outside edge, leaving an opening for turning, and catching the ends of the ties in the seam. Turn the cover right side out, taking care to push the corners out completely. Press.

Match up your odd chairs with a set of tailored slipcovers

Ruffled Chair Cover

A LOOSE COVER FOR A CHAIR WITHOUT ARMS IS EASY TO MAKE AND OFFERS A
SOLUTION TO SEASONAL DECORATING WITHOUT MAJOR COST.

Ruffles and swags make a charming dining setting. See page 168 for how to make the tablecloth

Before you begin

If you are new to making slipcovers, it is best to use a solid fabric or one with a small all-over print that does not need the pattern matched. Remember, if you are working with floral bouquets or a medallion print, center the pattern on the front of the chair back and on the seat.

Measuring

Measure the various planes of the chair (such as the width and depth of the back rest and seat, and the height of the seat from the floor) and mark these measurements on a sketch pattern of your chair.

MATERIALS

sufficient fabric (we used approximately 4½yds. (4m) for our chair, allowing for the fullness in the skirt)

paper and pencil

4" (10cm) Velcro® tape

pins

scissors

tape measure

tailor's chalk

matching sewing machine thread

sewing machine

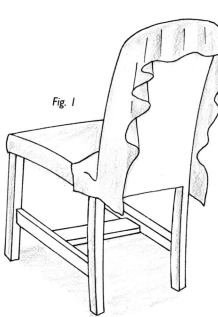

Fig. 1

Method

1 Cut out a rectangle of fabric each for the chair seat, the front of the back rest and the back of the back rest, using the measurements on your sketch pattern and following the grainlines of the fabric. Cut out the skirt the length required plus 1¼" (3cm) for the hem and one and a half times the distance around the chair seat. If necessary, join pieces with a flat fell seam. Add ⅝" (1.5cm) for each seam allowance. Make sure all prints match.

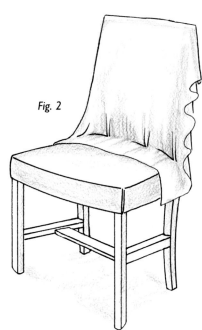

Fig. 2

2 Place the piece for the front of the back rest on the chair with the wrong side facing (figs. 1 and 2). Check the fit. If there is excess fabric, pin darts or gather the edge to make the fabric sit neatly. (See page 120 for how to deal with corners.) Treat the piece for the back of the back rest the same as for the front.

3 While the pieces are still on the chair, pin the outer and inner back rest pieces together with wrong sides up. Check the fit and re-pin the darts if necessary. Mark the seam lines with tailor's chalk. Remove the back rest pieces from the chair.

4 Stitch around the top and sides, leaving a 4" (10cm) opening on one

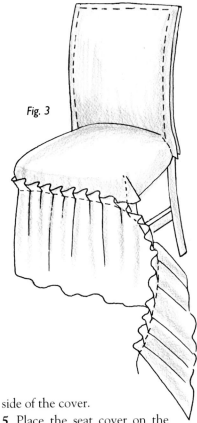

Fig. 3

side of the cover.

5 Place the seat cover on the chair and pin darts in the corners to reduce fabric bulk. Mark the seams and darts as before. Remove the seat cover from the chair. Stitch the darts, then join the inner back cover to the seat cover piece.

6 Press ½" (1.2cm), then ¾" (2cm) to the wrong side on the bottom and the ends of the skirt. Stitch the hems in place. Divide the top edge of the skirt into quarters and mark with a pin. Gather the top edge of the skirt.

7 Pin the skirt to the seat cover with right sides together and raw edges even, beginning and ending at one of the back corners (fig. 3). Pull up the gathering to fit, placing a pin mark at each corner. Adjust the gathering, making it a little fuller at the corners. Stitch the skirt in place. Press.

8 Sew Velcro® to the back opening or make ties from scraps of fabric and sew them to either side of the opening.

9 If you wish to create a very charming effect, make two bows from the same fabric and slipstitch one to each side of the chair back.

Instant Sofa Cover-up

INSTANT LOOSE COVERS REQUIRE LITTLE SEWING, ONLY A SMALL FINANCIAL INVESTMENT AND NOT A LOT OF TIME.

Before you begin Practise your skills by draping an old sheet on your chair or sofa. This way you will quickly be able to work out where fabric can be tucked into crevices to anchor it. If the existing sofa has torn covers and you are not likely to use it again in its present state, sew strips of Velcro® to the old sofa to match up with Velcro® on the fabric cover. The Velcro® will help the fabric to stay neatly in position and it will not crease as much.

Select a fabric, such as linen or another woven fabric, that is less likely to show creases. Fabric bows on the arms add a further decorative touch and can be attached with Velcro®, or stitched or pinned into place.

Use 54" (137cm)-wide fabric for a two-seater sofa cover, so fewer seams will be necessary.

MATERIALS
fabric
pins
tailor's chalk
Velcro® (if required)
cord, ribbon or sewn ties

Method

1 It may be necessary to join lengths of fabric together to achieve the required width. If this is the case, use flat fell seams for added strength and always carefully match the fabric pattern.

2 Remove the seat cushions. Drape and tuck the fabric piece over the base of the sofa. When you are happy with the draping, mark the hem line with tailors chalk. Remove the cover. Even out any great irregularities in the chalk marks, then trim the excess fabric from the hem. Press a double hem under and stitch the hem in place.

3 Tie sashes, ribbons or cords around the arms to hold the fabric in place. The ties can be attached with Velcro®, pins, or by topstitching them in place.

Pleat the fabric at the arms for a neat finish

Wrapped seat cushion

MATERIALS
sufficient fabric
pinking shears
safety pins (optional)
needle and thread (optional)

Method

1 Use pinking sheers to cut out a fabric square twice the width and length of your cushion plus 12" (30cm). Place the cushion in the center of the fabric on the wrong side.

2 Wrap the cushion as if it were a gift; first fold the fabric to the center, turning in the raw edges. Secure the fabric on the underside with safety pins or stitches. Place on your chair or sofa to complete the look (figs 1 to 3).

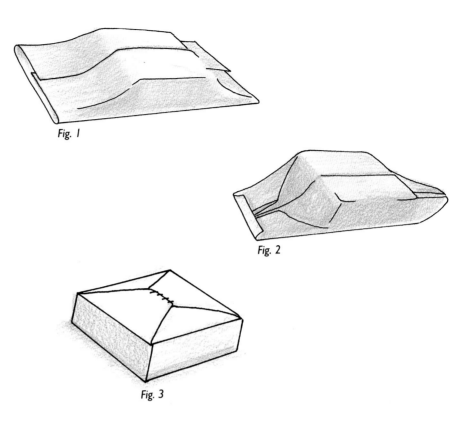

Fig. 1

Fig. 2

Fig. 3

No-sew pillow

MATERIALS
sufficient fabric
pinking shears

Method

1 With pinking shears, cut a rectangle of fabric three times the width of your pillow and twice as long (fig. 4).

2 Fold the fabric as indicated in the illustration, bringing both ends up to tie in a knot at the top of the pillow (fig. 5). Place the knot to the underside for a tailored look (fig. 6).

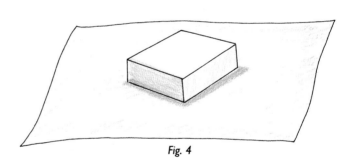

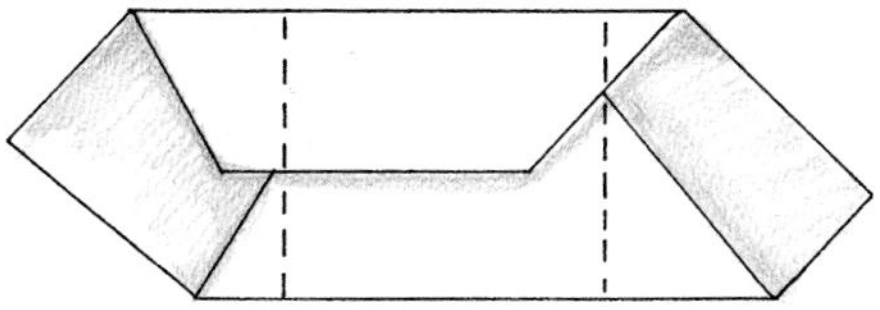

Fig. 4

Fig. 5

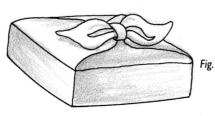

Fig. 6

Bed Linen

BED SHEETS

DUVET COVERS

RUFFLED BED SKIRT

BOX-PLEATED BED SKIRT

TIERED BED SKIRT

PILLOWCASES

COMFORTER

QUILTED SPREAD

TENT CANOPY

SHEER CANOPY

FRINGED BEDSPREAD

UPHOLSTERED HEADBOARD

NURSERY LINEN

Bed Linen

IN MEDIEVAL TIMES, SERVANTS IN NOBLE HOUSEHOLDS SPUN AND WOVE ELABORATE
SHEETS AND PILLOW SHAMS FROM SILKS AND PURE COTTONS.

Through the ages, bed linen has always been considered a great luxury and was an essential part of a young lady's trousseau. Exquisite bed linen was often traded as part of a dowry or bequeathed in a will. Threads of gold and silver were worked on handmade laces, satins and silks to create sumptuous trims on pillows and linens.

Today's bed linen, in its many colors and styles, was introduced into Europe during the 1960s. Up until this time, bed linen was predominantly white with a bedspread printed in traditional florals. Bed linen has come a long way from those austere times, providing not only warmth and comfort but great decorative possibilities for the bedroom as well.

The color scheme you select for your bed linen should reflect the total decorative scheme of your room. If you have a number of bed linen components to work with, combine different prints such as checks, stripes and florals, using a common element, such as the color, to link the patterns together.

If you prefer the clean crisp look of white linen, consider adding variations in texture to emphasize each of your components. Damask, with its silk and matte combination of weaves, provides wonderful textural qualities while the addition of lace edges on pillows and valances adds yet another variation.

Style is another consideration when planning your bedroom decor. A stately brass or wooden four-poster bed in a formal bedroom, can be shown to advantage with a box-pleated bed skirt, defining the height of the bed, or quilted bed shams in a Jacobean chintz with pillow shams in a coordinating smaller print. Both items can be easily removed to reveal subtle cotton sheets piped in one of the colors detailed in the bed shams. A decorative bolster or neck roll adds shape and proportion to the top of a bed.

Teenagers are often the hardest to select a bed linen scheme for. The great advantage of making your own bed linen is that you can quickly, and without too much expense, change the look as your children grow. For teenagers, it is always pretty safe to work with solid colors as the base of a bed, which can then be combined with plaids, stripes, paisleys, abstracts and florals.

For toddlers and babies, the nursery can be a wonderful place decorated in stimulating bold motifs or pastels. You will need to make all the items to size for your particular child's room; crib sizes can vary dramatically.

Openings & closures

You should always leave a generous opening on a duvet cover through which to insert your duvet. The opening is best placed at the bottom of the cover and, when used effectively, opening and closing mechanisms should be virtually invisible, and washable. Zippers are not recommended for duvet cover openings, because they will deteriorate over time with constant laundering. Velcro® or snaps are the best type of invisible closure; however, decorative closures, such as tailored buttons or a row of tied bows, will give a distinctive effect.

Fabrics

The availability of wide-width sheeting has made it very easy for the home decorator to achieve a totally coordinated look for a bedroom, at relatively low cost. A number of stores now supply wide-width sheeting which coordinates with curtain and upholstery ranges. Therefore, you have the option of covering your window, upholstering the bedroom chair or vanity stool in a coordinating fabric and then using the wide-width sheeting to make the bed linen or bedspread. A blend of fifty-percent cotton and fifty-percent polyester is recommended because of its easy-care qualities. However, a one hundred-percent cotton fabric, or any other fabric that can be easily laundered, dried and pressed may be used for bed linen.

The advantage of wide-width fabric is that there will be no joins or seams in the middle of your sheets or duvet cover, but you can successfully use fabric of any width for making bed linen.

For the ultimate in luxury, try the fresh feeling of damask or convert a lace tablecloth into a duvet cover. Crocheted doilies that have never been out of storage can now take pride of place as a trim for your new pillowcases or bed pillows. Laces can also be bought by the yard. One hundred-percent cotton lace complements damask bed linen beautifully, but remember to preshrink all the fabrics and trims before sewing.

Tied bows

Buttons

Velcro® tape

Snap tape

Measuring

❖

It is always important to measure the bed carefully before you purchase fabric – small differences won't matter for flat sheets, but accuracy is important for ruffles or valances. There is little uniformity in bed sizes; the depths of mattresses vary and the addition of castors changes the height from the top of the mattress to the floor. Likewise, pillowcases can vary in size.

Sheeting width varies from 91" (228cm) to 100" (254cm) from selvage to selvage. The quantities given in the instructions in this book are calculated on standard sizes of manufactured sheets and duvet covers. You may need to adjust these for your own use.

Duvet covers should be made to fit individual duvets or comforters, so measure your own before purchasing fabrics. Consider using contrasting or complementary colors or prints for the front and back of your duvet cover.

When measuring for a pillowcase, add 1¼" (3cm) for the seams to the required finished width and 8¼" (21cm) to the length for the seam allowance and flap, if desired.

To measure a bed, measure the flat surface from the top of the bed to the bottom edge of the bed (A to B) and the flat surface from side edge to side edge (C to D). The depth of the bed is measured from the flat surface at the side edge to the floor (B to E and D to F) (fig. 1).

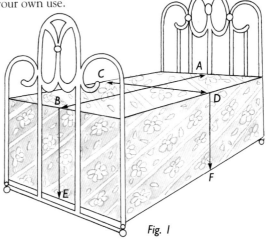

Fig. 1

fabric requirements

❖

	Queen	Double	Single
Flat sheet	3yds. (2.8m)	2½yds. (2.3m)	1¾yds. (1.6m)
Fitted sheet	2⅞yds. (2.7m)	2⅜yds. (2.2m)	1⅝yds. (1.5m)
Duvet cover	4⅝yds. (4.2m)	4yds. (3.6m)	3yds. (2.8m)
	to finish at	to finish at	to finish at
	2⅓yds. (2.1m)	2yds. (1.8m)	1½yds. (1.4m)
	by the width of the sheeting (for all sizes)		

Fabric required for pillowcases:

Plain pillowcase	½yd. (.5m)
Ruffled pillowcase	¾yd. (.7m)
Flanged pillowcase	¾yd. (.7m)

Bed Sheets

Before you begin For sheets, select a cotton or poly-cotton blend fabric that will survive the rigours of frequent laundering.

The cutting and sewing methods described apply to all sizes. Use ⁵/₈" (1.5cm) seams, unless otherwise instructed, and finish all raw edges.

French seams are commonly used for sewing bed linen. To sew a French seam, pin and stitch a ⁵/₈" (1.5cm) seam with the wrong sides facing. Trim the seam allowance back to ¹/₄" (6mm). Press the seam closed along the seam line with the right sides together. Pin and stitch the seam again with a ³/₈" (1cm) seam allowance, enclosing the raw edges. For more information on how to sew French seams, see page 32.

Cut the fabric according to the dimensions of your bed. If joins are necessary, match the pattern so that the print runs uniformly across the total width of the fabric. To match patterns, cut one piece of fabric to the required length and lay the piece flat. Mark the pattern repeat with two pins or tailor's chalk. Fold under the selvages of the fabric piece to be joined then find the beginning of the next pattern repeat and measure your length from this point, allowing for any necessary seam or hem allowances. Trim the selvages, then baste the two pieces together before sewing. A more detailed method for matching fabrics can be seen on page 43.

Fitted sheet

MATERIALS
sufficient fabric
³/₈" (1cm)-wide elastic
matching sewing machine thread
tape measure
pins
scissors
sewing machine

Method

1 Cut the fabric for the sheet as wide as the mattress plus the depth of the mattress plus 12" (30cm) for the tuck-under on each side and 1¹/₄" (3cm) for the hem, and as long as the mattress plus the depth of the mattress plus 12" (30cm) for the tuck-under on each side and 1¹/₄" (3cm) for the hem.

2 Cut squares from each corner of the fabric as illustrated (fig. 1). Note that A to B is the depth of the mattress plus 12" (30cm) for the tuck-under and ⁵/₈" (1.5cm) for the hem. Pin the sides of the square together, joining the A points. Sew from the outside edge to the inner corner, forming an angle at each corner of the sheet.

3 Press ¹/₄" (6mm) to the wrong side around the outside edge. Stitch the hem in place. Sew the elastic to the hem on each corner, starting and finishing 16" (40cm) on either side of the corner seam, using a zigzag stitch and stretching the elastic as you sew (fig. 2).

Above: Brightly colored cotton is great for a child's fitted sheet

Right: A flat sheet can be trimmed with lace, ribbon or braid

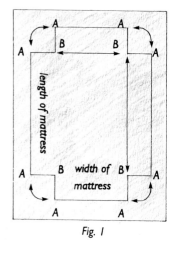

Fig. 1

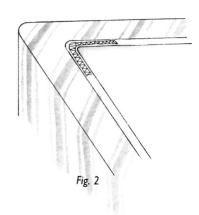

Fig. 2

Flat sheet

MATERIALS
sufficient fabric
matching sewing machine thread
pins
tape measure
scissors
sewing machine

Method

1 Press ¹/₄" (6mm) then ³/₈" (1cm) to the wrong side on the side and bottom edges. Note that the selvages should be at the top and bottom edges of your sheet. Stitch the hems in place.

2 Press a 2" (5cm) hem at the top and stitch in place.

3 Trim the top edge with a panel of lace, if desired.

❖

Flat sheet with contrast panel

MATERIALS
sufficient fabric
contrasting fabric, 12" (30cm) x the sheet width
contrasting corded piping, the width of your sheet plus 1" (2.5cm) for turnings
matching sewing machine thread
pins
scissors
tape measure
sewing machine

Method

1 Turn in and press ¹/₄" (6mm) to the wrong side along the under side edges. Press ³/₈" (1cm) under twice on the bottom edge.

2 Make the piping following the instructions on page 21. Pin the piping to one long side of the contrast panel with the right sides together and the raw edges even. Stitch the piping in place, stitching as close to the piping as possible. Press under the raw edges of the piping and the contrasting panel at the piped edge.

3 Pin the plain edge of the contrasting panel to the top edge of the sheet so that the right side of the contrasting panel is facing the wrong side of the sheet. Stitch along the top edge and down the sides. Trim any excess bulk and clip across the corners.

4 Turn the contrasting panel to the right side of the sheet. Press. Pin, then machine-stitch along the piping line.

5 Press another ³/₈" (1cm) under on the sides. Stitch the side and bottom hems. Press.

Contrasting bands of fabrics add interest to a sheet

Duvet Covers

Basic duvet cover

Before you begin Finish all the seam allowances on the inside of your duvet cover with a serger. If this is not possible, consider using French seams. (See page 32 for how to sew French seams.)

MATERIALS
sufficient fabric
approximately 4¹/₂ yds. (4m) of ⁵/₈"
(1.5cm)-wide
cotton tape (optional)
Velcro®, snaps, or snap tape
matching sewing machine thread
sewing machine
tape measure
pins
scissors

Method

1 If you are using cotton or poly-cotton fabric, join lengths to achieve the required size, taking care to match any pattern. Cut a top and a bottom for your duvet cover 1" (2.5cm) larger than the duvet.
2 Place the two pieces with right sides together. Pin and stitch the top, two sides and the bottom, leaving a 39" (100cm) opening in the center of the bottom edge (fig. 1). Begin sewing at the bottom edge, work along one side to the top and then back down along the remaining side and the bottom edge. Trim the seam allowances and clip the corners.
3 Press in and stitch down the seam allowances at the opening, then sew on the closure of your choice.
4 You may like to sew ties of cotton tape inside the cover at each corner and a corresponding tie on to each corner of the duvet. Tie these together to keep the duvet in place within the cover. Decorative ties sewn to the outside corners of the cover can be used to tie it to the bedposts.

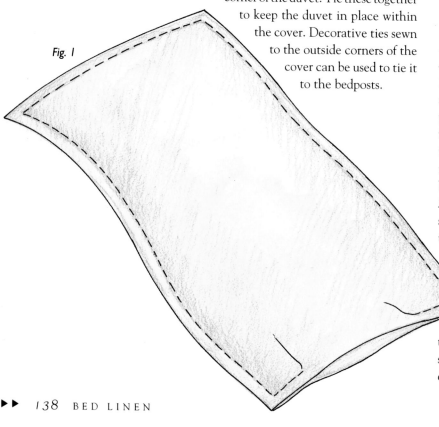

Fig. 1

Buttoned duvet cover

Before you begin Make the buttons a decorative feature of this duvet cover. Choose interesting buttons, such as mother-of-pearl or covered buttons. If you are going to cover buttons, allow additional fabric for each button.

MATERIALS
sufficient fabric
four buttons for a single and six to eight buttons for a double, queen or king size duvet cover
matching sewing machine thread
sewing machine
scissors
pins
tape measure
sewing machine

Method

1 If you are using sheeting, place the selvages at the top and bottom edges. If you are using cotton or poly-cotton fabric, join lengths to achieve the required size, taking care to match any pattern. Cut a top and a bottom for your cover.
2 Sew a ⁵/₈" (1.5cm) hem along one short side of each of the two pieces for the bottom end of the cover. With right sides together, pin and stitch the three remaining sides together with a flat seam, starting from the bottom, working up one side to the top, then back down along the remaining side. To prevent fraying, serge or zigzag each of the raw edges individually. Trim

the seam allowances and clip the corners. Turn the cover right side out and press.

3 Press an additional 2" (5cm) to the wrong side along each bottom edge. Stitch the hems in place, then stitch the ends together for 12" (30cm) on each side.

4 Make buttonholes, evenly spaced, and approximately 1¼" (3cm) from the folded edge.

5 Sew the buttons in corresponding positions, 1¼" (3cm) from the folded edge. Use buttons with shanks or make thread shanks (fig. 2).

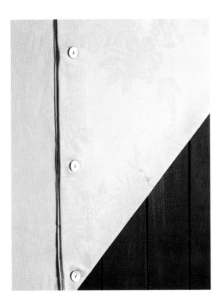

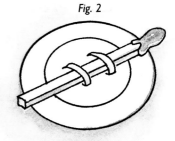

Fig. 2: Stitching over a matchstick which is later removed produces a thread shank for a button

A simple buttoned duvet cover complements a tailored, pleated bed skirt and an array of pillow styles

Reversible piped duvet cover

Before you begin The measurements given here are for a single bed; adjust the measurements to fit your own bed Finish all the seam allowances on the inside of your cover with a serger or zigzag stitching.

MATERIALS

1½yds. (1.4m) of each of two different fabrics

3yds. (2.8m) of 2³/₈" (6cm)-wide contrasting bias binding (see page 20 for how to make continuous bias binding)

3yds. (2.8m) medium piping cord,

3yds. (2.8m) of 4³/₄" (12cm)-wide bias binding in a second contrasting color (see page 20 for how to make continuous bias binding)

3yds. (2.8m) thick piping cord

matching sewing machine thread

tape measure

pins

scissors

sewing machine

Velcro® tape, or snap tape

Method

1 If you are using sheeting, place the selvages at the top and bottom edges. If you are using cotton or poly-cotton fabric, join lengths to achieve the required size, taking care to match any pattern. Cut the duvet cover top from one fabric and the bottom from the other fabric.

2 Pin and baste the smaller piping to the top fabric along two long and one short sides, with the right sides together and the raw edges even. Place the larger piping over the smaller piping, basting it in place. Stitch both rows of piping to the top of the duvet cover at once.

3 Place the top and bottom pieces together with the right sides together. Stitch the two pieces together, leaving a 39" (100cm) opening in the unpiped end. Trim the seam allowances and clip the corners.

4 Press ¼" (6mm), then ³/₈" (1cm) to the wrong side of the opening. Stitch. Sew on the Velcro® or snap tape.

Jumbo piping in bright colors defines the edges of this cheerful duvet cover for a child's bed

Ruffled reversible duvet cover

This is a great way to ring the changes in your bedroom – floral one day, stripes the next; country checks one day and traditional white the next. Teamed with an array of reversible pillowcases you can achieve two totally different looks for the price of one.

Make the duvet cover in exactly the same way as the basic duvet cover, cutting the top and bottom from different fabrics.

Ruffles can also be added to a reversible duvet cover. Ruffles should always be doubled, so that the ruffle is finished on both sides. For this duvet cover, the ruffle strips were cut 9½"

Top: Choose a crisp geometric print to team with a floral for two very different looks

Above: Make pillowcases, bed skirt and sheets to match the duvet cover

(24cm) wide to finish at 4" (10cm) wide. Make sure the color and the fabric you select for the ruffle complement both sides of the duvet cover. (See pages 23 to 24 for how to make and apply ruffles.)

Ruffled Bed Skirt

Before you begin To calculate the width of fabric needed for the ruffle, measure the depth of the bed from the top of the box spring to $3/8$" (1cm) above the floor and add $1^1/4$" (3cm) for the top and bottom hems. The length should be at least twice the length of the two longer sides plus the width of the mattress plus $5/8$" (1.5cm) for any joining seam allowances and side hems.

You will also need a rectangle of fabric, the same dimensions as the top of the mattress plus $5/8$" (1.5cm) for seam allowances.

MATERIALS
sufficient fabric

matching sewing machine thread

pins

scissors

tape measure

sewing machine

$31^1/2$" (80cm) of $1/4$" (6mm)-wide elastic
(optional – if you have a posted bed)

*eight 12" (30cm)-long fabric ties
(optional – if you have a posted bed)*

A ruffled bed skirt adds charm to a bedroom

Method

1 Cut out the rectangle of fabric for the deck. For beds with no bedposts or board at the foot cut the length of fabric required for the ruffle, joining pieces as necessary to achieve the total length. Hem the top of the deck piece with a double hem, pressing $1/4$" (6mm), then $3/8$" (1cm) to the wrong side. Hem the short ends and the bottom edge of the ruffle as for the deck piece (fig. 1).

Gather the remaining raw edge of the ruffle with two rows of gathering stitches. Pull up the gathering so that the ruffle fits around the deck piece (fig. 2). Pin the ruffle to the deck piece with the raw edges matching and the right sides together. Adjust the gathering, then stitch into place.

2 For beds with bedposts and/or boards, hem the head end of the deck piece. Cut the ruffle strip to finish on either side of the posts or board. Hem the short ends and the lower edge of the ruffle by turning $1/4$" (6mm), to the wrong side, then $3/8$" (1cm). Gather the upper edges of each ruffle piece separately with two rows of gathering stitches. Pull up the gathering so that each ruffle piece fits the matching side of the deck piece. Adjust the gathers, then pin and stitch the ruffles to the deck piece.

3 Sew ties to the ruffles on either side of the bedposts or the legs of the box spring, if desired. Make the ties from scraps of fabric, then sew a 4" (10cm) length of elastic to one end of each tie and the other end of the elastic to the corner of the ruffle. The elastic will take the strain off the ties and prevent the stitching from breaking.

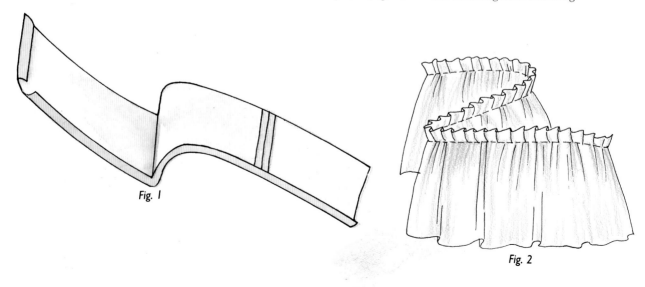

Fig. 1

Fig. 2

Box-pleated Bed Skirt

Before you begin Box-pleating can be done by hand or with tape. Just as there are tapes to give you different heading styles for your curtains, similar gathering tape can be used to achieve box pleats. Here, we have used tape that automatically makes an 8" (20cm) wide box pleat.

Measuring

To calculate the width of fabric you need for the bed skirt, measure the depth of the bed from the top of the box spring to $^3/_8$" (1cm) above the floor (B to E) and add $1^1/_4$" (3cm) for the top and bottom hems. The length should be at least two and a half times the length of the two longer sides of the mattress (C to D) plus the width of the mattress plus $^5/_8$" (1.5cm) for any joining seam allowances and side hems needed (fig. 3).

You will also need a rectangle of fabric, the same dimensions as the top of the mattress plus $^5/_8$" (1.5cm) all around for seam allowances.

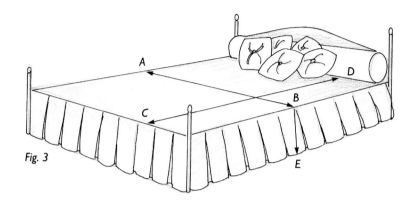

Fig. 3

fabric for the bed skirt, joining pieces as necessary to achieve the total length. Finish the bed skirt bottom and the two short sides with a rolled edge or a double hem.

2 Pin the tape to the top edge of the wrong side of the bed skirt and sew in place. Pull up the tape from one end to form the box pleats. Press the pleats. Stitch over the pleats at the top edge of

the tape. Some tapes can be removed once the pleats are set and can be used again later.

3 With the right sides together, pin and sew the box-pleated bed skirt to the deck piece. Double hem the top edge of the deck piece. Press.

4 For beds with posts make a separate bed skirt for each side and the bottom of the bed.

A plain cotton box-pleated bed skirt works well for a child's bed

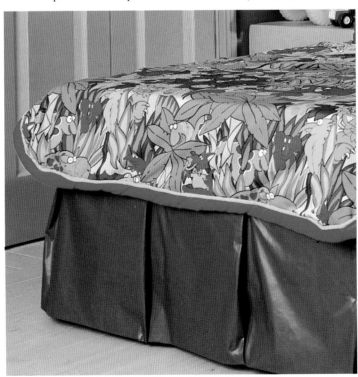

MATERIALS
sufficient fabric

box-pleating tape, the same length as the two long sides of the mattress plus the width

matching sewing machine thread

pins

scissors

tape measure

sewing machine

$31^1/_2$" (80cm) of $^1/_4$" (6mm)-wide elastic (optional – if you have a posted bed)

eight 12" (30cm)-long fabric ties (optional – if you have a posted bed)

Method

1 Cut out the rectangle for the deck piece. For beds with no bedposts or board at the foot, cut the length of

Tiered Bed Skirt

YOU CAN ADD A TOUCH OF EXTRAVAGANT GLAMOUR WITH TWO, OR
EVEN THREE LAYERS OF RUFFLES OF VARYING LENGTHS, MIXING
DIFFERENT TEXTURES, COLORS AND PRINTS.

Before you begin Calculate the width of the first base ruffle in the same way as for the standard bed ruffle or bed skirt. For each additional ruffle, subtract 4"-8" (10cm-20cm) from the depth, depending on the height of your bed. Make sure you have enough of each contrasting ruffle showing. All other measurements remain the same.

MATERIALS

sufficient fabric for each contrasting ruffle

matching sewing machine thread

pins

scissors

tape measure

sewing machine

*31¹/₂" (80cm) of ¹/₄" (6mm)-wide elastic
(optional – if you have a posted bed)*

*eight 12" (30cm)-long fabric ties
(optional – if you have a posted bed)*

Method

1 Cut out the rectangle of fabric for the deck piece. For beds with no bedposts or board at the foot, cut the required length of fabric for each ruffle, joining pieces as necessary to achieve the total length required. Hem the headboard end of the deck piece with a double hem, pressing ¹/₄" (6mm), then ³/₈" (1cm) to the wrong side.
2 Hem the short ends and the bottom edge of each ruffle as for the deck piece.
3 Lay the ruffles on top of one another with the deepest ruffle on the bottom, so that all the top raw edges are even and the right sides of all ruffles are facing upwards. Gather all the top raw

Choose a combination of solid and patterned fabrics

edges together through all thicknesses. Pull up the gathering so that the ruffle fits around the deck piece. Pin the ruffle to the deck piece with the raw edges even and the right sides together. Adjust the gathering evenly. Stitch the ruffles into place.
4 For beds with posts, make a separate tiered bed skirt for each side and the bottom of the bed.

Pillowcases

THERE ARE MANY STYLES OF PILLOWCASES THAT YOU CAN ACHIEVE
WITH JUST A LITTLE TIME AND SOME INSPIRATION.

Basic pillowcase 1

Before you begin This pillowcase is made out of one continuous piece of fabric with a turned flap which covers the pillow. Fabric for the pillowcase is cut to the dimensions of your pillow: the width of the pillow plus $5/8$" (1.5cm) for each seam allowance and twice the length of the pillow plus $5/8$" (1.5cm) for each turning and hem plus 6" (15cm) for the flap.

MATERIALS
sufficient fabric
matching sewing machine thread
pins
scissors
tape measure
sewing machine

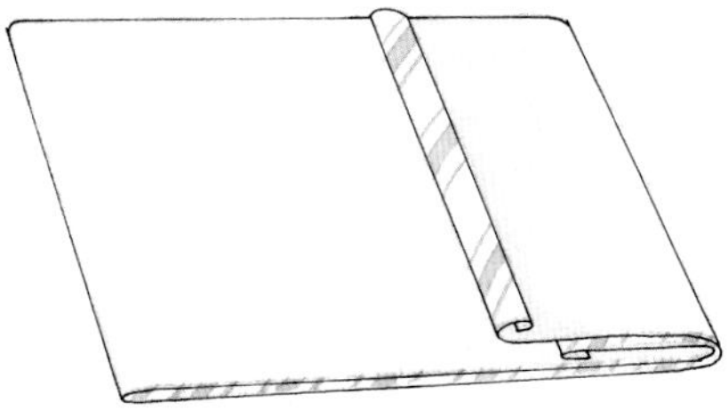

Fig. 1

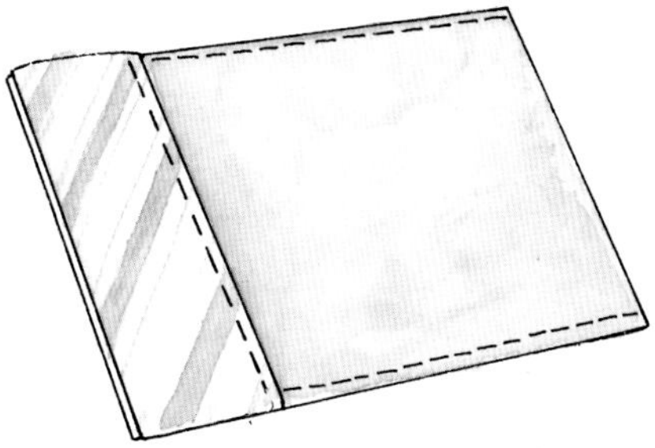

Fig. 2

Method

1 Cut the fabric to the required size. Press $1/4$" (6mm) to the wrong side on both short raw ends. Press another $3/8$" (1cm) under and stitch the hems in place.
2 With right sides together, fold back one end of the fabric to measure approximately the length of the pillow. Press with a warm iron to form a crease.
3 Place the fabric with the shorter side on the bottom. On the top section, fold back the 6" (15cm) flap as shown in fig. 1. Stitch along both long sides through all thicknesses. Trim and finish the raw edges if necessary. You can use French seams if you prefer. (See page 32 for how to sew French seams.)
4 Turn right side out and press.

Basic pillowcase 2

Before you begin This pillowcase resembles a bag without a flap and is ideal if you want to use buttons or ties. You will need a piece of fabric cut to the dimensions of your pillow: the width of the pillow plus $5/8$" (1.5cm) for each seam allowance and twice the length of your pillow plus $5/8$" (1.5cm) for all hems, plus 6" (20cm) for the cuff turnings at the opening.

MATERIALS
sufficient fabric
matching sewing machine thread
pins
scissors
tape measure
sewing machine

Method

1 Cut the fabric to the desired size. Press $1/4$" (6mm) to the wrong side on the short raw ends. Fold the fabric in half widthwise with right sides together. Sew the sides with a $5/8$" (1.5cm) seam. Serge or zigzag the raw edges.
2 Press 4" (10cm) to the wrong side around the open end for the cuff. Stitch the cuff in place, close to the fold with one continuous line of stitching (fig. 2).
3 Turn the pillowcase right side out and press. Add the closure of your choice – buttons, snaps or ties.

Use either method for making a basic pillowcase

Pillowcase with bows

Before you begin

Braids and ribbons are both suitable for the bows, but you will need to finish the ends to stop them fraying. Preshrink ribbons or braids and test for colorfastness.

Measuring

You will need a piece of fabric cut to the dimensions of your pillow: the width of the pillow plus $5/8$" (1.5cm) for each seam allowance and twice the length of your pillow plus $5/8$" (1.5cm) for all turnings and hems plus 6" (15cm) for the cuff turnings at the opening.

MATERIALS
sufficient fabric

six strips, each 3" x 12" (7.5cm x 30cm), for the bows

matching sewing machine thread

pins

tape measure

scissors

sewing machine

tailor's chalk

turning hook or knitting needle

Method

1 Make the basic pillowcase, using method 2.

2 Fold the ribbon for the ties in half. Sew one short end and one long side with a $5/8$" (1.5cm) seam. Trim the seam and turn right side out with the turning hook or knitting needle. Slipstitch the remaining end closed. Press each tie flat.

3 Mark three evenly spaced positions on the right side of the front cuff.

4 For three ties, sew the end with the slipstitches to the inside edge of the front cuff at the markings. Sew another tie to correspond on the inside edge of the back cuff.

Pristine white in a variety of textures works well in a bedroom

Buttoned pillowcase

MATERIALS
two pieces of fabric, one $19^1/2$" x 60" (50cm x 152cm) and one $5^1/2$" x $19^1/2$" (14cm x 50cm)

five buttons (if you are going to use covered buttons, allow additional fabric for each button)

matching sewing machine thread

contrasting piping

pins

tape measure

scissors

sewing machine

tailor's chalk

turning hook or knitting needle

Method

1 Place the two pieces of fabric together along a $19^1/2$" (50cm) end with the right side of the small piece facing the wrong side of the larger piece and the raw edges even. Stitch. Press the small piece to the right side of the larger piece.

2 Press $3/8$" (1cm) under on the opposite raw edge of the small piece. Tuck the contrasting piping under the pressed edge and stitch the edge in place, through all thicknesses.

3 Press $3/8$" (1cm), then 2" (5cm) to the wrong side on the $19^1/2$" (50cm) raw edge of the larger piece. Stitch.

4 Fold the pillowcase with right sides together and matching the short ends. Stitch the sides, securing the stitching at the opening edge. Turn the pillowcase right side out and press.

5 With tailor's chalk, mark the positions of five evenly spaced buttonholes across the front edge of the opening, $1^1/2$" (4cm) down from the opening. Stitch the buttonholes then sew the buttons on the other side of the opening to correspond.

6 Bind the opening edges if desired.

Flanged pillowcase

MATERIALS

one piece of fabric, 28" x 34" (71cm x 86cm), for
the pillowcase front

two pieces of fabric, one 26" x 28" (65cm x 71cm) and one 14" x 28" (35cm x 71cm), for the pillowcase back

sewing machine thread in a contrasting color and a matching color

pins

scissors

tape measure

tailor's chalk

sewing machine

Method

1 Narrow hem one 28" (71cm) end of each back piece. Place the back pieces on the front piece with the right sides together, the hemmed edges of the back pieces overlapping and all the raw edges even. Stitch around the outside edge. Trim the seams and turn the pillowcase right side out. Press.
2 With tailors chalk, mark a guideline 3" (7.5cm) from the outside edge all around the pillowcase. Stitch along this line to form the flange.

Ruffled pillowcase

MATERIALS

one piece of fabric, 20" x 31" (51cm x 78cm), for the pillowcase front

two pieces of fabric, one 20" x 28" (51cm x 71cm) and one 8" x 20" (22cm x 51cm), for the pillowcase back

2³/4yd. (2.5cm) of 8" (20cm)-wide fabric, for the ruffle strip

matching sewing machine thread

pins

scissors

tape measure

sewing machine

tailor's chalk

A checked flanged pillowcase and a floral ruffled pillowcase complement each other

Method

1 Join the short ends of the ruffle strip to form a loop. Fold the ruffle strip in half with the wrong sides together and raw edges even. Gather the raw edges with two rows of gathering stitches. Pull up the gathering to fit around the front piece.
2 Pin the ruffle around the front, with right sides together and raw edges even. Adjust the gathering. Baste in place (fig. 1).
3 Narrow hem one 20" (51cm) edge of each back piece. Place both back pieces on the right side of the front piece (over the ruffle) with the right sides together, overlapping the hemmed edges and having all the outside edges even. Stitch around the outside edge through all thicknesses. Turn right side out and press.

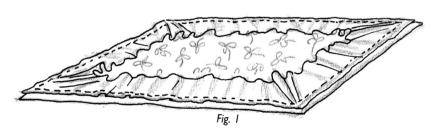

Fig. 1

European pillowcase

Before you begin These instructions are for a flanged European pillowcase but a European pillowcase can also be trimmed with ruffles, lace inserts, or piping in the same way as other pillows in this section.

MATERIALS
*28" (71cm) square of fabric,
for the pillowcase front*

*two pieces of fabric, one 18" x 28" (46cm
x 71cm) and one 15" x 28" (38cm x
71cm), for the
pillowcase back*

matching sewing machine thread

25" (63cm) square pillow form

tailor's chalk

tape measure

pins

scissors

sewing machine

Method

1 Press ¼" (6mm) then ⅜" (1cm) to the wrong side along the 28" (71cm) edges of both back pieces. Stitch the hems in place.

2 Place the two back pieces on the front with right sides together and back pieces overlapping at the center. Baste the overlapped edges together.

3 Stitch along all sides through all thicknesses. Trim the seams and corners. Remove the basting. Turn the pillowcase right side out and press.

4 With tailor's chalk, mark a line 2" (5cm) from the edge on all four sides of the pillowcase. Stitch along this line to form the flange.

Above: A collection of plump European pillows

Below: Make this child's charming pillow by attaching cotton lace to the ruffle strip before gathering. The pillowcase is then made in exactly the same way as the one on page 147.

A lace tray cloth slipstitched on the front of a pillowcase is an easy way to appliqué

Scalloped pillowcase

Method

1 Cut out the lace pattern to be embroidered. Look for strong solid lines. Pin the lace pattern to the pillowcase front. Using a small zigzag stitch, embroider the lace design on to the pillowcase front.

2 Make a template for the scalloped pattern, by drawing around the outline of the small plate on to the piece of cardboard and cutting it out. Our scallops are approximately 2¹/₂" (6.5cm) wide and ⁵/₈" (1.5cm) deep. Using the template and disappearing marker, draw a row of scallops along each side of the pillowcase front. Alternatively, set your machine for scallops close to these sizes.

3 Stitch along the pattern with satin stitch. When the stitching is complete, use sharp scissors to snip into the scallops and cut away the excess fabric along the raw edge.

4 Stitch a narrow double hem on one long edge of the smaller back piece. Repeat this process on one short edge of the larger back piece.

5 Press ¹/₄" (6mm) to the wrong side on the remaining three sides of the smaller back piece. Place this piece (right side up) on to the wrong side of the embroidered front piece. Topstitch it in place, stitching 2" (5cm) in from the scalloped edge.

6 Press ¹/₄" (6mm) on the three remaining sides of the larger back piece. Pin the hemmed edge of the back piece to match the topstitched edge of the smaller back piece. This will form the side opening. Stitch the three sides into place, 2" (5cm) in from the scalloped edges. The larger back piece should completely cover the smaller back piece form the pillowcase flap.

Comforter

THESE FEATHER- OR DOWN-FILLED COMFORTERS,
ARE THE IDEAL SOLUTION FOR COLD WINTER NIGHTS. THEY PROVIDE THE
WARMTH OF SEVERAL BLANKETS WITHOUT THE WEIGHT.

Comforters make bedmaking a breeze

Before you begin The size of your comforter is entirely up to you. Generally a double bed comforter should be approximately 81" x 81" (2m x 2m) and a single bed comforter 81" x 63" (2m x 1.6m).

Use a tightly woven fabric like a down-proof cambric or a tightly woven furnishing chintz or cotton. Don't use sheets – feathers can work their way through the weave and escape.

If you are joining lengths of fabric use flat fell or French seams.

The choice of filling is up to you. Down is more expensive than feathers, but is warmer, lighter and bulkier. A combination of feathers and down is a good compromise. Polyester fiber is suitable for anyone allergic to feathers.

Generally, filling is sold in packs, by weight. Approximately 3.3lbs (1.5kg) of a feather-and-down-combination filling is needed for a double bed comforter. Polyester fiber weighs slightly more than feathers. Experiment until you are happy with the weight of your own comforter. Tape is used to create channels for the

filling. Choose firm cotton twill tape, not bias binding. The quantity of tape will depend on the number of channels you make. For this double bed comforter, 8" (20cm)-wide channels suited the fabric pattern. This gave us nine rows of tape (giving us ten channels), so we used 20yds. (18m) of twill tape. The length of tape required is equal to the number of rows of tape multiplied by the length of the comforter. Decide on the width of channels best for your fabric.

A feather comforter is, theoretically,

washable – but the bulk is daunting when hanging it out to dry. Dry-cleaning is effective. Hanging your comforter out regularly to air in the sun will keep it smelling clean and fresh.

Experienced comforter makers say that one should only work with feathers and down in the bathroom with the door shut! When filling your comforter, place the opened bag of feathers in the bath. This helps to confine the flyaway feathers to a relatively draught-free area with little for them to stick to. (Remember to remove the towels!)

MATERIALS
sufficient fabric to cut a front and back of the required size plus 4" (10cm) all around for turnings

fabric strip, 12" (30cm) wide, for the ties

filling of your choice
(see Before you begin)

2" (5cm) wide cotton twill tape
(see Before you begin)

pins

tape measure

matching sewing machine thread

scissors

sewing machine

Method

1 Press 4" (10cm) to the wrong side all around each piece to mark the final fold line for the hem. Fold the fabric along the tape lines at predetermined distances for the channel widths. Press along each line to make a sewing guide. This step is not necessary if you have striped fabric as the stripes provide a guide for the channel widths.
2 Stitch one edge of the tape along one stripe/crease on the wrong side of one piece (fig. 1). Then stitch the other side of the tape to the same stripe/crease on the wrong side of the other piece. Be sure to stitch very close to the edges of the tape. Do this for all the channels.
3 Press 1¼" (3cm) to the wrong side twice on the sides and lower edge. Topstitch the hems in place through all

Ties at the corners allow you to bundle up the comforter neatly for storage

thicknesses, closing it at the same time. Fill the channels evenly, smoothing the filling right down the channels. When you are satisfied with the quantity of filling, fold over the top edge and hem the same as for the sides (fig. 2).
4 Attach ties to the bottom end of your comforter for attaching it to your bed or for tying it into a bundle for storage when not in use, if desired.

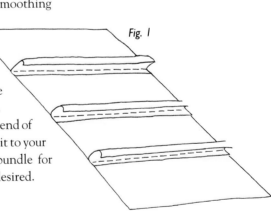

Fig. 1

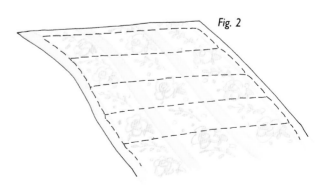

Fig. 2

Quilted Spread

A QUILTED SPREAD IS ANOTHER ATTRACTIVE DECORATIVE COVER YOU CAN MAKE FOR YOUR BED.

Before you begin

Providing only minimal warmth but high fashion appeal, a decorative spread is thinner than a comforter and is filled with polyester batting rather than the bulkier down and feathers. A decorative spread made in the same fabric as a comforter, or in a fabric that coordinates with it, makes an ideal summer/winter combination in any bedroom. A spread can also be reversible, giving a different look if the spread is rolled down over a bedspread showing the contrasting fabric beneath.

Use the same dimensions as those given for the comforter.

The quilting can be done by machine or by hand and there are many different quilting patterns you can use. Remember, busy or ornate fabrics work best with simple quilting patterns, but with solid fabrics a more intricate quilting design can be used. If you are unsure about quilting, have your fabric professionally quilted. Check quilting magazines and fabric stores for professional machine-quilters.

MATERIALS
two pieces of fabric cut to the required dimensions plus ³/₈" (1cm)
all around to allow for quilting shrinkage

polyester batting

quilting thread

2³/₈" (6cm)-wide bias strips for binding the edge

matching sewing machine thread

pins

scissors

tape measure

tailor's chalk or disappearing marker

quilting pattern

sewing machine

Method

1 Make sufficient bias binding. See pages 20 to 21 for how to make and join bias binding.

2 Mark your quilting pattern on the top fabric with tailor's chalk or disappearing marker. Prepare the quilt sandwich by placing the batting between the two pieces of fabric, smoothing out any wrinkles. The batting should run vertically down the fabric. Pin with safety pins or baste all three layers together, laying in a grid of horizontal and vertical lines 12" (30cm) apart. Baste around the outside edges.

3 Machine or hand quilt the pattern (fig.1). Press.

4 Finish the raw edges with bias binding. Finish the ends by turning under.

This spread has been quilted with diagonal rows of stitching

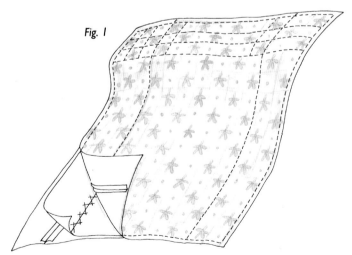

Fig. 1

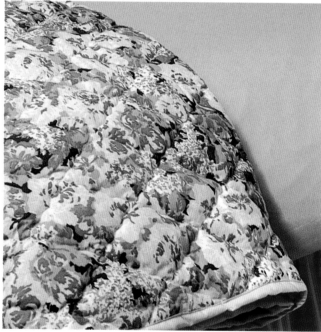

Tent Canopy

PURELY DECORATIVE, THIS STYLE OF CANOPY CAN BE SUSPENDED FROM THE CEILING ON POLES, REPLACING A HEADBOARD AND CREATING A STUNNING VISUAL EFFECT.

Before you begin To calculate how much fabric is needed, measure from the floor over the pole and back to the floor, plus 12" (30cm) for extra draping. The fabric should be approximately 28" (71cm) wide by this measurement long. If you need to join lengths allow $5/8$" (1.5cm) for each seam allowance and 2" (5cm) for the finished hem.

MATERIALS

decorative pole, approximately 30" (75cm) long

two contrasting pieces of fabric of the required size

sufficient $2^3/8$" (6cm)-wide contrasting bias strips to bind the long edges of the canopy

matching sewing machine thread

curtain mounting bracket

ceiling hook for attaching the cord

decorative cord and tassel

tape measure

pins

scissors

sewing machine

Method

1 Place the two fabrics with wrong sides together and the raw edges even. Baste them together along all the edges.
2 Make continuous bias binding following instructions on page 20. Pin and baste the bias binding along two long sides, enclosing the raw edges and turning under the ends of the bias tape. Stitch in place.
3 Fold the fabric in half lengthwise. Stitch across the width of the canopy at this point and then stitch again to

form a casing. The casing should be the diameter of the pole plus $3/8$" (1cm).
4 Fit the canopy on the pole and mark the hem position. Trim any excess length before pressing $1/4$" (6mm) then another $1^3/4$" (4.5cm) to the wrong side. Stitch the hems.
5 Fit the canopy on the pole. Tie the decorative cord and tassel to the front end of the pole and attach the other

end of the cord to a hook in the ceiling. Make coordinating tiebacks, if desired.

Far left: A close-up of the quilted spread
Above: Contrast color and fabric for a coordinated decor

Sheer Canopy

CANOPIES WERE ORIGINALLY USED IN THE TROPICS TO ALLOW PEOPLE TO ENJOY THE
COOL NIGHT AIR PROTECTED FROM BITING INSECTS.

Before you begin You will need a round hoop on which to hang your canopy, as well as a strong hook that can be mounted into a beam in the ceiling to support the canopy.

Fabric and trims will vary depending on the effect you are trying to create. Our canopy is made from a printed voile and trimmed with cotton lace. Sheer netting and any suitable pre-shrunk lace will give a similar whimsical effect.

Measuring

Measure around the base of the bed to determine the diameter that the fabric must cover. Divide this number by the width of your fabric to determine how many drops of fabric you will need. Add one additional drop to ensure that there is still some gather in the canopy when it is closed around the bed.

MATERIALS
hook
*cane, wood or plastic hoop,
12"-16" (30cm-40cm) in diameter*
fabric
lace for trimming
*fishing line or strong twine for suspending
the hoop from the ceiling*
19^1/$_2$" (50cm) narrow cotton tape
cord for attaching the canopy to the ceiling
matching sewing machine thread
pins
scissors
tape measure
sewing machine

Today, canopies are largely decorative, with a romantic feel

Method

1 Fix the hook to the ceiling. With the twine or fishing line, suspend the hoop from the hook. Experiment to find the hanging length that suits the proportions of the bed and the room. Measure the drop from 12" (30cm) above the hoop to the floor, adding 19½" (50cm) for proper coverage of the bed.

2 Stitch the drops of fabric together, using French seams for a neat finish.

3 Fold the fabric in half, in the direction of the seams, with the wrong sides together. Pin the two edges for 8" (20cm) from the top and stitch together with a French seam.

4 Pin and attach lace to the front opening edges (if desired) with French seams or a serger for a neat finish. Stitch a narrow hem around the base of the canopy.

5 Mark the position where the canopy should fall over the hoop, about 12" (30cm) below the top edge. From this point taper the fabric up to make a circle measuring 6"-8" (15cm-20cm) in diameter. Make a hem at the top edge of the canopy to form a casing and thread the cord through the casing. Pull up the fullness of the fabric. Stitch a loop of tape at the casing. Thread the cord through the loop and attach it to the hook in the ceiling. Slipstitch lace to the outside edge of the hoop, if desired.

Fringed Bedspread

Before you begin For the length of the bedspread, measure from the floor to the top of the bed, including the height of your pillows. Add an additional 24" (60cm) for the tuck under the pillows. The finished width of your bedspread will be the width of the top of the bed plus the drop to the floor. You may wish to add a little extra to allow the finished bedspread to "puddle" or hang loosely on the floor. If you are using a lightweight fabric that requires lining, allow for a ⅝" (1.5cm) seam allowance all around. If the bedspread is to be unlined, allow 1" (2.5cm) on each side for a double hem.

We were lucky enough to find some antique damask to which we added a 4" (10cm) bullion fringe. To show the fringe to its best advantage, this bedspread finished 3¼" (8.5cm) above the floor before the fringe was attached.

MATERIALS
sufficient fabric, approximately
4¾yds. (4.2m)
for a double bed
6 yds. (5.5m) of bullion fringe
matching sewing machine thread
pins
scissors
tape measure
sewing machine

Method

1 Cut out the fabric, allowing a 2" (5cm) seam allowance at the top end.

2 Press 1" (2.5cm) to the wrong side twice along the top edge. Stitch. On the remaining three sides, ¼" (6mm), then ⅜" (1cm) under and stitch.

3 Pin the bullion fringe ⅜" (1cm) above the hem of the bedspread, with the right side facing out. Stitch the fringe in place along the woven band.

Dress a simple rectangle of fabric with a luxurious fringe to make a stylish bedspread

Upholstered Headboard

INEXPENSIVE PLYWOOD CAN BE USED FOR THIS STYLISH HEADBOARD.

Before you begin The headboard can sit behind the bed, be attached to the wall or fixed to the mattress base with corner brackets. The bottom can be left flush so that it sits evenly on the floor or you can add legs.

The height of the headboard should be 10"-24" (25cm-60cm) above the bed. It can be shaped to any style.

The quantities given here are for a single bed headboard.

MATERIALS
plywood
spray adhesive
woodworking glue
staple gun and staples
push pins
tailor's chalk
main fabric, enough to cover the headboard back and front plus an allowance for overlaps and turnings
contrasting fabric 12" (30cm) wide x three times the perimeter of the headboard for the shirred strip
6¹/₂yds. (6m) hi-loft polyester batting
needle and quilting thread or sewing machine and matching sewing machine thread
tape measure
scissors

Method

1 Cut out the wood to the desired shape. Glue the batting to the entire board with spray adhesive. Trim any excess even with the edge of the board.
2 Using the board as a pattern, cut out the front fabric with the grain of the fabric running down the board and allowing extra to fit over the edge to the back. Cut another piece of fabric in the same manner for the back that is

the same size and shape as the headboard. Spray the adhesive on the back of the front fabric piece then glue it over the batting. Hold the fabric in place with occasional push pins, then staple or tack the fabric in place on the back of the headboard. Turn the bottom raw edge on the back piece under, then glue it on to the back of the headboard over the raw edges. Staple the edges in place over the front piece.
3 With tailor's chalk, mark the fabric on the front of the headboard at 4" (10cm) intervals and 6" (15cm) in from the edge. Join the marks to form an arc.
4 Join the pieces for the shirred strip with flat fell seams, if necessary, to achieve the required length. Gather both long sides of the strip and pull up the gathering so the strip is the right length required to go around the headboard. Final adjustments can be made

when the shirred strip is tacked in place.
5 Place the middle of the shirred strip in the middle of the top edge of the headboard with the right side of the strip facing the right side of the front of the headboard and the bottom gathering line on the chalk line. Staple the bottom edge of the shirred strip to the chalk line, placing the staples end to end. Continue stapling down one side, turning the raw edge under at the end and stapling it in place.
6 Cut the remaining batting into 1¹/₄" (3cm)-wide strips. Working from the back, begin stuffing the area behind the shirred fabric with the batting strips, puffing out the shirring. At the same time, bring the edge of the shirred panel over the stuffing on to the back of the headboard, stapling it in place.
7 Repeat steps 5 and 6 for the other side of the headboard.

Nursery Linen

MAKING YOUR OWN NURSERY LINEN OFFERS A GREAT OPPORTURNITY
TO DECORATE WITH FABRIC.

Nursery quilt

Before you begin You will need ½yd. (.5m) of 45" (115cm)-wide fabric in each of two contrasting fabrics for the quilt front and 2¾yds. (2.5m) of a third contrasting fabric for additional squares, the quilt back, ruffles and bows.

Preshrink and press all fabrics before cutting out.

MATERIALS
sufficient fabric
batting
matching sewing machine thread
pins
scissors
tape measure
sewing machine

Method

1 Cut eleven 8" (20cm) squares from two of the fabrics and ten 8" (20cm) squares from the third fabric.

2 Arrange the squares in eight rows of four squares each. To form the diagonal pattern, make sure you begin each row with the same fabric as the end of the previous row. Sew squares into rows with ³/₈" (1cm) seams. Sew the eight rows together to form the quilt top. Press all the seams.

3 From the third fabric, cut a strip 8" (20cm) wide and one and a half times the circumference of the quilt top for the ruffle. Join strips if necessary to achieve the total length. Sew the short ends of the ruffle strip together to form a loop. Press the ruffle strip in half

with wrong sides together. Gather the raw edges.

4 Pin the ruffle to the quilt top with the right sides together and the raw edges even. Adjust the gathering to fit around the quilt top with more in each corner, then stitch the ruffle in place.

5 Cut the batting the same size plus a ³/₈" (1cm) allowance all around. Baste to the wrong side of the quilt top.

6 Cut the quilt back the same size as the batting. Place the quilt top and the quilt back together with the right sides together and the raw edges even. Stitch around the outside edge, leaving a 12" (30cm) opening in the center of one side for turning. Turn the quilt right side out. Press, then slipstitch the opening closed.

7 Make 10" (25cm) lengths of decorative cording, knot the ends, then stitch them to the meeting points of the squares. Tie it into bows.

Choose a combination of pastel solids and prints in easy-care cotton blends for a totally coordinated nursery. Make the ruffled pillowcase following the instructions on page 147

Fitted crib sheet

Before you begin As crib mattresses vary a great deal in size, it is often difficult to buy a sheet that fits your crib. Sometimes, it is easier to make your own fitted crib sheet to ensure the best fit possible. Stretch terry cloth, poly-cotton or cotton are suitable fabrics. Preshrink and press the fabric before cutting out.

Measuring
Measure the width, length and depth of the mattress and add 10" (25cm) for the tuck-under.

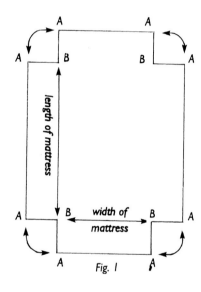

Fig. 1

MATERIALS
sufficient fabric
15" (38cm) of ¼" (6mm)-wide elastic,
cut into four equal pieces
pins
tape measure
matching sewing machine thread
scissors
sewing machine

This crib quilt can be enlarged by adding extra squares

Method

1 Cut the fabric for the sheet, as wide as the mattress plus twice the depth of the mattress plus 10" (25cm) for the tuck-under on each side and 1¼" (3cm) for the hem, and as long as the mattress plus twice the depth of the mattress plus 10" (25cm) for the tuck-under on each side and 1¼" (3cm) for the hem.

2 Cut squares from each corner of the fabric as illustrated (fig. 1). Note that A-B is the depth of the mattress plus 10" (25cm) for the tuck-under and ⅝" (1.5cm) for the hem. Pin the sides of the squares together, joining the A points. Sew from the outside edge to the inner corner, forming an angle at each corner of the sheet.

3 Press ¼" (6mm) to the wrong side around the outside edge, then another ⅜" (1cm). Sew the hem in place. Sew the elastic to the seam allowance on each corner, starting and finishing 8"

(20cm) on either side of the corner seam, using a zigzag stitch and stretching the elastic as you sew (fig. 2).

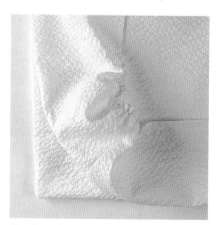

Stitching elastic around the corners will keep the sheet in place

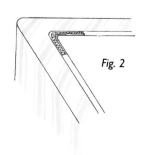

Fig. 2

Baby basket

MATERIALS

paper for making the templates

pencil

scissors

*fabric tape – to measure the
circumference of the basket*

*one piece of fabric, the size of the
base template plus ³/₈" (1.5cm) for seam
allowances*

*batting, the depth of the
basket x the circumference*

*two pieces of fabric, the depth of the basket
x the circumference plus 4" (10cm)*

*fabric for the ruffle, twice the circum-
ference of the basket x 8" (20cm) wide*

*2yds. (1.8m) of 1" (2.5cm)-wide ribbon
if basket has handles*

*sufficient elastic to go around the
basket, stretched tightly*

quilter's thread

quilter's chalk

matching sewing machine thread

pins

scissors

tape measure

ruler

sewing machine

Method

1 Make a paper template of the base of your basket. Cut out the template and place it inside the basket to check the fit. Trim if necessary.

2 Using the template, cut two base pieces adding a ³/₈" (1cm) seam allowance all around. Cut a piece of batting the same size.

3 Mark the quilting design on the fabric with chalk. A grid of squares or diamonds works very well. Sandwich the batting between two layers of fabric, smoothing out any wrinkles. Baste the layers together, laying in a grid of horizontal and vertical lines. Machine-quilt the design. Remove the basting stitches.

4 Make a paper template for the sides of the basket. Using the template, cut out two pieces of fabric, adding 2¹/₂" (6cm) around the top edge for turning and ³/₈" (1cm) seam allowance around the bottom edge. Cut the batting the same shape as the template without any seam allowances.

5 Mark the quilting design on the fabric with chalk. Vertical lines are easy and work well, spaced about 3" (7.5cm) apart. Sandwich the batting between the fabrics as before. Baste through all the thicknesses around the top and bottom edges, using quilting thread. Machine-quilt the design, stitching from the bottom edge up to 1¹/₄" (3cm) from the top edge. Note that the batting does not go all the way up to the top. Remove the basting stitches.

6 Hem the short ends of the ruffle strip, with a double ¹/₄" (6mm) hem.

7 Make a double ruffle by folding the ruffle strip in half with the wrong sides together. Gather the raw edges together. Adjust the gathering to fit the top edge of the quilted side piece. Pin the ruffle to the top edge of the side piece with the right sides together and the raw edges even. Stitch.

8 Insert the elastic into the ruffle through the open ends.

9 If your basket has handles, slit the fabric where the handles are joined to the basket and narrow hem the edges. Attach ribbon ties to the edges.

10 Pin the base to the side piece at the raw edges. Stitch, then serge or zigzag to finish the raw edges. Place the liner into the basket, bringing the elasticised ruffle over the side and passing the handles through the slits.

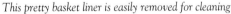

This pretty basket liner is easily removed for cleaning

Table Linen

STENCILED LINENS

CIRCULAR TABLECLOTHS

TABLE TOPPERS

PLACE MATS AND NAPKINS

QUILTED ACCESSORIES

FESTIVE SETTING

SCALLOPED LINENS

FRINGED TABLE SET

Table Linen

A grand table set with flowers, china, crystal and silverware can be quite breathtaking. Crisp white linen tablecloths provide the perfect backdrop against which all the other elements are placed. Linen napkins provide an additional touch of elegance as well as serving a more practical purpose at the dinner table.

All tablecloths and table linens are functional in that they protect your furniture and your clothes from soiling. They can be as decorative as you wish and, depending on the time and place of their use, they can be either casual or formal in style. Their plain, no-fuss construction often means they can also be reversible.

Everyday table linens should be made from easy-care washable fabrics, so that they can survive the stresses of frequent use and the resultant wear and tear. Cotton, polyester and cotton, cotton sateen, gingham and cotton linens are all suitable for casual table linen. Damask and silks add a sense of formality and luxury to a dining table, while a vivid combination of textured fabrics provide a touch of drama.

Contrast and textures create exotic effects even with the most simple of fabrics. Try mixing fabrics, such as linen and satin, to create truly elegant table napkins. Incorporate appliqué or embroidery stitches for an individual look. You can stencil muslin napkins with a variety of prints to take you from breakfast to an afternoon tea with a country feel.

Instructions for making these elegant table linens are on page 178

The finish you choose will add interest to your table. Layers of mitered corners in a variety of colored fabrics and textures create a look and style that will leave your guests wondering where you bought the extravagant display.

In a more formal dining room, try to match the table linen to the overall room scheme. For example, use the background color of your curtains as the base color for a cloth on a side table to create an interesting harmony of color and shape in your room. On the other hand, if you want the table to blend into the room, so that a prized vase or collection of china is the focus, select a fabric in a similar color to your walls, then create an accent with a cloth topper in a similar texture.

Measuring for tablecloths

When making tablecloths always try to get fabric that is wide enough to cover the width of the table without seams. You will also need to decide how deep you wish the overhang to be – to your lap or near the floor, or somewhere in between.

Square tablecloth
Measure across the width of the table. To this measurement add twice the desired overhang measurement and the hem allowances.

Rectangular tablecloth
Measure across the table. To this measurement add twice the overhang to find the width of the tablecloth. Measure the length of the table and add twice the overhang. Add the hem allowances to both measurements (fig. 1).

Round tablecloth
Measure the diameter of the table through the middle. To this measurement add twice the desired overhang and the hem allowances.

Oval tablecloth
Measure across the table. To this measurement, add twice the overhang to find the width of the tablecloth. Measure the length of the table and add twice the overhang. Add hem allowances to both measurements.

If the width of the table is greater than the fabric width and fabric widths need to be joined, it is important that these joining seams be placed along the table edges and not in the middle.

Joining fabric

You may need to join fabric to achieve the required length and width for a tablecloth. It is important to place these joining seams where they will be as unobtrusive as possible. Usually this means placing them along the table edge (fig. 2). For an oval or a round table place the seams as shown in figs. 3 and 4 below. Always use a flat fell seam when joining fabric to avoid thick seams.

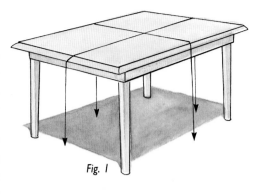

Fig. 1

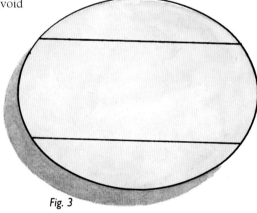

Fig. 2

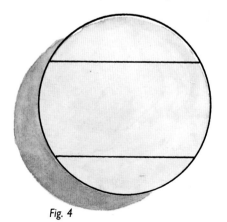

Fig. 3

Fig. 4

Stenciled Linens

MATERIALS

sufficient fabric for the tablecloth

24" (61cm) square of fabric for each napkin

matching sewing machine thread

pins

scissors

sewing machine

tape measure

purchased stencil or firm plastic for making a stencil

pencil

permanent marker

craft knife for cutting a stencil

cutting board for cutting a stencil

fabric paints

stenciling brushes

masking tape

Before you begin Sometimes fabric can be so wide that you do not have to join pieces to achieve the required size. If this is not the case, join three pieces together with seams that run close to the table edges, not two pieces joined with a seam down the center of the table.

It is best to choose a one-hundred-per-cent cotton fabric with a smooth finish for a tablecloth and napkins. Cotton launders well and is pleasant to handle. If you prefer the wearing qualities of synthetic fibers, try using a polyester/cotton mix.

There are many ways to position the stencil design on your tablecloth, depending on the size of the cloth, the particular design you have chosen, and your own preference. You could place the design at each place setting, as a continuous border around the edge of the cloth, or positioned to sit in from the edge of the table. Bear in mind when planning your design and the layout, that the edge of the tablecloth is not likely to be visible when you are seated at the table so much of the effect of any stenciling along the edges could be lost.

Measuring

Measure your table, following the steps given in measuring for tablecloths on page 163. Calculate your fabric requirements using these measurements.

Method

1 Miter the corners of the tablecloth as shown in the diagrams (figs. 1 to 3) and on page 22.
2 Press 1/4" (6mm) to the wrong side on all raw edges, then another 5/8" (1.5cm). Stitch the hems in place.
3 If you are making your own stencil from the bow design on page 165, trace the stencil design on the plastic and cut out the stencil with the craft knife.
4 Position the stencil on the fabric. Paint in the first color, using a dabbing action, then apply any other colors separately. With masking tape, cover any area that you wish to paint a different color.
5 To set the colors, press on the wrong side of the fabric with a dry iron.

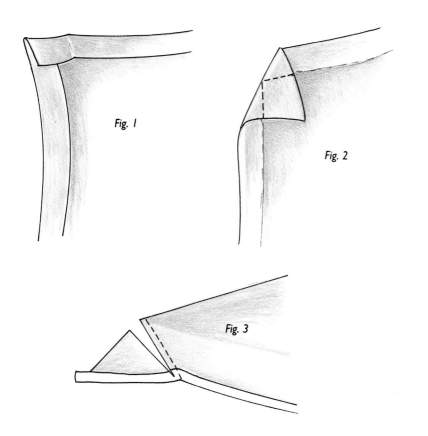

Fig. 1

Fig. 2

Fig. 3

Stencil the same bow design around the edge of the tablecloth

Circular Tablecloths

CIRCULAR TABLES ARE A PRETTY WAY TO FILL AN EMPTY CORNER. THERE IS NO GREAT MYSTERY TO MAKING CIRCULAR TABLECLOTHS. THE SECRET LIES IN MEASURING AND CUTTING ACCURATELY, THEN THE SEWING IS SIMPLY A STRAIGHT LINE.

Round tablecloth

Before you begin Measure from the center of the table to the floor. Add extra for a hem if you plan to turn the edge under rather than add a ruffle or lace. Take the edge trimmings into consideration and add or subtract accordingly. This will be your basic measurement. Purchase four times this basic measurement in fabric plus 4" (10cm). Omit the extra 4" (10cm) if your fabric is as wide as twice the basic measurement or your table is small. Wide sheeting is ideal for a tablecloth on a small bedside table because no seams are necessary.

MATERIALS
sufficient fabric
matching sewing machine thread
pins
scissors
tape measure
tailor's chalk
sewing machine
trims and ruffles as desired

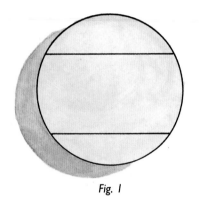

Fig. 1

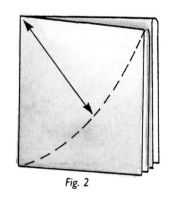

Fig. 2

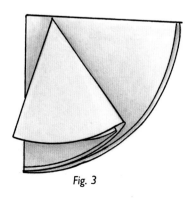

Fig. 3

Method

1 Join your fabric to make one piece large enough for the circle. To do this, cut two pieces each twice the basic length plus 4" (10cm). Place one piece aside. Cut the other piece in half lengthwise, parallel with both selvages. Trim all the selvages. Using a flat seam, join the trimmed edges of the cut pieces to the large uncut piece (fig. 1).

2 To cut out the tablecloth, fold the fabric in half, then in half again, so that the fabric is now folded into quarters. Place one end of the tape measure at the folded point and mark the basic measurement point at one edge of the fabric. Swing the tape measure around, marking out the arc of the circle with the chalk, following the basic measurement point on the tape measure (fig. 2). Cut through all the thicknesses of fabric along the chalk line (fig. 3).

3 If you are adding lace, measure around the circumference of the cloth to determine the quantity of ungathered lace or bias binding required. If you are gathering lace or making a fabric ruffle, use at least one and a half times this measurement. For a simple hem, press a $^5/_8$" (1.5cm) double hem under on the edge and stitch. You can stitch narrow piping cord into the hem using the zipper foot on your sewing machine.

Welted
round cloth

Before you begin Measure your table as for the round tablecloth on page 166. Subtract 1³/₄" (4.5cm) from this measurement for the width of the welting. This is the length of fabric you will require. If necessary, join lengths to achieve the width, using flat fell seams along the edges of the table.

MATERIALS
sufficient fabric

7 yds. (6.5m) of extra-thick piping cord

7 yds. (6.5m) of 4" (10cm)-wide bias-cut fabric plus ⁵/₈" (1.5cm) for each seam allowance

matching sewing machine thread

sewing machine

scissors

tape measure

Method

1 Cut out the fabric as for the standard tablecloth. The raw edges can be serged or zigzagged to prevent fraying.
2 Make a continuous bias strip as instructed on page 20. Join the ends of the bias strip to form a loop.
3 Fold the bias-cut fabric in half with wrong sides together. Place the piping cord inside the fold. Using the zipper foot on your sewing machine, sew a row of stitching as close to the cord as possible. Interweave the cord ends where they meet (figs. 4 to 6).
4 With the right sides together and the matching raw edges, pin the welting around the outer edge of the tablecloth, then stitch it in place, following the first stitching line. Trim away any excess seam allowance if necessary. Finish the raw edge by serging or zigzag stitching.

Silk taffeta is the perfect choice for this elegant round cloth with a welted edge

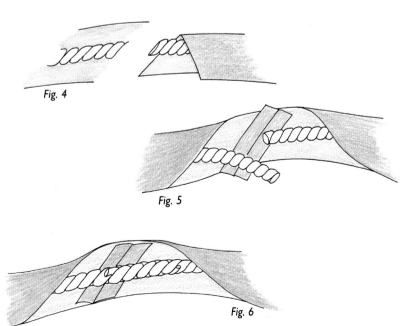

Fig. 4

Fig. 5

Fig. 6

Table Toppers

Square table topper

Before you begin

Plan how large the table topper should be. Make sure the proportion of the table topper is right for the circular cloth that will be beneath it.

Measuring

To calculate the quantity of fabric needed, measure the diameter of your table top and add 12" (30cm) for the overhang. For the bias trim, you will need a bias strip of fabric in contrast color, $1\frac{1}{2}$" (4cm) wide and the same length as the sides of the square.

Method

1 Make and join the continuous bias strip as shown on page 20. Press $\frac{1}{4}$" (6mm) under on both sides of the bias strip.

2 Cut a perfect square from the fabric to your required measurements. Turn in and press $\frac{1}{4}$" (6mm), then turn in and press another $\frac{1}{4}$" (6mm). Stitch the hem in place. Make sure the corners are stitched into neat points. (See page 22 for stitching corners.)

3 Pin a length of bias strip to two opposite edges of the tablecloth with both the right side of the bias and the right side of the tablecloth facing upwards. Turn in $\frac{3}{8}$" (1cm) on each end of each of the bias strips and secure the ends under the cloth with a pin. Stitch down each side of the bias strip close to each edge. Repeat the process on the other two sides. Press.

For a simple country look, checked cotton can be bias-trimmed following the instructions given here

---

Swagged table topper

Before you begin

You can attach matching or contrasting fabric bows to the cloth with Velcro® for a romantic effect. Measure the diameter of the table and add to this measurement the overhang and hem allowance. You may need to join the fabric as instructed on page 166.

Method

1 Make the table topper, following the method for the round tablecloth on page 166. Press $\frac{1}{4}$" (6mm) then $\frac{3}{8}$" (1cm) to the wrong side around the outer edge. Stitch the hem.

2 Mark quarter points on the circumference. On the wrong side of the fabric at each quarter point and beginning at the edge of the cloth, sew a 3" (7.5cm) length of bias binding perpendicular to the edge to form a casing. Thread 4" (10cm) of elastic through each casing, stitching the end of the elastic to the casing at the cloth edge. Leave the inner end of the casing open. Stitch another length of elastic to the wrong side of the tablecloth just above the top of the casing. Draw up the elastic to gather up the casing and tie the ends of the two pieces of elastic together. Release the elastic for washing and pressing the tablecloth.

Festoon table topper

MATERIALS
sufficient fabric
*fabric strip for the ruffle, 4³/₄"
(12cm) wide and twice the
circumference of the finished table
topper*
*fabric, strips 4³/₄" (12cm) wide,
for the bows*
*12" (30cm) of ³/₈" (1cm)-wide
bias binding*
*15" (40cm) of ³/₈" (1cm)-wide
elastic*
matching sewing machine thread
pins
scissors
tape measure
sewing machine

Method

1 Make the table topper, following the method given for the round table-cloth on page 166.

2 Join the ruffle strip with a flat seam to form a loop. Fold the ruffle strip in half with the wrong sides together. Serge or zigzag the raw edges together, then gather them.

3 Pin the ruffle around the bottom edge of the table topper with right sides together and raw edges even. Adjust the gathering and stitch the ruffle in place.

4 Mark the circumference into quarters. At each of the quarter points stitch a 3" (7.5cm) length of bias binding perpendicular to the edge of the wrong side of the table topper, beginning at the ruffle seams, to form a casing. Thread 4" (10cm) of elastic through each casing, stitching the end of the elastic to the outer end of the casing at the cloth edge. Leave the inner end of the casing open. Stitch another length of elastic to the wrong side of the table topper, just above the top of the casing. Draw the elastic in the casing to gather it and tie the ends of the two pieces of elastic together. Release the elastic for washing and pressing the table topper.

5 Cut the strip for the bows into four 19¹/₂" (50cm) lengths. Fold the strips in half with right sides together and raw edges even. Sew along one long side and one short side of each strip. Turn the strips right side out and press. Tie the strips into bows and slipstitch them in place over the gathering.

Above left: Ruffles and bows make this a charming table topper for a small table

Left: Team the swagged table topper with chair covers in the same fabric. Make the chair covers following the instructions on page 128.

Place Mats and Napkins

Place mat with contrast border

MATERIALS
two pieces of fabric, each
17$^{1}/_{2}$" x 22$^{1}/_{2}$" (44cm x 57cm)

batting, 17$^{1}/_{2}$" x 22$^{1}/_{2}$" (44cm x 57cm)

approximately 2$^{3}/_{8}$yds. (2.1m) of contrast-
ing fabric for the border

1$^{1}/_{2}$yds. (1.35m) purchased bias binding
or 1$^{1}/_{4}$" (3cm)-wide bias-cut fabric strip
in a contrasting color

matching sewing machine thread

pins

scissors

tape measure

sewing machine

Method

1 Place the fabric rectangles with wrong sides together and the batting sandwiched between them. Baste. Quilt through all thicknesses in a pattern of your choice.

2 From the contrasting fabric, cut four strips, two 4" x 17$^{1}/_{2}$" (10cm x 44cm) and two 4" x 22$^{1}/_{2}$ (10cm x 57cm). Press $^{3}/_{8}$" (1cm) under on one long edge of each strip. Cut the ends of the strips to perfect diagonals with the folded edge on the inner edge. Join them together with mitered corners (fig. 1).

3 Place the right side of the border on the wrong side of the back with the raw edges even. Stitch the border to the main piece. Trim the corners, then turn the place mat right side out and press.

4 Press the bias binding in half with the wrong sides together. Tuck the bias binding under the inner pressed edge of the border, leaving $^{1}/_{4}$" (6mm) of the bias binding protruding. Stitch the inner pressed edge in place, stitching through all thicknesses.

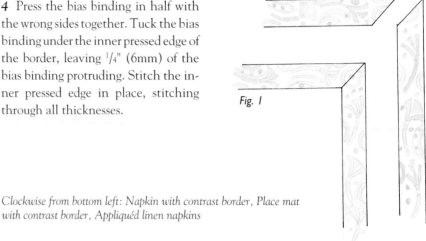

Fig. 1

Clockwise from bottom left: Napkin with contrast border, Place mat with contrast border, Appliquéd linen napkins

Appliquéd linen napkins

MATERIALS

24" (61cm) square of linen for each napkin

fabric motifs for the appliqué

fusible web

matching sewing machine thread

pins

scissors

tailor's chalk

tape measure

sewing machine

Method

1 Cut out the motifs, ¹/₄" (6mm) be-yond the edges. Following the manu-facturer's instructions, apply the web to the back of the motifs. Trim close to the motif.

2 Position the motifs on the napkin. Fuse in place.

3 Adjust your sewing machine stitch to a satin stitch. Stitch around the motif, enclosing the raw edge as you stitch.

4 Make a narrow double hem around all sides of the napkin. Press.

Primary brights in crisp cottons are the perfect choice for these satin-stitched napkins, place mats and tablecloth

Satin-stitched table linens

Before you begin Measure the size of your table and determine the drop you require, then add 1" (2.5cm) for the hem allowance. Refer to page 163 for further instructions on measuring your table and determining the size of your tablecloth.

MATERIALS

piece of fabric, 13" x 17" (33cm x 42.5cm) for each placemat

13" (33cm) square of fabric for each napkin

sufficient fabric for the tablecloth, cut to size

matching or contrasting sewing machine thread

sewing machine

scissors

tape measure

Method

The method is the same for all items.

1 Press 1" (2.5 cm) to the wrong side on all the raw edges, mitering the corners (figs. 2 to 4).

2 Machine-stitch a satin stitch border around all sides over the raw edges and across the mitered corners. Remember to pivot at the corners

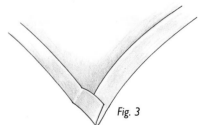

Fig. 2

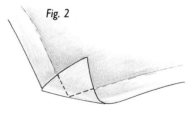

Fig. 3

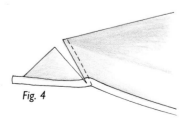

Fig. 4

Napkin with contrast border

MATERIALS

18¹/₂" (47cm) square of fabric

four strips of contrasting border fabric, each 3¹/₂" x 18¹/₂" (7.5cm x 47cm) (vary the width to suit the fabric pattern)

2yds. (1.8m) of purchased bias binding or 1¹/₄" (3cm)-wide bias-cut fabric strips

matching sewing machine thread

pins

scissors

tape measure

sewing machine

Method

1 Press ³/₈" (1cm) to the wrong side along the long inner edge of each border strip. Cut the ends to perfect diagonals, then join them together with mitered corners.

2 Place the right side of the border and the wrong side of the square together. Stitch around the outside edge. Trim the corners, then turn the napkin right side out and press.

3 Press the bias binding in half with the wrong sides together. Tuck the bias binding under the inner pressed edge of the border, leaving ¹/₄" (6mm) of the bias binding protruding. Stitch the inner pressed edge in place, stitching through all thicknesses.

4 If you are using ribbon or braid which has finished edges, use this simple method to achieve the same result. Press a ³/₈" (1cm) double hem on the edges of the napkin. Stitch. Pin the ribbon or braid around the edge of the napkin, folding the corners as shown (figs. 1 to 3). Stitch close to both edges of the ribbon or braid.

The red and green checked place mat has been made in the same way, without the bias binding trim. It has no batting and is not quilted.

Tartan with a contrasting fabric works well for this place mat and napkin

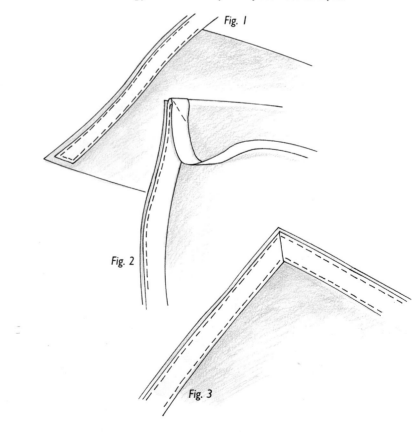

Fig. 1

Fig. 2

Fig. 3

Pleated place mat

MATERIALS
*piece of fabric, 12" x 54" (30cm x 137cm),
for the pleated body*

*piece of fabric, 4" x 63" (10cm x 160cm),
for the border strip*

*fusible interfacing, 12" x 36"
(30cm x 91.5cm)*

matching sewing machine thread

sewing machine

pins

thread

tailor's chalk or water-soluble marker pen

ruler

Method

1 With the chalk or marker, mark every $5/8$" (1.5cm) along both long sides of the fabric piece for pleating. Begin to fold in the pleats with your fingers and secure the pleats with pins as you work. Pressing with a warm iron will also help to hold the pleats in place. Baste along both long edges. The pleated panel should be about 12" x 15" (30cm x 38cm) when it is complete.

2 Cut the border into two strips 4" x 12" (10cm x 30cm), and two strips 4" x 20" (10cm x 51cm). Cut fusible interfacing the same size and fuse it to the wrong side of the border strips.

3 Press $1/4$" (6mm) to the wrong side along the long edges of each border strip. Fold each strip in half lengthwise with wrong sides together and press. Sandwich the pleated center piece between the folded edges of the border strips. On the wrong side, overlap the border pieces at the ends so the short and long border pieces meet in an L-shape at the corners (fig. 4). Pin the edges to hold them in place.

4 On the right side, fold the corners to form miters. Baste through all thicknesses, then machine-stitch in the following way: Begin at the outer edge of one mitered corner, stitch toward the center down the angle of the miter then back to the outside edge of the next mitered corner. Repeat the process on the opposite side and then stitch the two remaining inside border edges individually.

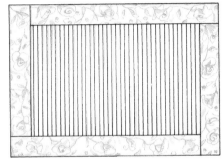

Fig. 4

This unusual pleated effect is very easy to achieve

Quilted Accessories

SIMPLE QUILTING IS A FEATURE OF THIS MATCHING TABLE SET.

Before you begin You can quilt your own fabric, using a quilting guide to plan the squares and spaces. The guide looks like an arm that extends from behind the sewing machine's presser foot into the center of the machine. The first row of stitching is made, then the guide is adjusted to sit along this stitching. Further rows of stitching are made, each the same distance from the previous one, as measured by the guide.

Place mat

MATERIALS
piece of fabric, 13^1/$_2$" x 19^1/$_2$" (34cm x 50cm)
batting, 13^1/$_2$" x 19^1/$_2$" (34cm x 50cm)
piece of fabric or contrasting fabric, 13^1/$_2$"
x 19^1/$_2$" (34cm x 50cm), for the backing
2yds. (1.8m) of corded piping
matching sewing machine thread
pins
scissors
tape measure
sewing machine

Method

1 Place the batting on the wrong side of the fabric. Pin or baste the layers together and quilt through all thicknesses as desired.
2 Using the rim of a cup as a guide, round off the corners of the front and back pieces.
3 With the right sides together and the raw edges even, pin the piping around the quilted front, clipping the seam allowance at the curves. Overlap the ends of the piping where they meet.

Draw out a little cord from the piping and cut it off to eliminate bulk. Stitch the piping in place.
4 Place the front and the back with right sides together and the raw edges even. Stitch around the edge, following the previous stitching line and leaving an opening for turning. Turn the place mat right side out and press. Slipstitch the opening closed.

Napkin

MATERIALS
19^1/$_2$" (50 cm) square each of cotton
fabric and contrasting cotton fabric
2^1/$_4$yds. (2m) corded piping
matching sewing machine thread
19^1/$_2$" (50cm) bias binding in the same
color as the corded piping
pins
scissors
tape measure
sewing machine

Method

1 Using the rim of a cup as a guide, round off the corners of both the fabric pieces.
2 Make the napkin same as for the place mat, without the quilting.
3 Fold the bias binding in half lengthwise. Stitch along the folded edges. Knot the ends of the bias binding then stitch the center 5" (13cm) down from one corner of the napkin.
4 Fold the side with the tie attached in half, with wrong sides together. Roll the opposite side of the napkin toward the end with the tie. Wrap the

tie around the rolled napkin and tie it in a bow.

Bread napkin

MATERIALS
piece of fabric, 15" x 19^1/$_2$" (38cm x 50cm)
matching sewing machine thread
scissors
tape measure
sewing machine

Method

Serge or zigzag the fabric edges or turn the hem under and zigzag it in place. Knot the napkin around the bread.

Tea cozy

Before you begin Measure the height and width of your teapot. On a piece of paper, mark the dimensions, allowing an additional 4" (10cm) for seams. You will need contrasting bias binding, 2^3/$_8$" (6cm) wide by the circumference of the tea cosy plus the length of the arc (see step 1).

MATERIALS
paper
pencil
sufficient quilted fabric
contrasting piping and bias binding
matching sewing machine thread
pins
scissors
tape measure
sewing machine

Method

1 With the dimensions you have calculated, draw a teapot pattern. Draw an arched shape from the center point to each side point. Cut a front and a back for the tea cozy following the pattern.

2 Pin and baste the piping around the front piece with right sides together and raw edges even. Pin the front and back together with right sides together and the raw edges even, Stitch, catching the piping in the seam.

3 Press ¼" (6mm) to the wrong side on the bottom edge, then another ¾" (2cm). Stitch.

4 Bind the bottom edges with the bias binding.

Clockwise from left: Tea cozy, Place mat, Napkin, Bread napkin

Festive Setting

SMART AND CHIC, THESE SLIPCOVERS AND TABLECLOTHS MAKE A FESTIVE TABLE FOR A SPECIAL OCCASION.

Make the meal a real celebration with this tablecloth and matching chair covers

Tablecloth

Before you begin

Cloths and slipcovers like these can also be used where the furniture is worn or the chairs are mismatched. Napkins and placemats can be added to complete the setting.

Measuring

Measure your table and on a sheet of paper sketch the pattern pieces A to G, marking in the following measurements:

A and B (short side overlay swags) = table width x 23" (59cm) for the scallops + 1$^1/_4$" (3cm) for the hems.

C and D (long side overlay swags) = table length x 23" (59cm) for scallops + 1$^1/_4$" (3cm) for the hems.

E and F (long side tablecloth panels) = length = as for piece G, width = drop to floor + 1$^1/_2$" (4cm) for hem and seam. Cut 5$^1/_4$" (13.5cm) into the panel on one side where the marks fall on panel G. G (table top plus floor drops) = length = table top length + 2" (5cm) for seams + twice the drop. Mark where the floor drop meets the table top on each side.

MATERIALS

paper and pencil

sufficient fabric (we used approximately 10yds. (9m) of 54" (137cm)-wide fabric for a table 36" x 60" (91.5cm x 152cm)

matching sewing machine thread

pins

scissors

tape measure

tailor's chalk

sewing machine

Method

1 Using your drawings as a guide, cut out the pieces from the fabric. Place the main piece G on the table and mark a line with tailor's chalk where the drop begins at each end of the table so you will know where to attach the side overlays (fig. 1). Place pieces E and F on the table and mark them in the same way.

2 Press a narrow double hem on one long and both short edges of each of the side overlay pieces A, B, C and D. Stitch the hems. Sew a row of gathering stitches along the short sides of all the overlay pieces but do not pull up the gathering.

3 Stitch overlay pieces A and B to the main table top piece G along the marked line, leaving $^1/_4$" (6mm) free at each end so the ends can be pulled up later to form the scalloped corner.

4 Join the long side overlay piece C to the side panel F and the long side overlay piece D to the side panel E between the marked lines.

5 Gather up the ends of all the side overlay pieces, so that they pull up to approximately 6$^1/_4$" (16cm) at the corners to form the swags. Slipstitch the gathered sections to the side panel pieces.

6 Join the side panels E and F (with the overlays attached) to each side of G (fig. 2).

7 Place the cloth on the table, arranging the corners attractively over the gathering.

Fig. 2

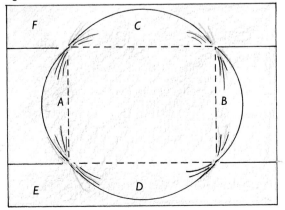

Fig. 1

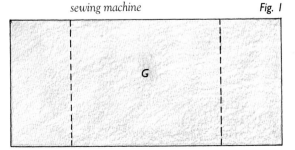

Chair bow

Before you begin

This chair cover is made in the same manner as the one on page 128.

MATERIALS

approximately 2$^1/_2$yds. (2.3m) of 54" (137cm)-wide fabric

Velcro® dots (optional)

matching sewing machine thread

pins

scissors

tape measure

sewing machine

Method

1 Cut fabric for the bow, 24" x 47" (61cm x 120cm) plus $^5/_8$" (1.5cm) seam allowance. Fold in half with right sides together and raw edges even. Sew around all sides, leaving an opening for turning. Turn right side out and press.

2 Cut a tie 12" x 24" (30cm x 61cm) plus $^5/_8$" (1.5cm) for seam allowances. Make the tie same as the bow, cutting the ends at an angle.

3 Cut a loop, 2" x 4" (5cm x 10cm) plus $^5/_8$" (1.5cm) seam allowances. Make the loop as for the bow and the tie.

4 Baste the bow ends to the center. Baste the center of the tie behind the bow center. Wrap the loop around and stitch in place. Stitch the bow to the chair cover, or attach with Velcro®.

Scalloped Linens

THIS SIMPLE BUT ELEGANT TABLECLOTH IS VERY EASY TO MAKE.

MATERIALS
54" (137cm) square of fabric
for the tablecloth
15" (38cm) square of fabric for each napkin
matching sewing machine thread
cardboard
marking pen
cup
large coin
disappearing marker
sharp-pointed scissors
pins
scissors
stabilizer
tape measure
sewing machine

Method

1 To make a template of the scallops on the cardboard, use the coin to draw continuous half circles across the edge of the cardboard. Make another template the same way using the cup. Cut out the templates.

2 Cut out a round tablecloth following the instructions on page 166. Place the larger template on the edge of the fabric and mark the pattern along the edge with the marker.

3 Place the stabilizer under the fabric and follow the manufacturer's instructions for use. Using satin stitch, work along the scalloped pattern, turning the fabric between each scallop. Use a pre-set scallop if your machine has one.

4 Using the sharp scissors, cut close to the edge of the stitching, snipping into the scallops as you go. It may be necessary to run a second row of stitches over the first, for a more dramatic effect.

5 Make the napkins in the same way using the smaller template.

The scalloped edge creates a very elegant finish

Fringed Table Set

UNEVEN WEAVE FABRICS, INCLUDING LINENS AND LOOSELY WOVEN
COTTONS, PROVIDE THE BASE TO CREATE INTERESTING YET VERY SIMPLE
TABLE NAPKINS AND CLOTHS WITH FRINGED EDGES.

This technique works well on a patterned fabric

Before you begin Measure the size of your table. Determine the drop you require for the tablecloth and add 1¼" (3cm) for the fringing allowance. Fringing only works on a rectangular or square tablecloth.

MATERIALS
piece of fabric, 12¹/₂" x 16¹/₂" (32cm x 42cm) for each place mat
11" (28cm) square of fabric for each napkin
sufficient fabric for the tablecloth, cut to size
scissors
pin or needle

Method

1 Ensure that all the fabric edges are as straight as possible.

2 Using a pin or needle, pull out the threads along one side at a time on each piece to make approximately ³/₄" (2cm) of fringing on each side. For the tablecloth, make the fringing 1¹/₄" (3cm) wide.

The Finishing Touch

LINED BASKET

WASTEPAPER BASKET

BAND BOXES

LAMPSHADES

DECORATIVE SCREEN

TOWELS WITH FLAIR

PICTURE BOWS

PHOTO FRAMES

DRAWSTRING BAG

FABRIC-COVERED BOX

Lined Basket

FABRIC LINED BASKETS HAVE MANY USES AROUND THE HOME.

Before you begin If you want the basket to hold books or magazines, ensure that it is wide enough so that books can be laid flat without buckling. If you don't wish to display the contents of your basket, make sure it has high sides or, better still, a lid.

MATERIALS

fabric strip for the side panel, equal to the inside depth of the basket plus 2⅜" (6cm) x twice the inside basket circumference

cardboard and batting, the same size as the base of the basket

fineline permanent marker

piece of fabric, 1" (2.5cm) larger than the inside base of the basket

matching sewing machine thread

ribbon or cord, the same length as the inside circumference of the basket plus 2" (5cm)

fabric strip, 3" x 19½" (7.5cm x 50cm), for the bow

turning hook or knitting needle

sewing machine, or needle for handsewing

scissors

tape measure

pins

spray adhesive

craft glue

Method

1 Turn the basket over so that the base is facing up. Using the cardboard and marker, draw, then cut out a template of the base. Place it inside the basket to check the fit. Remove the template.

2 Using the base template, cut batting the same size. Glue to the cardboard with a light spray of adhesive. Using the same template, cut out the fabric

for the base 1" (2.5cm) larger all around. Lightly spray the batting with adhesive and fix the fabric to the batting.

3 When the base cover is dry, turn it over. Snip into the 1" (2.5cm) allowance around the edge of the fabric, then glue the edge of the fabric to the cardboard with the craft glue.

4 Stitch the short ends of the side panel with right sides together to form a loop. Press ¼" (6mm) to the wrong side along the top edge, then another 1¾" (4.5cm). Stitch the hem in place, leaving a 1¼" (3cm) opening.

5 At the bottom raw edge, stitch two rows of gathering stitches ¼" (6mm) apart and ⅜" (1cm) from the edge. Pull up the gathering to fit

around the base of the basket. Glue the gathered area of the strip under the base.

6 Thread the length of ribbon or cord through the casing. Place the fabric inside the basket, then using the ribbon or cord, gather in the casing and adjust the gathers evenly around the top edge of the basket. Slipstitch the casing seam closed and the casing to the basket.

7 Fold the fabric strip for the bow in half with right sides together and raw edges even. Stitch one short edge and along one side. Trim the seams and clip the corners. Turn the strip right side out. Press. Slipstitch the remaining edge closed. Tie the bow around the handle of the basket.

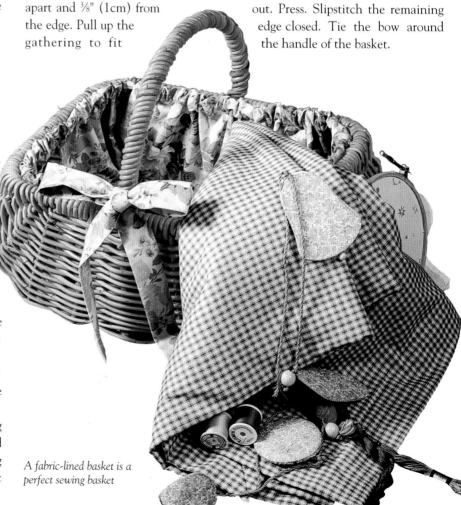

A fabric-lined basket is a perfect sewing basket

Wastepaper Basket

ADD TRIMS AND BRAIDS IF YOU ARE FOLLOWING A THEME FOR YOUR
ROOM AS AN ADDED DASH OF INTEREST.

MATERIALS

wastepaper basket

*fabric strip, equal to the inside depth
plus 6" (15cm) x twice the inside basket
circumference, for the side panel*

*cardboard and batting, the same size as the
base of the basket*

*piece of fabric, 1" (2.5cm) larger than the
inside base of the basket*

fine permanent marker

matching sewing machine thread

1" (2.5cm)-wide ribbon for the bow

*elastic, ³⁄₈" (1cm) wide x the
circumference of the basket top*

sewing machine, or needle for handsewing

scissors

tape measure

pins

spray adhesive

craft glue

Method

1 Turn the basket over so that the base is facing up. Using the cardboard and marker, make a template of the base. Cut out the template and place it inside the basket to check the fit; trim if necessary. Remove the template.

2 Cut out batting the same size as the base template. Glue the batting to the cardboard with a light spray of the adhesive. Using the same template, cut out the fabric for the base 1" (2.5cm) larger all around. Lightly spray the batting with adhesive and fix the fabric to the batting.

3 When the base cover is dry, turn it over. Snip into the 1" (2.5cm) allowance around the edge of the fabric, then glue the edge of the fabric to the

cardboard with the craft glue.

4 Join the short ends of the side panel with the right sides together to form a loop. Press the seam open.

5 Press ¼" (6mm) then another 1" (2.5cm) to the wrong side along the top edge. Stitch the hem in place to form a casing leaving a ¾" (2cm) opening for the elastic.

6 At the bottom raw edge, stitch two rows of gathering stitches ¼" (6mm) apart and ³⁄₈" (1cm) from the edge. Pull up the gathering to fit around the base

piece. Glue the gathered area of the strip under the base piece.

7 Thread the elastic through the casing, securing the ends with a knot or with slipstitches. Slipstitch the opening closed. Place the fabric liner in the basket. Tie the ribbon in a bow and slipstitch it in place.

A fabric-lined wastepaper basket will find a place in many rooms of the house

Band Boxes

BAND BOXES PROVIDE EXCELLENT STORAGE FOR A VARIETY OF BITS AND PIECES.

Before you begin The amount of fabric and batting you need will depend on the size of your box and whether you are covering it and/or lining it. For our fabric-covered box, we used approximately 1½yds. (1.3m) of 45" (115cm) wide fabric and a small amount of batting for the lid. Allow an extra ⅝" (1.5cm) to turn under and overlap around the edges of all the fabric unless instructed otherwise.

MATERIALS
sturdy box with a lid

one strip of cardboard, the width of the outer lip of the lid and the same length as the circumference of the outer lip

craft glue

spray adhesive

small paintbrush to apply the adhesive

sufficient fabric

polyester batting

strip of a complementary fabric or ribbon, 8" x 35" (20cm x 89cm), for the bow (optional)

braid, ribbon, masking tape or fabric to cover the joins (optional)

Method

1 Cut one lid from the fabric, 1" (2.5cm) larger than the top of the lid all around. Cut one lid from the batting without any allowances. Cut one strip of fabric the circumference of the base by the depth of the box plus 2" (5cm). Cut one strip of fabric the circumference of the lid by the depth of the lid plus ⅜" (1cm). Cut one strip of cardboard the circumference of the lid by the depth. Cut a circle of fabric for the base, 1" (2.5cm) larger all around than the base. Cut one base from the cardboard, without any additional allowance.

2 Glue the batting to the lid and center the fabric piece on top. Clip into the 1" (2.5cm) allowance of the fabric. Glue the clipped allowance down to the sides of the lid, pulling the fabric tight. Trim away excess fabric.

3 Glue the strip of fabric for the side of the lid to the corresponding strip of cardboard with the ⅜" (1cm) allowance all around. Clip into the allowance, then glue the fabric on one long side and both short ends to the wrong side of the cardboard. Glue the fabric-covered cardboard strip to the outside lip of the lid with the covered edge at the top.

4 Press under one short edge of the fabric for the side of the box. Place the base fabric around the outside of the box with the turned edge covering the raw edge and a 1" (2.5cm) allowance at the top and bottom. Glue into place. Clip into the allowances at the top and bottom.

5 Turn the allowance at the bottom of the box over on to the base, glue into place. Turn the top allowance to the inside of the box and glue in place.

6 Place the fabric circle for the base face down on a protected surface. Clip 1" (2.5cm) into the allowance all around. Spray the wrong side of the fabric with adhesive. Place the corresponding cardboard circle on the adhesive and press down. Turn the clipped allowance to the wrong side and glue it in place.

7 Spray the base of the box with adhesive and glue the fabric-covered cardboard circle on to the base, covering all the raw edges.

8 Cover the joins on the inside of the box with braid, ribbon, masking tape or fabric. Make a bow in the complementary, fabric or ribbon, if desired, and glue it to the lid of the box.

Lampshades

LAMPSHADES ARE AN ESSENTIAL ELEMENT OF MANY DESIGN SCHEMES. AVAILABLE IN AN ARRAY OF SHAPES AND SIZES, THEY ADD INTEREST TO A DULL CORNER.

Before you begin

The three styles of lampshades shown here are variations on a basic shade, but with individual finishing treatments. Lampshade frames can be bought from a craft store or, if you have existing shades that could do with an update, it's simple to remove the old shade and re-cover the frame yourself. Measure the existing frame to determine quantities of fabric needed.

Always buy a wire lampshade frame that is plastic-coated to prevent it from rusting over time.

All frames that are to be covered in fabric must be bound with a white or cream cotton tape so that the shade fabric can be stitched to the frame.

Binding the frame

To determine how much binding tape you will need, measure the circumference of the two circles to be covered and all the vertical supporting spokes that connect the two circles. Do not measure the wire or supporting wires where the bulb is to be inserted as these wires will not be covered. Multiply your total by three to obtain the total length of tape needed.

To bind the frame: First cover the vertical spokes, tucking the tape under and around the frame (fig. 1). Tuck one end of the tape under the last loop to secure it. Repeat the process for the top and bottom circles so that all the external parts of the frame are covered. In some instances it is easier to secure the tape ends with pins until the binding is complete and then stitch or glue the ends in place.

Stiffened shade

MATERIALS
metal lampshade frame, stripped bare

approximately 1⅛yds. (1m) of 45" (115cm)-wide fabric

approximately 1⅛yds. (1m) of 45" (115cm)-wide iron-on buckram interfacing

bias strip, 1½" (4cm) wide and as long as the combined circumferences of the top and bottom circles plus ¾" (2cm) allowance

craft glue

clothespins

pins

cotton binding tape to cover the frame (see Before you begin)

strong handsewing needle and thread

large piece of paper for the pattern

scissors

fine marker

tape measure

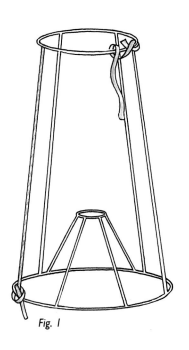

Fig. 1

This elegant shade needs no embellishment

Method

1 Bind the frame with tape.

2 Place the frame at one end of the sheet of paper, then roll the frame across the paper, marking the outline of the pattern. Cut out the pattern (fig. 1). Check that it fits your frame before cutting out the fabric.

3 Cut out the fabric, adding ¼" (6mm) seam allowances on either end and at the top and bottom edges. Cut the interfacing the same size.

4 With a warm iron, fuse the interfacing to the wrong side of the fabric, leaving the side allowances free.

5 On both long sides of the bias strip, press ¼" (6mm) to the wrong side.

6 Stitch the bias binding to the top and bottom raw edges of the fabric, with the right sides together, leaving a ⅜" (1cm) seam allowance on the fabric and stitching in the fold line of the bias binding. If you prefer, you can bind the edges by hand after the fabric has been attached to the frame (fig. 2).

7 Press the raw edges of the fabric over the interfacing and fit the shade to the frame. Use clothespins to keep the shade in place until all the stitching is complete. Fold ¼" (6mm) to the wrong side on one short end and overlap the raw edge with the fold. Glue the overlap in place. Slipstitch the fabric to the binding on both top and bottom circles.

8 Fold the free side of the bias binding over the frame and slipstitch or glue it into place on the wrong side.

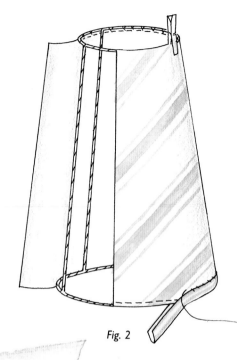

Fig. 2

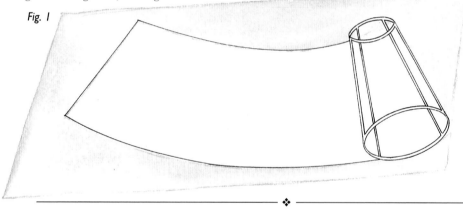

Fig. 1

Pleated shade

Before you begin Measure the circumference of the frame and multiply that measurement by one and a half to give the length of fabric required. Cut bias strips 1½" (4cm) wide x the circumference of both circles plus ¾" (2cm) for turnings.

MATERIALS

sufficient fabric for the shade and for bias strips or purchased bias binding

metal lampshade frame, stripped bare

craft glue

clothespins

pins

scissors

cotton binding tape to cover the frame

strong handsewing needle and thread

Method

1 Bind the frame with cotton tape. (See page 185 for instructions.)

2 Using your measurements, cut a rectangle of fabric, adding ¾" (2cm) allowances to each side. Fold the fabric with the right sides together, then stitch the short ends together in a ¾" (2cm) seam. Press the seam open and turn right side out.

3 With needle and thread, gather along the top and bottom edges but do not

pull up the gathering.

4 Divide the fabric into four equal sections and mark at the top and bottom edges with pins. Place the fabric over the frame, drawing in the gathering threads so that the four pairs of pins are equally spaced around the frame. Use clothespins to hold the fabric in place. Arrange the gathered fabric into pleats, evenly spaced around the frame. With your fingers, press the pleats all in one direction and secure them with pins before stitching the pleats into place. Trim any excess fabric.

5 Remove the shade from the frame. Stitch the bias binding to the top and bottom raw edges of the fabric, with the right sides together, leaving a ⅜" (1cm) seam allowance on the fabric and stitching in the fold line of the bias binding.

6 Place the shade on the frame. Turn the free edge of the bias binding over the frame and slipstitch it in place.

❖

This is a very effective lampshade for a formal living room

We have created this very formal lampshade following our basic lampshade pattern. Use matching bias binding for the top and bottom trim and a subtle contrasting color for the center trim. Apply the two smaller rows of piping so that their seam allowances are touching. Make a third length of 2" (5cm)-wide bias binding, turning in and pressing ¼" (6mm) on each side. Use the wider bias strip to cover a length of foam cording available from your craft store. Glue the bias to the flat back of the cording and then center and glue it directly over the top of the bias binding already attached at the base of the shade. Neatly fold under all the ends of the bias to cover any joins.

Lined shade with ruffle

MATERIALS
metal lampshade frame, stripped bare
approximately 1⅛ yds. (1m) of 45"
(115cm)-wide fabric for the cover
approximately 1⅛ yds. (1m) of 45"
(115cm)-wide lining fabric
contrasting fabric for 2⅜" (6cm)-wide
bias binding
ruffles can be cut from scraps,
but if in doubt allow another ½ yd. (.5m)
of fabric for ruffles
large sheet of paper for the pattern
fineline marker
craft glue
approximately 6¾ yds. (6m) narrow
cotton tape
handsewing needle and strong
sewing thread
masking tape
scissors
tape measure

Method

1 Bind the frame as instructed on page 185.

2 Place the frame at one end of the sheet of paper, then roll the frame across the paper, marking the outline of the pattern. Cut out the pattern (see fig. 1 on page 186). Check that it fits your frame before cutting out the fabric.

3 Using the pattern, cut out the lining and main fabric, leaving a 2" (5cm) allowance all around.

4 Fit the lining around the frame, pinning it to the tape. Pin the ends closed as a seam. Remove the lining from the frame and sew the seam as it is pinned. Trim the seam allowance to ⅜" (1cm). Repeat this process for the main fabric.

5 Place the lining inside the frame with the seam following the line of one upright strut. Pin it to the binding tape.

6 Cut sufficient bias strips to go around the top and bottom rings. Press ⅜" (1cm) to the wrong side on both long edges of the bias strip, then fold it in half with the wrong sides together. Stitch the binding to the main shade fabric, ⅜" (1cm) from the edge and stitching in the fold line of the bias binding. Replace the shade on the frame. Turn the free edge of the bias binding to the inside and slipstitch it in place.

7 Cut sufficient 4" (10cm) wide ruffle strips which when joined measure at least one and a half or twice the total circumference of the top and bottom rings, depending on the thickness of your fabric. Make each ruffle in the following way: Join the ends of the strip to form a loop. Fold the strip in half with the wrong sides together and the raw edges even. Serge or zigzag the raw edges then gather them. Draw up the gathering to fit inside the bias-trimmed top and bottom rings. Glue the ruffle into place. Glue the bias binding over the gathered edge, tucking the ends under at the overlap.

8 Cover the raw edges inside the shade with masking tape.

A ruffled shade has very little sewing in its construction

Decorative Screen

FABRIC-COVERED FOLDING SCREENS CAN BE MADE FROM ANY TYPE OF WOOD THAT IS STURDY ENOUGH TO SUPPORT ITS OWN WEIGHT.

Before you begin

If you wish to shape the top of the screen, you will need a jigsaw and a paper pattern to follow when cutting.

MATERIALS
large sheet of paper

pencil

3 panels of plywood, each 16mm x 19¹/₂" x 63" (16mm x 50cm x 1.6m)

jigsaw

5⅝yds. (5m) of 45" (115cm)-wide fabric

1½yds. (1.3m) of ⅝" (1.5cm)-wide braid

11¼yds. (10m) of 24" (61cm)-wide polyester batting or ¼" (6mm) thick foam

6 brass hinge brackets and screws

screwdriver

scissors

wood glue

craft glue

spray adhesive

staples and staple gun, or upholstery tacks

Method

1 Make a paper pattern for the curved top of the screen panels. Using the pattern, mark the curve in pencil on top of each panel of plywood, then cut out with the jigsaw.

2 Cut two pieces of fabric, each 21" x 63" (55cm x 16cm) for each panel. Cut two pieces of batting or foam, each 19¹/₂" x 63" (50cm x 160m). Using the spray adhesive, glue the batting or foam to the front and back of each panel.

3 Lightly spray the adhesive on to the batting, then lay the fabric on top, trimming the top edge in the curved shape of the wood panels with a 1" (2.5cm) allowance.

4 Staple or tack the fabric edges in place. Trim away the excess fabric.

5 Starting at the bottom, staple or tack the braid over the fabric edge, then proceed to glue the braid all around each panel, covering the raw edge of the fabric. At the other end, turn under the raw edge of the braid and staple or tack it in place.

6 Attach the hinges. The hinges should be about 8" (20cm) from the top and bottom of the screen.

Use a screen to divide a room, provide a private space or hide those things you don't want seen

Towels with Flair

AN ELEGANT AND LUXURIOUS ADDITION TO ANY BATHROOM IS A STACK
OF PRETTY TRIMMED TOWELS ON AN OPEN SHELF OR DRESSER.

A lace trim turns a plain towel into a very special one

Trimmed towels

Before you begin Across the ends of most towels is a flat, woven band. This is the ideal place to stitch rows of ribbon or braid. You can also stitch lace or scalloped trims under the edge of a length of ribbon or fabric.

Always wash laces and trims before stitching them on so that they do not pucker after washing. Remember to trim your wash cloths, bath mats and hand towels to match for a truly coordinated bathroom look.

Prewash dark-colored towels in cold water with salt added to allow for any dye loss. This is especially important if you are working with light-colored contrasting trims. Prewash the trims to allow for any shrinkage.

To determine how much trim is required for each towel, measure the width of the towel and add 2" (5cm) for turnings.

MATERIALS
towel or item to be trimmed
trim
matching handsewing or machine thread
needle
pins
scissors
sewing machine (optional)

Method

1 If you are using a trim with one finished edge, such as lace, pin the trim on the woven band with the wrong side of the trim facing upwards. Tuck in both raw ends, then stitch along the straight side of the trim close to the edge (or at the distance that best suits the design of the trim).

2 Turn the trim to the right side and press. Topstitch along the folded edge, leaving the lacy edge free. Stitch the ends in place.

3 If you are using a fabric strip as a trim, press all the raw edges under, then topstitch the trim in place by stitching close to the pressed edges.

Elegant lace-trimmed towels are a feature of this traditional bathroom

---

Appliquéd hand towel

Before you begin For an adjoining bathroom, try this quick and easy appliqué method to coordinate your towels with your bedroom decor, using your bedspread or curtain fabric for the appliqué.

Using fusible web is a quick and easy way to fuse two layers of fabric together without sewing and it is available from most fabric and craft stores.

MATERIALS
towel, hand towel, wash cloth
fabric with a suitable motif
fusible web
sewing machine thread
scissors
sewing machine

Method

1 Roughly cut out an interesting motif from the fabric.

2 Following the manfacturer's instructions, fuse the web to the wrong side of the motif.

3 Carefully cut around the motif. Peel off the backing paper and position the motif on the towel. Press for ten seconds.

4 Outline the motif with a tight zigzag stitch around the outer edge.

Any simple motif can be appliquéd on to a towel

Picture Bows

THESE LOVELY ACCESSORIES ARE THE PERFECT FINISHING TOUCH,
BUT DON'T FORGET THEY ARE PURELY DECORATIVE
AND NOT INTENDED TO SUPPORT A WEIGHT.

Bow 1

Before you begin This picture bow has been made so that the lining fabric is visible around the edges of the main fabric. Determine the length you wish your bow to be, measuring between the point where you would like the bow to sit and 2" (5cm) down behind the picture frame. Allow an extra 2" (5cm) at the top end for the turned casing that will become the center of the bow. Determine the width of your bow relative to the frame.

MATERIALS
½yd. (.5m) of 45" (115cm)-wide main fabric
½yd. (.5m) of 45" (115cm)-wide contrasting fabric
matching sewing machine thread
fabric glue
small hook or ring
sewing machine
pins
scissors
tape measure

Method

1 To make the bow tails, cut one main strip to the required width plus ¾" (2cm) for seam allowances. Cut the contrasting fabric ¾" (2cm) wider.

2 Pin the main fabric and the contrasting fabric with the right sides together and raw edges even. Stitch the two long sides (fig. 1) and one short side. Trim the seams. Turn right side out and press. There should be a narrow border of the contrasting fabric showing on the right side. Slipstitch the open end closed.

3 To make the center of the bow, fold the top end of the tail piece over to the front, forming a loop. Topstitch the loop in place; the tighter the loop, the fuller the finished bow will be.

4 Cut a piece of the main fabric, 10" x 19½" (25cm x 50cm), and of the contrasting fabric, 11" x 19½" (28cm x 50cm), for the bow. Join the pieces in the same way as for the tail. At the back of the bow center, pin and stitch the closed end over the slipstitched end. Slide the bow through the loop on the tail section, centering it with the seam under the loop at the back. Secure the bow with stitches at the back. Sew the hook or ring to the back of the loop.

5 Glue the bottom edge of the tail section to the back of the picture frame. Hang the picture, then attach the bow to a hook on the wall.

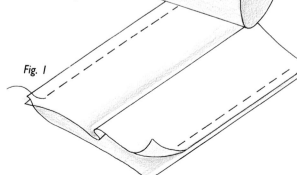

Fig. 1

Method

1 Cut a strip for the bow loop to the required length and width, adding ¾" (2cm) for seam allowances. Cut another strip for the bow tails, the same width and length you have calculated, allowing for the turned casing that wraps around the bow loop.

2 Fold both strips in half with right sides together and raw edges even. Sew the long sides. Turn the strips right side out through the open ends. Press.

3 Fold the ends of the bow loop so that they meet at the center back and slipstitch them together.

4 Fold the tail section in half. Fold 3" (7.5cm) at the top over to the front to form the casing. Slipstitch the casing into place. The smaller the casing, the tighter the bow center will be. Experiment until you are pleased with the effect. Pass the bow loop into the casing so that the slipstitching on the back of the loop falls inside the casing. Slipstitch the loop into place. Sew the ring or hook to the back of the bow.

5 Glue the ends of the tails to the back of the picture. Hang the picture first, then position the bow and attach it to the wall above the picture.

Method

1 Make the tail section the same as for bow 1 on page 192.

2 Cut the additional pieces of the main and contrast fabric for the bow center as for bow 1, cutting four pieces. Make two bow centers as for bow 1.

3 Place the second bow center over the first and at right angles to it. Stitch them together through the center. Gather in the bow centers to form a series of tiny gathers in the middle.

4 Gather the square of contrasting fabric and cover the button with it. Stitch the button over the gathers. Secure the bow with a few stitches from the back. Sew the hook or ring to the back of the double bow.

5 Complete as for bow 1.

Bow 2

Before you begin Determine the length you wish your picture bow to be, measuring between the point where you would like the bow to sit and 2" (5cm) down behind the picture frame. Allow an extra 2" (5cm) at the top end for the turned casing that will become the center of the bow. Determine the width of your picture bow relative to the width of the frame.

MATERIALS
½yd. (.5m) of fabric
matching sewing machine thread
small hook or ring
sewing machine
pins
scissors
tape measure

Bow 3

MATERIALS
½yd. (.5m) of main fabric
½yd. (.5m) of contrasting fabric
matching sewing machine thread
fabric glue
small hook or ring
sewing machine
one button to cover
2" (5cm) square of contrasting
fabric to cover the button

Photo Frames

WE ALL HAVE PHOTOGRAPH COLLECTIONS OR A FAVORITE CROSS STITCH
OR EMBROIDERY PROJECT THAT WE WOULD LIKE TO FRAME.

Before you begin Use your decorative talents to make a special frame by covering the mounting board with fabric, or you can cover the frame in a suitable fabric to make its own statement. This can be especially effective in children's rooms where a favorite nursery print can be placed inside a frame which is covered in gingham or brightly colored fabric.

Fabric-covered mats

Before you begin The mat fits inside a photograph or picture frame, so select a fabric that is suitable for the frame as well as for the picture it contains. A natural- or ivory-

Choose a small print fabric that will not overwhelm the photograph to cover the mats

colored silk will add a subtle textured look to a silver frame, while a mat covered with a small cottage print will add interest to a floral cross stitch. Select a pattern that is in proportion to your frame. A large print or one that is too sparse will lose its detail if used on a small mat.

MATERIALS

*stiff self-adhesive craft board or purchased
self-adhesive mat*

metal ruler

craft knife

pencil

fabric

fabric glue

craft glue

scissors

clothespins or large paper clips

Fig. 1

Fig. 2

Method

1 Draw the desired shape and size of the mat on the craft board and then cut it out, using the metal ruler and sharp craft knife.

2 Cut out the fabric, using the mat as the pattern, allowing at least ⅝" (1.5cm) all around. Peel the protective backing from the board and then place the fabric over the top. Make sure that there are no wrinkles in the fabric.

3 With the craft knife or the scissors, trim the fabric from the inside of the frame to ⅝" (1.5cm) from the board edge. Do the same for the outside edge, if necessary. On the inside edge, snip into the fabric at each corner at an angle of 45 degrees (fig. 1). Turn the fabric to the back and glue down all the sides and edges with craft glue (fig. 2). On the outside clip across the corners, level with the frame. Hold the fabric in place with clothespins or paper clips until all the glue is dry.

This is a clever way to smarten up an old picture frame. Glue ribbon inside the freshly-painted frame, mitering the corners

Drawstring Bag

A DRAWSTRING BAG CAN BE USED FOR MANY DECORATIVE
AND PRACTICAL APPLICATIONS.

Choose a fabric that suits the purpose of your bag

Before you begin Choose a fabric appropriate for the proposed use of the bag; coated fabric could be used for toiletries, and a light sheer fabric could be used for lingerie. A brightly coloured children's print could be used to take toys to grandma's, or used as a library or book bag. You can make the bag any size you like; the measurements given here are for a toiletry bag.

MATERIALS
⅔yd. (.6m) fabric
drawstring cord or ribbon
matching sewing machine thread
tailor's chalk
sewing machine

Method

1 Fold the fabric in half lengthwise, with the right sides together. Stitch the sides together in a ⅝" (1.5cm) seam. Finish the raw edges with serger or zigzag stitching.

2 Turn the bag right side out. Press ¼" (6mm) to the wrong side at the top edge, then another 2" (5cm). Stitch through all thicknesses along the fold and again ⅝" (1.5cm) away, forming a casing.

3 Open the stitching at the side seams for approximately ⅝" (1.5cm). Thread a length of cord or ribbon in one opening through the whole casing and out the same opening. Repeat for the other opening. Knot the ends of the cord or ribbon together.

Fabric-covered Box

THIS PADDED, CHINTZ-COVERED BOX STARTED LIFE AS A TOY BOX
THAT HAD BEEN HEAVILY USED.

Before you begin Decide on your fabric. Stripes are attractive, but you will have to match them carefully from the front to the back and over the lid. The easiest fabric is one with a small print or an all-over pattern that does not require matching.

Measuring

Measure your box carefully. You will find it easier to measure each panel of the box and draw these outlines and measurements on paper. Using these drawings, you can calculate the fabric quantities you will require, adding extra for turning and overlapping. For

Provided your box is solid and has suitable timber for holding the fabric, looks don't matter.

our box we needed 5yds. (4.5m) of main fabric and 4½yds. (4m) of lining fabric. We also used 5yds. (4.5m) of furnishing braid.

MATERIALS

sufficient main fabric and lining fabric

the same quantity of hi-loft polyester batting

narrow furnishing braid

approximately 60" (1.5m) strong cord or fine chain

four screw-in eye hooks

staples and staple gun

craft glue

handsewing needle and thread

decorative upholstery tacks

pliers

decorative handles

three hairline hinges (these are less visible than conventional hinges)

strong dressmakers pins

small tack hammer

Method

1 Cover the box completely with batting, using staples to secure the edges. Cover the top of the box with extra batting if you want it to be more softly padded. Make sure the edges are neat and that you use enough staples to keep the batting edges flat.

2 Line the box with the lining fabric, covering each panel of the box with fabric pieces cut to size plus a turning allowance. Glue these carefully into place. Take the lining all the way up to the lip of the box.

3 Cover the outside of the box with cut-to-size (plus turnings) pieces of the main fabric, as for the lining, allowing sufficient fabric to come over the top of the box and down into the inside of the box to overlap the lining and down on to the outside base of the box. Hold the fabric in place with pins, until you have secured the side edges with decorative tacks. Space these tacks at ¾" (2cm) intervals. When you have folded the main fabric into the inside of the box, secure the edges with staples placed in a row about 1¼" (3cm) down from the lip of the box. Fold the fabric neatly into the corners. If necessary, sew the

Cover any joins with decorative braid

edges together by hand to hold the pieces together. Glue braid over the line where the fabrics meet, securing it with a few tacks.

4 Take the main fabric on to the inside base of the box, folding the corners as necessary. Cover the base with lining fabric and braid, if desired.

5 Cover the outside of the lid, bringing the fabric inside the lid as for the box. Cover the inside of the lid with a panel of lining fabric and cover the line where the fabrics meet with braid. Tack the corners.

6 Screw the hinges to the box and lid to hold the lid evenly in place. Screw eye hooks inside the lid and the sides of the box. Establish a suitable angle at which the lid remains open and cut two lengths of the cord or chain to hold the lid at this point. Tie a length of cord between the eye hooks on each side of the lid and the box. Knot and glue the ends of the cord neatly, perhaps bind-

ing over the raw edges of the cord with a band of thread or stiffening them with glue. If you are using chain, open a link at each end with pliers and then reclamp them around the eye hooks on the box and the lid.

7 Attach decorative handles to the sides and the center front of the box, if desired.

8 Any overlap of fabric inside the box that does not sit flat can also be tacked.

Index

Acetates 14
Acrylics 14
Adhesives 28
Appliqué 94
Appliquéd pillow 98, 101
Appliquéd towel 191
Appliquéd linen napkins 171
Appliquéd tieback 65
Austrian shades 76, 84-85
Bag, drawstring 196
Band boxes 184
Baskets
    baby 159
    lined 182
    wastepaper 183
Basting 30
Bay window 37
Bed linen
    see also Comforter; Duvet cover;
        Pillowcases; Sheets; Valances
    bedspread 155
    fabrics 134, 135
    measuring for 135
    nursery 157-59
    quilted spread 152
Bed skirt
    box-pleated 117, 143
    ruffled 117, 142
    tiered 144
Bedspread 155
Bias binding 20
Binding 20-21
Blanket stitch 30
Bolsters
    gathered-end 104-05
    piped flat-end 105
Box-pleated curtain heading 40
Box-pleated valance 117, 143
Boxes
    fabric-covered 197-98
    hat 184
Braid 18
Bread napkin 174
Buckram valance 68-69
Buttoned pillow 110-11
Buttoned pillowcase 146
Buttonhole stitch 31
Buttons 26, 95
Café curtains 53-56
Canopies
    sheer 154
    tent 153
Cartridge-pleated curtain heading 40
Chair covers
    director's chairs 123-25
    festive 177
    ruffled 128-29
    tailored 126-27
Chair cushions
    tailored 126-27
    with deep ruffle 108
    piped 109
Circular tablecloths 166-67
Color 11-12
Color wheel 12
Comforter 150-52
Corner window 36
Corners 22-23

sewing on covers 120
Covers
    see also Chair covers; Valances
    easy chair 118-21
    edge treatments 116-17
    fabric 114
    pattern 115
    sewing corners 120
    sofa 130-31
    trimming 115
Crib sheet 158
Curtains
    see also Tiebacks; Valances
    café 53-56
    decorator scarf 58
    fabric requirements 41-44
    headings 39-40
    lined 50-52
    linings 42
    measuring for 40-41
    panel joining 43
    pattern matching 43
    pencil-pleated 51-52
    poles for 38-39
    rod pocket 45-46
    sash 57
    scale and proportion 44
    shirring tape 46-4
    swags 60-61
    tails 60-61
    tie-on 48-49
    trims 59
    unlined 45-47
    window shapes 36-37
Decorative trims see Trimming
Decorator scarf 58
Director's chair covers 123-25
Dormer window 37
Double-hung window 36
Double ruffles 59
Draped rectangular pelmet 70-71
Drawstring bag 196
Drop (curtains) 41
Duvets covers
    basic 138
    fabric requirements 135
    openings and closures 134
    reversible piped 140-41
    ruffled reversible 141
Easy chair cover 118-21
Edgestitched seams 33
Equipment 28-29
    shades 74
European pillowcase 148
Fabrics
    bed linen 134-35
    color 11
    covers 114
    curtains 41
    cushions 91
    selection 13
    shades 76
    types and qualities 14
Fastenings 25-27
Festive setting 176-77
Festoon table topper 169
Fitted sheets 136
    crib 158
    fabrics 134-35
Flanged pillowcase 147
Flat fell seam 32
Flat seam 32
Flat sheets
    fabric 134-35

instructions 137
French doors 37
French seam 32
Fringed table linens 179
Fusible web 28
Gathered curtain heading 39
Gathered-end bolster 104-05
Gathering 30
Headboard, upholstered 156
Heading tape 39-40
Headings, curtain 39-40
Heirloom cushions 100-01
Hemming 31
Hook-and-eyes 25
Hook-and-loop fastenings 25
Jabots 60-61
Joining panels see Panel joining
Lace patchwork pillow 100
Ladder stitch 32
Lampshades
    lined, with ruffle 188
    pleated 186-87
    stiffened 185-86
Lapped seam 33
Lined basket 182
Lined shade 80-81
Lined curtains 50-52
Linen see Bed linen; Table linen
Lining (curtains) 42
    detachable 51-52
    loose 50-51
Lock stitch 31
Measuring
    for bed linen 135
    for curtains 40-42
    for shades 75
    for tablecloths 163
Mitered corners 22
Napkins
    appliquéd linen 171
    bread 174
    with contrast border 172
    quilted 174
    stenciled 164-65
Needles 28
No-sew pillows 131
Nursery linen 157-59
Oversewing 30
Panel joining 17
    curtains 43
    tablecloths 163
Pattern 13, 15-16
    covers 115
Pattern matching 17
    curtains 42, 43
Pencil-pleated curtain 51-52
Photo frames 194-95
Picture bows 192-93
Picture windows 36
Pillows
    see also Bolsters; Chair cushions
    appliquéd 94
    with contrast band 98
    covering 121
    fabrics 91
    fillings 91
    hand-appliquéd 101
    heirloom 100-01
    lace patchwork 100
    machine-appliquéd 98
    no-sew 131
    openings and closures 94-95
    piped 96-99
    round buttoned 110-11

ruffled piped 97
stenciled 102-03
triangular 99
trimming 91-93
wrapped cover 131
zippers 95
Pillowcases
basic 145
with bows 146
buttoned 146
European 148
fabric requirements 135
flanged 147
ruffled 147
scalloped 149
Pinch-pleated curtain 50-51
Piped pillows 96-99
chair 109
Piped flat-end bolster 105
Piping 21
covers 115
curtains 59
inserting zippers with 27
pillows 91
Place mats
with contrast border 170
pleated 173
quilted 174
Pleated placemat 173
Pleated shade 186-87
Pocket tape 42
Poles, curtain 38-39
Quilted bedspreads 152
Quilted table linens 174-75
Quilts
nursery 157
Reversible piped duvet cover 140-41
Rod pocket curtain 39, 45-46
Rod pocket valance 71
Roller shades 76, 78-81
Roman shades 76, 82-83
Round buttoned pillow 110-11
Round tablecloths 166-67
Ruffled chair cover 128-29
Ruffled pillowcase 147
Ruffled piped pillow 97
Ruffled piped valance 66-67
Ruffled tieback 64
Ruffled valance 117, 142
Ruffles 23-24
curtains 59
pillows 92-93
Sample boards 16
Satin-stitched table linens 171
Scalloped café curtains 55-56
Scalloped table linens 178
Scalloped pillowcase 149
Screen 189
Seams 32-33
Self-bound seams 33
Sewing machine 28-29
Shades
Austrian 84-85
bonded roller 78-81
equipment 74
fabrics 76
lined 80-81
measuring for 75
mounting 76
Roman 82-83
tie-up 86-87
trimming 77
Shaped piped tieback 63
Sheer canopy 154

Sheets
crib 158
fabrics 134
fitted 136
flat 137
measuring for 135
Shirred curtain 57
Shirred tape curtain 46-47
Sliding doors 37
Slipcovers 112
Slipstitch 31
Snaps 25
Sofa cover 130-31
Square table topper 168
Stenciled pillows 102-03
Stenciled tablecloth and napkins 164-65
Stiffened lampshade 185-86
Stitches 30-32
Style 10
Swagged table topper 168
Swags (curtain) 60-61
Synthetic fibers 14
Table linen
see also Napkins; Place mats; Tablecloths
quilted 174-75
Tablecloths
circular 166-67
festive 177
fringed 179
measuring for 163
satin-stitched 171
scalloped 178
stenciled 164-65
Table toppers
festoon 169
square 168
swagged 168
Tailored chair cover 126-27
Tape, curtain 39-40
Tea cozy 174-75
Tent canopy 153

Texture 13
Thread eyes 25
Tie-on curtains 48-49
Tie-up shade 86-87
Tiebacks
appliquéd 65
ruffled 64
shaped piped 63
Tiered valance 144
Tools see Equipment
Towels
appliquéd 191
trimmed 190
Triangular pillow 99
Trimming 18-21
covers 115
curtains 59
pillows 91-93
shades 77
Triple-pleated curtain heading 39
Turning hook 28
Upholstered headboard 156
Valances
buckram 68-69
draped rectangular 70-71
with jumbo piping 67-68
rod pocket 71
ruffled piped 66-67
Velcro® 25
cushions 94-95
duvet covers 134
Wastepaper basket 183
Welted round cloth 167
Windows
measuring for curtains 40-41
measuring for shades 75
proportions 44
shapes 36-37
Zigzag 33
Zippers 26-27
pillows 95

Acknowledgements

LOCATIONS in Australia: Brian and Marie Livingstone, Kedron homestead; John and Michele Dounan, Topiary Farm; Brian and Helen Dounan; Judy and Jim Poulos

ADDITIONAL PHOTOGRAPHS: Maurice Kain Textiles, Sanderson Fabrics, Ashley Wallpaper, P. Rowe Fabrics, Wilson Fabrics, Design Plus (All of Australia)

MAKERS: Judy Timmins, Shelagh Dounan, Ivy Skrabanich, Christine Aggar, Adele Horsfall

SET DESIGN: Phillip Skrabanich

PROPS: Victoria Amos, Paul White, Louise Grimes

The publishers would also like to thank the following Australian ompanies and organisations who helped with the preparation of this book: Maurice Kain Textiles Limited; Design Plus; Curtain Industry Association of Australia and New Zealand; Ashley Wallpapers; Instyle; Sekers/Jawatex; Fieldcrest Cannon; Sanderson Fabrics; Waverly Fabrics; P. Rowe Fabrics, Sheridan Textiles; Marco Fabrics; David Whitehead and Sons; World of Curtains (workroom); Mathvena Imports (accessories); Domestications Decore (accessories); Pan Pacific Distributing Co. (trims and braids); The Sleep Doctor, Sans Souci (beds); A. and G. McKinnon (cane furniture)